Cambridge Series on Judgment and Decision Making

Psychological Investigations of Competence in Decision Making

The premise of this book is that most activity in everyday life and work is based on tasks that are novel, infrequent in our experience, or variable with respect to the action to be taken. Such tasks require decisions to be made and actions taken in the face of ambiguous or incomplete information. Time pressure is frequently great, and penalties for failure are severe. Examples include investing in markets, controlling industrial accidents, and detecting fraud. The environments in which such tasks occur defy a definition of optimal performance, yet the benefits of successful decision making are considerable. The authors refer to domains without criteria for optimal performance as "competency-based" and describe the able behavior of individuals who work in them by the term "competence." The chapters of this book examine the propositions that metacognitive processes – thinking about the kind of thinking that a task requires – give structure to otherwise ill-structured tasks and are fundamental enablers of decision-making performance.

Kip Smith is Research Professor of Industrial Ergonomics at Linköping University, Sweden. After a first career as a geophysicist, Professor Smith received a Ph.D. in Information and Decision Science from the University of Minnesota. Currently, his research focuses on delineating the dynamic and neural constraints on models of individual and economic decision making and of team performance. Among his applied interests are foreign currency trading, air traffic control, and the Future Force warrior.

James Shanteau, Professor of Psychology at Kansas State University, received his Ph.D. in Experimental Psychology from the University of California at San Diego. His research interests include analysis of expertise in decision makers (including expert systems) and investigation of consumer health-care choices (especially organ donation/transplantation decisions). A cofounder and past president of the Judgment/Decision Making Society, he is former director of the Decision, Risk, and Management Science (DRMS) program at the National Science Foundation. Professor Shanteau is also the coauthor of many books, including *Emerging Perspectives on Decision Research* with Sandra L. Schneider (Cambridge University Press).

Paul Johnson is Carlson Professor of Decision Sciences and Adjunct Professor of Psychology and Computer Science at the University of Minnesota. He is also a member of the faculty in the Minnesota Centers for Cognitive Sciences and Political Psychology. Professor Johnson's research focuses on the role of variability and expertise in health-care decisions, the decision failures that arise from the misperception or misrepresentation of information (e.g., deception), and the use of knowledge resources and decision technologies in business and professional settings.

Cambridge Series on Judgment and Decision Making

The purpose of the series is to convey the general principles of and findings about judgment and decision making to the many academic and professional fields to which these apply. The contributions are written by authorities in the field and supervised by highly qualified editors and the Publications Board. The series will attract readers from many different disciplines, largely among academics, advanced undergraduates, graduate students, and practicing professionals.

Psychological Investigations of Competence in Decision Making

Edited by

Kip Smith
Linköping University

James Shanteau
Kansas State University

Paul Johnson
University of Minnesota

CAMBRIDGE
UNIVERSITY PRESS

PUBLISHED BY THE PRESS SYNDICATE OF THE UNIVERSITY OF CAMBRIDGE
The Pitt Building, Trumpington Street, Cambridge, United Kingdom

CAMBRIDGE UNIVERSITY PRESS
The Edinburgh Building, Cambridge CB2 2RU, UK
40 West 20th Street, New York, NY 10011-4211, USA
477 Williamstown Road, Port Melbourne, VIC 3207, Australia
Ruiz de Alarcón 13, 28014 Madrid, Spain
Dock House, The Waterfront, Cape Town 8001, South Africa

http://www.cambridge.org

First published 2004

Printed in the United States of America

Typeface Palatino 10/13 pt.   *System* LATEX 2_ε [TB]

A catalog record for this book is available from the British Library.

Library of Congress Cataloging in Publication Data

Psychological investigations of competence in decision making / edited by
Kip Smith, James Shanteau, Paul Johnson.
p.   cm. – (Cambridge series on judgment and decision making)
Includes bibliographical references and index.
ISBN 0-521-58306-3

1. Decision making.   I. Smith, Kip, 1951–   II. Shanteau, James, 1943–
III. Johnson, Paul E. (Paul Erick), 1938–   IV. Series.
BF448 .P79   2003
153.8′3 – dc21   2002035181

ISBN 0 521 58306 3 hardback

Contents

Contributors

PETER AYTON Department of Psychology, City University, London

BETH CRANDALL Klein Associates, Inc., Fairborn, Ohio

CYNTHIA O. DOMINGUEZ Air Force Research Laboratory, Wright Patterson Air Force Base, Ohio

MARGARET DUNN School of Medicine, Wright State University, Dayton, Ohio

JOHN M. FLACH Psychology Department, Wright State University, Dayton, Ohio

RHONA FLIN Department of Psychology, University of Aberdeen

GERD GIGERENZER Max-Planck Institute for Human Development, Berlin

STEFANO GRAZIOLI Department of Information Technology, University of Virginia

DAVID HARDMAN Department of Psychology, London Guildhall University, London

ULRICH HOFFRAGE Max-Planck Institute for Human Development, Berlin

PAUL JOHNSON Carlson School of Management, University of Minnesota

PATRICIA M. JONES NASA Ames Research Center, Moffett Field, California

GARY KLEIN Klein Associates, Inc., Fairborn, Ohio

ELKE M. KURZ-MILCKE Max-Planck Institute for Human Development, Berlin

LYNNE MARTIN NASA Ames Research Center, Moffett Field, California

PATRICIA L. McDERMOTT Micro Analysis and Design, Inc., Boulder, Colorado

DANIEL M. McKELLAR School of Medicine, Wright State University, Dayton, Ohio

REBECCA M. PLISKE Department of Psychology, Dominican University

JAMES SHANTEAU Department of Psychology, Kansas State University

JAN SKRIVER Institute for Energy Technology, Halden, Norway

KIP SMITH Division of Industrial Ergonomics, Linköping University, Sweden

DAVID J. WEISS Department of Psychology, California State University, Los Angeles

Introduction: What Does It Mean to Be Competent?

Kip Smith, James Shanteau, and Paul Johnson

This book departs from the more traditional topics of judgment and decision-making research. It emphasizes neither the deficiencies of human cognition, nor heuristics and biases, nor behavior in carrying out tasks to which no one is particularly well adapted. Rather, it introduces two task-general sources of competent decision making in a wide variety of professional domains. In this introductory note, we summarize the genesis of this project and define what we mean by competence.

Recent summaries of work on expertise have focused on the measurement of expert (optimal) performance, its replication in laboratory settings, the mediating mechanisms for such performance, and the role of deliberate practice in achieving it. Clear examples of expertise in this sense occur in games, in athletic and musical performance, and in certain types of work.

The premise of this book is that much activity in everyday life and work is not of this sort. Many of the situations we encounter are novel, infrequent in our experience, or variable with respect to presenting conditions and the action to be taken. Such tasks require decisions to be made and actions taken in the face of ambiguous and/or incomplete information. Time pressure is frequently great, and the penalties for failure are often severe.

Examples of such situations include investing in a market, controlling an industrial accident, and detecting fraud. These are all environments that defy a definition of optimal performance. Practice may be beneficial but is unlikely to be the sole foundation for skilled performance. Indeed, the idea of optimal performance often does not apply, yet the benefits of successful decision making are considerable. Typically, in these domains there are also individuals who perform better than others.

In these and other, less dramatic situations like weather forecasting and probability estimation, individuals may use knowledge that is quite different from that of someone whose work is based on practice in achieving a known or computable standard (e.g., scheduling airline reservations). We refer to domains without criteria for optimal performance as *competency-based*, and we describe the behavior of individuals who work in them by the term *competence*.

In competency-based domains, we expect the mechanisms that govern actions taken to achieve goals to invoke task-general cognitive processes that redefine the role of the agent or the task constraints. For example, representational structures may be used to redefine the task or to distribute task components so that the agent is no longer taxed beyond her capacity. Alternatively, the task at hand may be recast as an instance of a broad class of tasks for which evolution has provided an adaptive metacognitive process.

We identify a pair of metacognitive processes that give structure to otherwise ill-structured tasks. The first we call *metacognition-self*, the second *metacognition-others*. Metacognition is thinking about the kind of thinking that a task requires. Metacognition-self is an introspective reevaluation of ongoing or planned cognitive activity and behavior. By taking this internal stepping-back, an agent may put herself within the situation and become able to identify herself as a source of task constraint. This task-general process may lead the agent to recast her role or to redefine the task, which may, in turn, facilitate performance. The chapter by Dominguez et al. illustrates the power of using metacognition-self in the operating room. Pliske et al. discuss how metacognition-self provides the flexibility needed when making a weather forecast.

The second metacognitive process is metacognition-others, thinking about others' thinking or, at the least, thinking about how others ought to be thinking. By jumping into others' minds, by taking a normative stance about how they should be processing information, an agent may be able to predict their thoughts, decision making, and behavior. This task-general process may lead the agent to update her goals or refocus her attention to critical cues, which may, in turn, facilitate performance. The chapter by Skriver et al. presents a study of a daunting situation in which metacognition-others saved many lives. Jones shows how metacognition-others is a key element in the successful design of human–computer systems. Grazioli et al. present empirical work in a pair of domains, fraud detection and spot currency trading, in which metacognition-others is the sole basis for agent differentiation and superior performance.

In addition to addressing the two central competence enablers – metacognition-self and metacognition-others – each chapter in this book enriches our understanding of the basis of skill and of success in the performance of decision-making tasks generally and in specific domains of work and society.

Jones and Pliske et al. discuss how addressing domain-specific constraints is a cornerstone of competent performance. The domains are quite different, but the approach is similar. Grazioli et al. and Kurz et al. identify sources of power in performance. The sources are neither processing speed, nor precision, nor the ability to remember large amounts of information. Rather, all four chapters illustrate that competency is an issue of adaptation and fit to task demands. As Simon argued in *Sciences of the Artificial*, once adapted, the agent simply does what the task requires. If we wish to understand the basis for an agent's success, we need to understand the structure of the task in which the behavior occurs. We must understand what the invariants are and how successful behavior is explained in terms of them.

A related issue is the problem of generativity. The chapters by Hardman and Ayton, Skriver et al., and Dominguez et al. address how far performance on familiar tasks can be extended when dealing with novelty. Task-general cognitive processes that redefine the role of the agent or the constraints of the task prevent performance from deteriorating dramatically as one moves away from the normal day-to-day routine.

The final three chapters in this volume address a more traditional competence enabler – representation that fits the demands of the task and the bounded rationality of the decision maker. Hardman and Ayton argue that argumentation provides fitting representations that support competent decision making under ambiguity and ignorance. In addition, argumentation explains several systematic deviations from the prescriptions of expected utility theory. The chapter by Kurz et al. addresses a topic that has been a mainstay of research in judgment and decision making: the representation of probabilistic information. They offer alternative accounts for procedures that reformulate the task and that markedly improve performance. Weiss and Shanteau address the issue of evaluating competence in domains in which not all agents working on a given task behave alike. Presumably, the learning history of each individual results in a specific adaptation to the task. However, each individual's adaptation results in unique performance. The authors show how we can understand competence in the face of variability.

As the editors of this book, our goal has been to open a new direction for judgment and decision-making research. Academic research generally and our society particularly have largely neglected the fact that sound judgment and decision making are the crux of many professions. By understanding and communicating what professional decision makers do and how they do it well, we make valuable contributions both to our field and to the professional community at large.

Part I

Metacognition-Self

1   The Conversion Decision in Laparoscopic Surgery: Knowing Your Limits and Limiting Your Risks

Cynthia O. Dominguez, John M. Flach,
Patricia L. McDermott, Daniel M. McKellar,
and Margaret Dunn

> Not in the past 100 years has such an upheaval in medicine occurred:
> The "discipline of surgery" is joining the technologic revolution and
> advancing the state of the art with laparoscopic surgery. This represents
> a radical shift in the concept of surgical practice. The "great leap of
> faith" has occurred; for the first time in history, surgeons are performing
> surgical procedures without physically seeing or touching the organs
> they are removing or repairing. (Satava, 1993, p. 111)

Day after day, all around the world, patients are wheeled into operating rooms to undergo procedures that they hope will restore them to
better health. Over the past 20 years, and especially in the past decade,
innovations in surgical technology and accompanying techniques have
led to a reduced level of access trauma (damage to healthy tissue from
the incision) for patients. Smaller incisions are made possible through
the use of tubular fiberoptic cameras. Images of the operative area are
displayed to surgeons on an external TV-like monitor, and the patients'
internal structures are manipulated with long-stemmed instruments.
As a group, these advances are called *minimally invasive surgery* and the
procedure itself *laparoscopy*.

Although patients and insurance companies are generally thrilled
about reduced hospital stays, quicker recoveries, and the greater convenience of minimally invasive procedures, there is a cost. Minimally
invasive surgery introduces significant challenges to surgeons. The new
surgeon–patient interface adds a barrier between the surgeon and the
work environment so that perceptual information surgeons need is de-
graded, and the motor skills required are more technically demanding
(Cuschieri, 1995). When a surgical procedure is especially challenging,
involving a patient with unusual anatomy and/or acute inflammation
of tissues, persisting with a minimally invasive approach may increase

the risk of major injury to a nearby structure. The surgeon has to evaluate the benefits and risks between continuing laparoscopically and converting to an open procedure. This ongoing evaluation is the conversion decision, to open or not to open.

General surgeons identified this evaluation as a critical decision that could be examined and better understood through cognitive field research. Benefits of opening include increased exposure, direct view and feel of the operative area, and often time efficiency whereby the operation can be done more quickly. Generally, 4% to 5% of laparoscopic cholecystectomy (gallbladder removal) cases are converted to open procedures (Schrenk & Woisetschlager, 1995; Southern Surgeons Club, 1991). This conversion decision, to open or not to open, was the focus of our research. However, it is important to understand that this "decision" is not typically presented to the surgeon as a distinct event, but happens over time in the context of a dynamically evolving situation.

The complexity of this decision cannot be overstated. It is not made by evaluating a static set of alternatives at just one point in time; on the contrary, it is extended in time, and it involves the integration of changing goals and information from many sources. Assessing the risk of unintended injury involves knowledge of one's own capabilities and those of other members of the surgical team. Further, it is clear that there is no consensus upon which to establish a normative or "right" decision. Twenty surgeons might describe 20 differing courses of thought and action in projecting how they would act in the best interests of a specific patient. Also, the outcome of the procedure is not a reliable measure of decision quality. In many cases, satisfactory outcomes follow despite questionable decisions, and occasionally negative outcomes may result despite reasonable choices. The current standards recommend a conservative approach, whereby surgeons convert to an open procedure whenever complications arise. However, there is great concern that a surgeon on any given case might not follow this standard – that a surgeon might persist in using minimally invasive procedures to the point where patient safety becomes compromised (Greene, 1995).

In this research, we used an exploratory approach to look at expertise in a commonly performed minimally invasive surgical procedure, laparoscopic cholecystectomy. Goals of this research were (1) to understand the decision to open during laparoscopic surgery and ultimately to develop a training intervention based on that understanding; (2) to understand perceptual expertise, including resident–staff differences and how both groups stay within the boundaries of safe performance; and

(3) to understand how metacognition interacts with expertise in this context. In this chapter, we will first discuss laparoscopic surgery in general, in the context of a particular challenging case, and in terms of analogous concepts that help us see relationships between surgery and other domains involving similar risks and complexities. Next, we will explain methods used in this research and findings related to metacognition. Finally, we will review other current writings and research pertaining to metacognition and suggest a new conceptualization that incorporates the findings of this research.

Laparoscopic Surgery: Challenges and a Case Study

Clearly, surgery is a profession well suited to the observation and study of risk, decision making, and various aspects of expertise. Surgeons must bring extensive medical knowledge, perceptual-motor skill, understanding of tools and their uses, and (last but certainly not least) good judgment to bear when they operate. To study the expertise of surgeons, we have found it useful to focus on a particular case, gallbladder removal in an 80-year-old woman. Gallbladder removal is a common bread-and-butter type of operation for general surgeons. This woman's case was chosen because it was a difficult one in which there was a wide range of opinion as to the appropriate course of surgical action. We used the background information and videotape from this patient's laparoscopic procedure to examine expertise in laparoscopic surgery and the role of metacognition in that expertise.

The Case

It was clear that this woman had an acutely infected gallbladder; the surgeon noted a palpable mass in the gallbladder's location when he physically examined her. She had a 2-day history of fever, pain in the right upper quadrant of her abdomen, and a high white blood cell count (leukocytosis). The ultrasound exam confirmed that she had a distended gallbladder with a thickened wall and gallstones. Pericholecystic fluid, indicating inflammation of gallbladder tissues, was also noted preoperatively.

Surgeons we interviewed had different opinions as to whether this woman's surgery should begin as an open or a laparoscopic procedure. Some surgeons reasoned that it should be done *open* because the patient was old; her aged lungs and heart would be less likely to withstand the pressure from insufflation[1] needed in laparoscopy and she certainly didn't need to return to work quickly. Ironically, other surgeons reasoned that the procedure should be done *laparoscopically* because the patient was old; she was more likely to develop pneumonia after an open procedure, and the bed rest needed to recover from the large incisions might decrease her likelihood of ever returning to full functioning. The conflicting opinions are difficult to reconcile, which is precisely why this case is a good one to study in the tradition of examining critical incidents (Klein, Calderwood, & MacGregor, 1989) to understand expertise and decision making.

Although these trade-offs were discussed by many of the 20 surgeons we interviewed, only 2 of them indicated that they would not begin the procedure laparoscopically; all of the others would "at least take a look" with the laparoscope. The procedure began with making the incisions and inserting the tubular ports through which instruments are inserted in the body. The surgeon first inserted the laparoscope in the umbilical port to survey the anatomy in the operative area. Three other ports were also placed and secured in the same manner, located roughly in a diagonal line from above the navel port toward the right hip. In general, placement of these incisions and ports depends upon where the surgeon believes the patient's biliary anatomy is located and how it can best be accessed. Port placement is quite important, because it may or may not afford proper visualization of the back side of an instrument when structures are clipped or cut.

When the laparoscope brought this patient's gallbladder into view, it was clear that the gallbladder was diseased. It was reddish-purple, with splotches of green and black. The greenish color was referred to as *classic dead tissue*. The distention of the gallbladder presented a problem. Grasping the gallbladder and retracting it would be impossible without somehow relieving the pressure (removing the gallbladder requires grasping it and pulling it up and out of the way while structures are identified and connective tissues are severed). An accepted method for dealing with this distention is to drain the fluid with a needle.

A strong concern of surgeons was whether the dead tissue on the wall of the gallbladder might cause the gallbladder to break apart, spilling infected bile into the abdomen; just how much tension might tear this tissue apart could be known with certainty only by trial and error. The

---

[1] Insufflation creates an air space for operating in the abdominal cavity; carbon dioxide gas is used at a pressure that is monitored by an insufflation machine.

risk of gallbladder tearing was treated as an acceptable one by some (but not all) surgeons:

> I know this is going to be very friable tissue, it's going to fall apart very easily in my forceps and [the procedure] may be very difficult to complete laparoscopically. But this is still one that I would give a fighting chance to, because I know her recovery will be that much more quick, and I can diminish her mortality from things like postoperative lung problems and so on. (Staff surgeon)

The alternative, but minority, viewpoint:

> It's going to shred. The gallbladder wall is dying. You're going to find yourself flailing. You're going to pull on the gallbladder to give yourself exposure to the cystic duct, and it's going to tear . . . you have torn the gallbladder, you've exposed their belly to everything the gallbladder has in it, you increase their risk of abdominal infection, increase their risk of a wound infection. The gallbladder is gangrenous; it's proba-bly so adherent to the surrounding tissue that you can easily just cut through something and not even know it, because the surrounding tissues are going to be just that inflamed. And again, the laparoscopic procedure is done to shorten the person's hospital stay. But this person has a sick gallbladder. Their concern is not just getting back to work in six days, this person could *die* from this disease. Your concern is doing what's best for the patient, not what leaves a minimal scar. (Fifth-year resident surgeon)

Even at this early point in the operation, the conflict about which ap-proach would inflict the least harm on the patient is apparent. The first surgeon felt that laparoscopy was best; the second surgeon felt that the potential harm of laparoscopy for this patient outweighed the problem of scarring, which was treated as a cosmetic issue.

Once the gallbladder was drained, the surgeons were able to grasp it, retract it, and get down to the business of dissecting and identifying structures. When the surgeons began dissecting, they found that the in-flammation of tissues surrounding the neck of the gallbladder made it difficult to tell what might be fat and what might be a duct or an artery. The inability to define the planes between important and unimportant tissues made for a dangerous situation; a wrong move could injure the common bile duct. The inflammation also caused blood to ooze contin-uously, which further obscured visualization.

Surgeons observing this situation on videotape cited operative tech-niques they would use to deal with the uncertainty. The two most common were (1) to begin dissecting closer to the gallbladder, so that work would progress from a known to an unknown area, and (2) to irrigate the area more to wash the blood off. Another strategy that could have been considered at this point is the use of an intraoperative x-ray, called a *cholangiogram*, to aid in identifying anatomy and to help avoid injuries.

Potential Injury

Bile duct injury is the most frequent negative outcome, or complication, of laparoscopic cholecystectomy (Stewart & Way, 1995; Way, 1992). The common bile duct connects the liver and the small intestine; if it is injured or severed accidentally in an 80-year-old woman, it is possible that she will not survive the ensuing operation to repair it. Identification of anatomical structures with 100% certainty is a key requirement that surgeons levy on themselves. Laparoscopic surgery has robbed surgeons of the opportunity to physically feel the structures they are manipulating, which makes the 100% certainty requirement all the more difficult to attain:

> We are training a new generation of surgical residents as "Nintendo" surgeons, adept at the video-assisted operation working in the two-dimensional world of television. Unfortunately, our patients' problems are three dimensional, and often judgment is enhanced by tactile response. Sometimes the real nature of the pathologic findings can be appreciated only by holding tissue between the fingers. (Munson & Sanders, 1994, p. 741)

Attaining certainty is clearly not a passive task. Perception and action are tightly coupled. Surgeons use a variety of active techniques to reduce their risk. For example, they might follow along a tubular structure to its origins or flip the gallbladder from side to side to get a better understanding of the anatomy. The biliary tree region of the body, where the gallbladder is located, has a high incidence of unusual anatomy (extra ducts or unusually attached ducts), which makes surgeons all the more cautious in identifying anatomy in this area.

Clipping and Cutting Structures

The two structures that must be identified, clipped, and cut in this procedure are the cystic duct and the cystic artery. As dissection proceeded for this patient, eventually two structures were seen. The surgeons separated the first, smaller one from surrounding tissue and brought a clip applier into the abdomen. Two clips were applied; it was difficult to determine exactly which structures were included in the clips, because there was no clear view of the back side of the clip appliers. Next, a scissor instrument was brought in and this structure was severed. A dissector was introduced again, and the surgeon worked to clear tissue away from the larger structure. These movements caused concern for several surgeons whom we interviewed; they felt that this area was too close for comfort to the area where the common bile duct should be.

Off to the left side, the gallbladder suddenly burst open and bile flowed out; it is likely that the tear occurred where a grasper was retracting the gallbladder. The surgeons reacted as though the gallbladder tearing was an expected event, requiring thorough irrigation and suction but eliciting little change in overall approach. A suction/irrigator was brought into the abdomen to rinse and clean out the spilled material.

The second structure was then isolated further, clipped with clip appliers, and divided with scissors. The field was very bloody at this point. Just beside the place where the dissectors were working, the double-clipped stump of the second structure could be seen. After a few seconds, *this structure began to pulsate*, indicating that what had been cut was a blood vessel, probably the cystic artery. This pulsating stump remained in the visual field for 30 seconds or so; about half of the surgeons (six staff and three residents) who watched this case on videotape noted the pulsation. Additional material was then stripped away so that a single strand of tissue, of unknown significance, was all that remained connecting the gallbladder and the biliary tree. The operating surgeons washed off this last bloody strand and then pulled at different parts of it, trying to identify it.

Two structures had already been clipped and cut, and now a *third* structure became evident. The surgeons were uncertain about what had already been cut and what this last structure was. It was at this point in the operation that the greatest number of "I would just open..." statements were made by surgeons thinking aloud while watching the videotape. Added to the uncertainty over identification and the possibility of unusual anatomy was concern that the actions taken previously had accidentally injured the common bile duct, because the tissue was inflamed and because it had been difficult to see the tips of the clip appliers and scissors.

Risk Assessment

Judging what was safe was an ongoing activity. Beginning with the initial "I would just take a look and see," an incremental, one-step-at-a-time approach was often described by surgeons interviewed. Confidence in identification and potential for injury were judged at each step. This type of ongoing, dynamic decision making, reflecting a complex mingling of facts and risk assessment, is not typically studied in medical decision literature, which tends to focus on diagnosis as an event. Sunk cost reasoning, such as "I've gotten this far, I might as well continue," was evident in some justifications given for continuing laparoscopically.

Surgeons we interviewed talked about this safety judgment in terms of their comfort level; comfort was a well-established part of their language to justify and explain decisions. "If you're not comfortable, you should open" was a ubiquitous creed among those we interviewed. Surgeons kept assessing whether events were beginning to move outside their limits of knowledge or capability or their comfort level during interviews; this pointed to a significant aspect of competence related to *calibration*, which will be discussed in greater detail later. Two essential elements of surgeons' comfort level were (1) whether they could identify structures with 100% certainty and (2) the perceived likelihood of injury, especially to the common bile duct. This awareness of comfort level is self-regulatory behavior, which we will refer to as *metacognition*; it was a consistent and significant theme throughout our interviews.

The Field of Safe Travel

We have already discussed the active process by which surgeons seek out information and strive to prevent injury during laparoscopic surgery. Top-level goals, such as removal of the gallbladder and doing no harm,[2] are pursued during surgery using a range of well-taught techniques. In 1938, Gibson and Crooks introduced a concept, the *field of safe travel*, to describe the space before an automobile driver in which the car may move without hitting anything. The driver may or may not be aware of this field; the field exists regardless. This concept likewise is useful

---

[2] These goals constitute the highest level of an abstraction hierarchy we developed for a "system" of surgery.

to describe the active way that surgeons determine and evaluate constraints and pursue a safe path of progress.

We have already illustrated, in describing the 80-year-old woman's case, several examples of how surgeons stay within a field of safe travel. First, along the dimension of physical location, working too far away from the gallbladder can result in injury to the common bile duct. This is the physical field. The physical field of safe travel can be defined better by using a cholangiogram to determine the patient's biliary tree structure.

Affordances of tissues, that is, whether the gallbladder wall affords retraction without tearing, is a second dimension of the field of safe travel in surgery. Determining the boundaries on affordances involves an interaction between the choice of instrument and the degree of force the surgeon exerts. Surgeons learn to use what the tissue looks like and how the tissue responds to exploratory manipulation to perceive the actions that are required to achieve their goal.

Third, a less obvious dimension of the field of safe travel involves appreciation of hidden dangers. An example is using visualization of the back tine of clip appliers and scissors to make sure that no structures are being injured unintentionally. Without that visualization, a nearby blood vessel can be inadvertently nicked and result in a free-flowing internal bleed, as occurred in one of the other challenging cases we used for this research. Hidden dangers would often be made explicit if the operation were an open, large-incision procedure affording direct three-dimensional visual and tactile feedback. We hypothesize that surgeons who have had extensive experience with open procedures, before laparoscopy became the standard mode of removing gallbladders (around 1990), are more cognizant of the hidden dangers. They have worked more frequently with the fully exposed space that can only be constructed piecemeal through a laparoscope. In general, the field of safe travel is restricted in laparoscopic surgery, and opening expands this field.

Fourth, evaluating how one's own ability level is commensurate with the demands of a particular ongoing procedure, as reflected by past experience and an appreciation for what one does *not* know, must overlay the previously described dimensions to maintain a safe field of travel. This is the calibration of competence mentioned earlier.

Staying within the safe physical boundaries, applying force through appropriate instruments so as to minimize injury to healthy tissue, and appreciating hidden dangers all involve *prediction* of what injury might result from straying outside of the field of safe operation. Sometimes the injuries are immediate, as when a torn artery bleeds massively. Sometimes they are seen only when the patient returns 5 days after surgery with symptoms indicating an injured common bile duct. The ability to predict injuries, or their likelihood, and the willingness to acknowledge *low* levels of certainty in identifying structures, are both essential to being well calibrated.

Environmental Factors

There are also environmental considerations in evaluating a field of safe travel, defined by constraints *outside* the patient or the operating surgeon. Surgery is a team effort, and there is a definite structure to the team. The surgeons we interviewed were part of a training community in which supervising surgeons (known as *staff* or *attending physicians*) functioned as teachers and role models during surgery to resident surgeons in an apprenticeship type of relationship. Staff surgeons who are uncertain about their residents' ability to perform a challenging procedure safely may decide to take over and perform it themselves. Confidence in the other members of the surgical team, from the scrub nurse (who sometimes holds and moves the camera, a critical function) to the anesthesiologist, also influences surgeons' stated willingness to open the patient.

The other environmental aspect worthy of note here is the upheaval in the relationship between years of surgical experience and proficiency in performing laparoscopic procedures. Highly experienced older surgeons have had to learn laparoscopic techniques late in their career. Although they have developed a keen appreciation for the three-dimensional space in the abdominal cavity, learning to manipulate this space without direct vision and touch, possibly under the supervision of a much younger surgeon, has posed problems (Gaster, 1993). On the other hand, a resident surgeon training today may have very few opportunities to remove a gallbladder with direct vision and touch. Having attending surgeons who may be uncomfortable performing open procedures could cause a new type of tension in the operating room: a generation gap with unforeseen consequences.

There are other influences upon a surgical field of safe travel, too numerous to mention, which include tools, technological failures, and higher-level organizational constraints. We have presented this concept to show the flavor and the breadth of the complexity that surgeons deal with in making decisions, as well as to identify common ground with other domains of similar complexity.

The key ideas we have highlighted in the context of this challenging laparoscopic case are the requirement to identify structures with certainty, the importance of comfort level and hence calibration, and the field of safe travel in surgery as a unifying concept. The challenges of identifying anatomy with certainty and preventing injury in an elderly patient with severe inflammation, and the range of environmental influences upon this decision, make this a rich domain and problem space within which to explore and understand competence. This is an environment that involves potentially life-and-death situations for thousands of people every day.

Methods

We conducted a series of 20 interviews with general surgeons. In this section, we will describe the surgeons we interviewed, the case events that stimulated the data collected, the interview methods used, measures or variables, and analysis of the resulting verbal protocols.

The Surgeons

Ten interviewees were senior residents; five of these were in their fourth postgraduate year, and five were in their fifth postgraduate year.[3] Because the surgeons in this group had 8 or 9 years of medical training, we considered them to be a *journeyperson* group rather than a *novice* group. The other 10 surgeons were on the staff at local hospitals and had a range of 2 to 28 years of experience since completing residency. The mean number of years since residency was 10.1. There was a bimodal distribution: Three of the staff surgeons had more than 20 years of experience since residency, and the other seven surgeons had 6 or fewer years. Of the latter group, five surgeons had between 4 and 6 years since residency, and two surgeons had less. Both groups estimated how many laparoscopic cholecystectomies they had done. The mean estimate for the resident group was 70, and the mean for the staff group was 255.

---

[3] Postgraduate year reflects the number of years since graduating from a 4-year medical school. The general surgery residency is a 5-year program; fifth-year residents are called *chief residents*.

Table 1.1. *Case Events in an 80-Year-Old Woman's Laparoscopic Cholecystectomy*

Decision point 1: comfort level ratings, questions
   Gallbladder first seen: angry, red, distended

Decision point 2: comfort level ratings, questions
   Aspiration of tense gallbladder: gallbladder graspable
   Beginning dissection: decision to obtain a cholangiogram
     First structure: small, uncertain, clipped/cut
     Gallbladder bursts open, spills bile
     Second structure: artery clipped/cut, pulsation
     Third structure: bloody, uncertain, surgeon discomfort

Decision point 3: comfort level ratings, questions

Stimulus: Case Events

We conducted interviews structured around three challenging laparo-scopic cholecystectomy cases taken from a video library of one of the authors who is a practicing surgeon. Our aim was to present tough cases, with the rationale that only by presenting a challenge could we find out how surgeons think and propose to act in risky situations. This approach is a variation of Klein et al.'s (1989) critical decision method. Using videotape allowed us to compare surgeons' responses to events shown in the videos, thus providing a common frame for evaluating whether and how staff and residents differ in perceptual expertise and in their assessments. Two of the cases were presented at each interview due to time limitations. Only one case was presented to all 20 surgeons, that of the 80-year-old woman described in the previous section. This is also the only case analyzed in this chapter.

The videotaped events served as stimuli for knowledge elicitation. The events in the 80-year-old woman's case are shown in Table 1.1. Before any videotape was shown, we gave the surgeons preoperative information (i.e., the patient is an 80-year-old female who has had fever for 2 days; the ultrasound exam showed fluid and a thickened gallblad-der wall). We asked what additional information the surgeons would want before proceeding with surgery and how each piece of information would be used. At three predetermined *decision points* selected by a sur-geon working on this research as natural stopping points, we stopped the video and asked a set of questions (see Table 1.2). In addition, we asked the surgeons to rate their comfort level on a 7-point anchored scale (shown in Table 1.3), ranging from having no concerns (1) to indicating

Table 1.2. *Questions Asked at Each Decision Point*

---

1. What do you think is going on here? Are there any alternative interpretations you could make?
2. Do you have any concerns at this time? What are they?
3. What errors would inexperienced surgeons be likely to make in this situation? Are there any cues they might miss?
4. Can you think of a time in your previous experience when you faced a similar situation? What was it?
5. Can you give me a numerical rating, from 1 to 7, of your comfort level with continuing this procedure laparoscopically, using the anchored scale shown here?
6. Can you give me a numerical rating, from 1 to 7, of the skill level you think would be needed to complete this procedure laparoscopically based on the anchored scale shown here?
7. If I told you that the surgeon decided to open at this point (decided to begin this procedure as an open one), would you think that was a reasonable course of action?
8. Given that your overall goal is to remove the gallbladder safely, what are your short-term objectives at this time?
9. Are there any alternative courses of action that might work? Would you do anything differently than these surgeons?
10. Are there any other cues you see that are influencing your actions that you haven't mentioned yet? Are there cues that you expect to see that are not present? As the attending surgeon, are you satisfied that the structures have been identified?

---

that they would open the patient immediately (7). Accordingly, larger numbers indicate greater levels of *discomfort*.

In Table 1.1, note that the decision points were not evenly dispersed throughout the case. Between decision points 2 and 3, there were

Table 1.3. *Anchored Scale for Measuring Surgeons' Comfort Level*

Comfort level at continuing (or beginning) this case laparoscopically
1. No concern whatsoever (0%)*
2. Little concern (5%)
3. Increased concern (25%)
4. Moderate concern; 50/50 chance that it will need to be converted (50%)
5. Many concerns (75%)
6. Very seriously considering converting/beginning as an open procedure (95%)
7. Would convert/begin as an open procedure now (100%)

---

* Percentage indicates level of concern and probability that this procedure will have to be done open. Larger numbers indicate greater levels of discomfort.

15 minutes of videotape during which the dissection of all three structures was shown. During this time, the videotape itself was the primary stimulus; the interviewer asked follow-up questions but did not point out anything for commentary.

The Interview Procedure

We interviewed surgeons in the hospitals where they worked, typically in a library or a conference room. The interviews combined structured and unstructured elicitation. Decision points were the structured portions of each interview, with the predefined questions shown in Table 1.2. Unstructured elicitation occurred as the videotape was being watched; surgeons were asked to think aloud and provide continuous commentary on events seen on the videotape. We requested that the surgeons role-play, imagining that they were actually doing the case.[4] We audiotaped and later transcribed each interview.

Measures

We developed two sets of measures (or dependent variables), those that were tied to specific videotape events and those that were noted any time they appeared in a transcript. Variables were developed initially and applied in a process whereby two readers evaluated each transcript, highlighting sections of text where a variable, such as *prediction* or *if/then rule* applied. Each variable was well defined for the reader. The two readers then compared results in a meeting in which each variable had to be justified, and a final analysis for that transcript was agreed upon. As we applied the set of variables, readers suggested new aspects of variables and entirely new variables in order to capture the verbal protocols more completely and descriptively. For instance, the metacognition variable was developed *after* analysis began to capture what we found to be consistent discussions of comfort level, risk, avoiding hidden dangers, or monitoring/controlling behavior. When all 20 transcripts had been initially analyzed and a final measurement scheme was in hand, one reader reread each transcript to apply these

---

[4] Getting into this role was difficult in the few cases in which the interviewees stated that they would not be in the situation shown on the tape. We handled this for residents by having them imagine that their attending physician directed this action, and for staff surgeons by having them imagine that they had been called in to help on this case in progress.

variables consistently. There were 23 variables in all, each of which had a range of responses identified with a particular code. In this chapter, we will limit the discussion to a cluster of variables related to metacognition findings.

Measures Tied to Specific Videotape Events. The variables tied to videotaped events that will be discussed here are comfort level ratings and whether surgeons saw the pulsation of the cystic artery after this structure was cut. The comfort level scale, as presented to the surgeons, is shown in Table 1.3. Seeing the cystic artery pulsate was significant because it was the only information available during this case for identifying one of the three structures with certainty.

Event-Independent Measures. Five general clusters of variables, comprising 15 variables, were applied throughout the transcripts: *conversion to an open procedure, constraints, metacognition, expertise,* and *goals.* The conversion and metacognition variables will be discussed in this chapter.

The conversion variables were used to note whenever the surgeons stated that they would convert the case or might be converting it right now. When the statement was made, the reason and the strength ("maybe" vs. "definitely") were documented. This (originally) dependent variable will be treated as a blocking variable in the results and discussion, contrasting the group of surgeons who said they would convert (the openers) with those who did not (the nonopeners).

Although metacognition will be defined and discussed in greater detail later, for illustrating the variable, consider it to refer to both self-knowledge and self-regulation of thinking (Gott, LaJoie, & Lesgold, 1991). Metacognition was operationalized as a variable to describe five general categories of verbalizations:

1. *General comfort level*: whenever surgeons mentioned their own or the operating surgeons' comfort level. For instance, "If surgeons don't feel comfortable doing acute gallbladders laparoscopically, then they should do what they feel comfortable with."
2. *Risk involved*: whenever surgeons discussed qualitative or quantitative risk, such as "She's got an increased risk of developing an infection postoperatively" or "Unrecognized duodenal injury has a forty to fifty percent lethality rate."

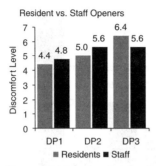
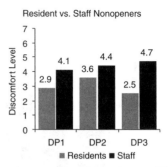

Figure 1.2 Mean comfort level ratings for openers and nonopeners. Higher numbers indicate greater levels of discomfort. At the left are the ratings for the five residents and four staff surgeons who decided to open. At the right are the ratings for the five residents and six staff surgeons who decided not to open. DP = decision point.

examining openers' and nonopeners' comfort levels at decision point 2 ($F(1, 19) = 15.1, p = .001$) and at decision point 3 ($F(1, 19) = 16.1, p = .001$) were significant. We also expected that staff surgeons would generally be more comfortable than residents in this case, reflecting their greater experience. However, there were no statistical staff–resident differences in comfort-level ratings at any of the decision points.

Figure 1.2 shows that both staff and resident openers became less comfortable across time, with the greatest discomfort at decision point 3. Two different trends are apparent for the nonopeners. The staff nonopeners were becoming progressively less comfortable over time, although they were still more comfortable than their counterparts who opened. The resident nonopeners, on the other hand, were more comfortable than any other group, and they were *most* comfortable at decision point 3; this was the *least* comfortable point for all of the other surgeons.

A two-way analysis of variance of comfort-level ratings was conducted at each decision point, contrasting the two levels of opener and the two levels of experience. At decision point 3, a marginal two-way interaction was found for surgeon type (resident vs. staff) and for openers versus nonopeners, $F(1, 15) = 3.7, p = .07$. The value of these numbers is questionable due to the small number of surgeons in the sample, but they illustrate what is visually obvious. That is, resident and staff openers are quite similar in comfort level at decision point 3, whereas resident and staff nonopeners are quite different from each other. Possible

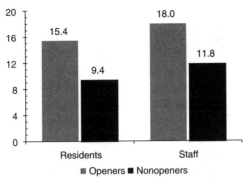

Figure 1.3 The mean number of metacognition statements by residents and staff surgeons.

reasons for this difference will be discussed shortly, in light of all the data presented in this chapter.

Metacognition Variable

We found no overall resident–staff differences in the number of metacognition statements made, but we did find differences between openers and nonopeners. A one-way analysis of variance showed that openers made more metacognitive statements than nonopeners, $F(1, 19) = 4.7$, $p = .04$. These differences are shown for residents and staff surgeons in Figure 1.3.

The resident opener group made more metacognitive statements on average (15.4) than the resident nonopener group (9.4). The same basic relationship holds between staff openers (18) and nonopeners (11.8). It makes sense that surgeons who said they would open made more statements that reflect an understanding of the risk involved in this case, as the metacognitive statements do, than did the nonopeners.

Pulsation of the Cystic Artery

In the earlier case description, the pulsation of the cystic artery provided the most concrete evidence for identification of any of the structures in this case. Staff surgeons noticed this pulsation more frequently than did residents: Six staff and three residents saw it. Figure 1.4 is a diagram breaking down the number of residents and staff into opener versus nonopener categories and showing how many in each group saw the

		Comfort level	Saw pulsation of artery?	Comfort level	Metacognitive statements
9 Openers	5 Residents	6.4	1 saw	7.0	19
			4 did not see	6.2	13
	4 Staff	5.6	1 saw	6.5	26
			3 did not see	5.3	14
11 Nonopeners	5 Residents	2.5	2 saw	3.0	13
			3 did not see	2.3	7
	6 Staff	4.7	5 saw	3.9	10
			1 did not see	6.0	16

Figure 1.4 Flow chart showing how the openers and nonopeners divided into subsets of staff and residents on seeing the pulsating cystic artery. The numbers in columns reflect the mean comfort-level ratings at decision point 3 of the group in each subset. Higher numbers indicate greater levels of discomfort. The numbers on the far right indicate the median number of metacognition statements for each subset or the number for the individual represented by the subset.

artery pulsation. Beginning with the resident openers at the top of the figure, one saw the pulsating artery and four did not. The staff openers showed a similar trend: One saw the pulsating artery and three did not. Because seeing the pulsation is a way to increase certainty about the identification of structures, we would expect that those who did *not* see the pulsation would have a less accurate situation assessment, would have a resultant lower comfort level, and would be more likely to say they would convert, as was the case. The left panel of Figure 1.2 shows that openers did indeed have greater discomfort than nonopeners.

If this logic holds, those surgeons who saw the pulsation would be more comfortable and less likely to open. Seeing the pulsation would tend to increase their comfort level with the identification and make them less likely to say they would open. The lowest section of Figure 1.4 shows that five out of six staff nonopeners did indeed see the pulsating artery. Thus, seeing the pulsation was clearly related to not opening for the staff surgeons. Overall, fewer openers than nonopeners saw the pulsating artery: 2 of 9 openers (22%) and 7 of 11 nonopeners (64%) saw it. Although five of six (83%) staff nonopeners saw the pulsation, no such trend is clear with the resident nonopeners (40%). The average comfort level ratings of this group, the resident nonopeners, reflected much *greater* comfort (see Figure 1.2).

Another part of the story can be seen in the number of metacognitive statements made by each of these four groups. Figure 1.4 shows the average comfort level ratings and the median number of metacognitive statements that each of the subgroups made.[5] The resident opener group, most of whom did not see the pulsating artery, made more metacognitive statements on average (15.4) than the resident nonopener group (9.4). The same relationship holds between staff openers (18.0) and nonopeners (11.8). This relationship is shown directly in Figure 1.2. Overall, a one-way analysis of variance showed that openers made more metacognitive statements than nonopeners, $F(1, 19) = 4.7, p = .04$. There were no statistical differences between resident and staff surgeons in the number of metacognition statements.

The three resident nonopeners who did not see the pulsating artery had a median number of metacognition statements of seven (see Figure 1.4); individual numbers were five, seven, and nine. These were by far the lowest number of all the subgroups, suggesting either that these surgeons are not aware of the risks that other surgeons see in this situation or that they are simply not verbalizing the risks. It might be argued that these resident nonopeners may not have the same level of competence as the other groups. This lower competence is reflected in an apparent insensitivity to potential risks. This insensitivity is indicated by the high degree of comfort and low level of self-monitoring without evidence of perceptual skill (e.g., identifying the cystic artery) that might justify that confidence.

Discussion

In laboratory research there is a tendency to parse cognition into elemental processes, and researchers tend to identify themselves with particular pieces of this cognitive puzzle. For example, laboratories or researchers focus on perception, motor control, decision making, problem solving, or metacognition. This reductionistic strategy has been very productive for analyzing a physical phenomenon where extrapolations from the pieces have increased our understanding of the whole. However, there is increasing evidence from numerous sources that this strategy may break down in the face of many natural phenomena. For these phenomena, the assumptions of linearity that support extrapolation from

---

[5] The variability in the number of these statements was large, ranging from 4 to 26; hence the median number was used to represent the group in Figure 1.4.

parts to the whole are not appropriate. For these nonlinear phenomena, essential emergent properties (such as competence) are not found among the pieces. Further, the pieces (such as metacognition) tend to lose their distinction when viewed within the whole. Early in our studies of the conversion decision, we began to frame the question in terms of metacognition. This decision was stimulated by the many comments that surgeons made about their comfort level. These comments indicated a kind of mindfulness or self-monitoring that is generally associated with the construct of metacognition. However, as the analysis progressed, it became harder and harder to distinguish metacognition from cognition. Was metacognition above the thought processes as an *executive control function*, as it is often termed (Gott et al., 1991)? Was it occurring after cognition, a reflection evaluating previous decisions? Was it a glue binding the cognitive processes together? Or was it simply the thought processes themselves?

Flavell and Wellman (1977) have suggested some ways to parse the concept of metacognition. They distinguish between metacognitive *experience* and metacognitive *knowledge*. Their article deals primarily with memory research and the concept of *metamemory*. They illustrate metacognitive experience with the "tip of the tongue" phenomenon, in which you are aware that you have the knowledge called for and that it will soon be recalled but you experience a temporary blockage. In surgery, an experiential in-the-moment reaction to a situation might be "I am really not comfortable with this situation" or "There is no way to identify structures in that bloody mess. I am completely lost." In these examples, the surgeon's feeling of discomfort or of being lost might precede the recognition of the source of those feelings.

The second aspect, metacognitive *knowledge*, is how we use what we already know (both declarative and procedural knowledge) to guide our thoughts and actions. Flavell and Wellman describe four general classes of metacognitive/metamemory knowledge derived from their studies of memory performance of children. The four classes (described using examples relevant to surgery) are (1) knowledge about tasks, such as knowing how difficult and time-consuming it can be to insert a small catheter into the cystic duct to perform a cholangiogram and how this may impact the decision of whether to do it; (2) knowledge of self (person variables), including knowledge about one's own knowledge, experience, capabilities, and proficiency; (3) knowledge of strategies that can be used to enhance performance, such as always dissecting from known to unknown structures; and (4) interactions between the preceding three categories of information, such as recognizing one's own inexperience in a particular task and therefore asking someone else to help perform it or choosing a strategy with reference to one's own ability.

Brown (1978) has extended Flavell and Wellman's idea of metacognitive knowledge and has discussed how it is either *static* knowledge, existing in factual form as it might be directly verbalized by someone who is asked about the task, or *strategic* knowledge, actively applied to regulate and correct thought processes. Strategic activities include *planning*, or deciding how to approach a problem; *predicting*, as when estimating the quantitative value of an outcome; *guessing* what might be the appropriate answer or decision; and *monitoring* how well a goal is being attained.

The breadth of metacognition, as Flavell and Wellman and Brown have conceptualized it, presents difficulties in trying to identify metacognitive statements in interview transcripts. Almost everything in these transcripts could have been framed to fit some form of the previous descriptions. More specific ideas about metacognition are needed, and they can be found in more recent work examining metacognition in training and in decision making.

For example, Baker and Brown (1984) abstracted two categories of activities that they feel are pivotal to understanding metacognition: (1) knowledge about cognition and (2) regulation of cognition. This distinction is acknowledged and supported in other, more recent descriptions of metacognition. For instance, McGuinness (1990, p. 302) states that metacognition "refers loosely to knowledge about, and control over, one's own cognitive system." Gott et al. (1991) call it a "broad term for both self-knowledge and self-regulation of thinking." Finally, Nelson and Narens (1994) present a framework of metacognition in memory (metamemory) in which a *metalevel* mechanism monitors and controls an *object level* of processing via a dominance relationship. Thus, these two aspects of metacognition, knowledge of our thought processes (monitoring) and control or regulation of them, seem to be universal in current conceptualizations of the topic.

In work that is particularly relevant to this study because it attempts to describe naturalistic behavior, Cohen et al. (1996) argue that using metacognitive skills for proficient problem solving and decision making involves two key activities corresponding to the monitoring–regulation distinction just described. The activities are (1) critiquing, which extends the monitoring aspect to *evaluation* of that knowledge, and (2) correcting, or regulating behavior through control actions. Cohen et al. explain situations involving time-stressed decision making in naval surface ship warfare with a *metarecognitional* model that extends recognitional decision processes (i.e., Klein, 1989) to account for how naval officers develop an explanatory story of a situation and modify it over time. Critiquing and correcting occur in an iterative, or cyclical, manner. These activities are assumed to be on a metalevel that is functionally but not structurally distinct from object-level processes (Nelson & Narens, 1994); at the object level, situation models and plans are developed. Critiquing activities in the Cohen et al. model include testing a situational model for incompleteness, discovering conflicts, and recognizing unreliable assumptions. Correcting involves collecting more data, activating additional information from long-term memory, adjusting assumptions, and/or selecting an explanation. In Cohen et al.'s research, goals of the domain include understanding the intentions of an enemy who could possibly be taking several different courses of aggression. Although some aspects of this model do not relate well to surgery, the idea of critiquing and correcting in a cyclical process is important.

It would seem that in order for metacognition to exist, it should have a separate function from "regular" cognition. This does not seem to be true: Few authors describe regular cognition as being separate from metacognition. Cohen et al. imply that object-level activities, such as planning and developing a situational model, are distinct from the critiquing and correcting functions. However, where does the plan development process end and the revision and critiquing processes begin?

Surgeons acquire knowledge about anatomy, physiology, boundaries of laboratory values, surgical techniques, and characteristics of illnesses that become part of their working knowledge, an object level of knowledge if you will. In our interviews, surgeons used this knowledge to assess the situation, make predictions, invoke rules, and assess risk and personal comfort level. In analyzing these interviews, we wonder whether it is useful to distinguish between functions of object-level knowledge and metalevel knowledge. Perhaps it is more useful to understand the *relationship between* self-knowledge and situation knowledge. Is metacognition entitled to a privileged executive status simply because it reflects knowledge of our own knowledge rather than knowledge of a system or situation? The manner in which personal comfort assessment and risk assessment integrate knowledge of the surgeon's state with knowledge of the patient's state and other situational factors highlights the relative nature of perception and action. Self-monitoring and situation monitoring are mutually dependent in determining the

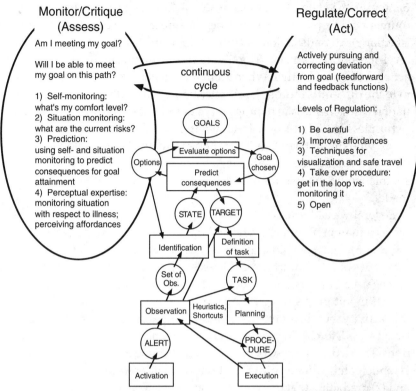

Figure 1.5 Rasmussen's decision ladder illustrates that metacognition is a useful way of viewing goal-directed action in complex work environments. The framework of monitoring and regulating depicts the relationship between the variables in the interview study. Perceiving, thinking, and acting are shown relative to assessing the situation and the self with respect to goal achievement. The left side, assessing, corresponds with the left side and the uppermost levels of the decision ladder, while the right side, acting, corresponds with the right side of the ladder. (Decision ladder figure from Rasmussen et al., 1994; reprinted by permission © John Wiley & Sons, Inc.)

safe field of operation. The meaning or significance of an event, action, or situation is determined by a relationship between the situation and the actor's capabilities, as reflected in constructs such as Gibson's (1979/1986) *affordance*.

Figure 1.5 illustrates the dynamic coupling between monitoring and regulating that was evident in the surgeons' verbal protocols. First, consider monitoring. Cohen et al. (1996) call this *critiquing*. It can also be called *assessing*. It involves being attuned to, and evaluating, task-relevant information. We observe information, assess it, and form a picture of the state of the system. As awareness of the external environment develops, we develop a personal reaction to it: a degree of satisfaction or dissatisfaction, whether things are as expected or not, or a level of comfort or anxiety. The situation assessment and the personal reaction feed on each other. When a situation generates discomfort, tuning in to the discomfort through self-attention in turn influences further situation assessment. When things seem normal, there may be a tendency to turn less attention toward the self; it is possible that surgeons in our study who did not say they would open saw the 80-year-old woman's case as meeting the criteria for a normal laparoscopic approach. If so, this would explain the lower number of metacognitive statements made.

Several variables used in this research to code surgeons' transcripts reflect situation monitoring and self-monitoring (refer to the left oval in Figure 1.5). The most obvious one is the metacognition variable, with its categories of (1) comfort level, (2) assessing risks, (3) predicting injuries or negative outcomes that could result from a particular action, and (4) self-monitoring strategies. All of the prediction variables fall within this activity, because predicting and anticipating are monitoring projected ahead, foreseeing the natural consequences of current states or actions. The two main types of prediction that emerged from our analyses – (1) anticipating difficulty in dissection and/or identification of structures and (2) predicting that this patient would sustain an unintended injury – illustrate how surgeons monitor a current situation to predict possible consequences.

Another variable was perceptual expertise; this variable overlapped with prediction of consequences. Two areas also emerged from statements coded under this variable: (1) using information about the progression of disease to add to or update a model of the situation and (2) using perceptual information to infer whether the situation would afford dissection, exposure, grasping, and other actions necessary to complete this procedure. These perceptual statements reflect monitoring of the patient's state and of the implications of the patient's state for desired action. This latter activity provides a bridge to regulation activities, shown on the right side of Figure 1.5.

When monitoring one's own state and the situation revealed either a disconnect from a desired state or a projected disconnect, surgeons referred to what can be called *regulation activities* as means of correction. The levels of regulation shown in Figure 1.5 do not constitute a hierarchy, but merely show that there is a range of the *extent* of action that is taken for regulation, from simply being more careful to converting to an open procedure. The interaction between monitoring and regulation is continuous. When surgeons said, for instance, "I would be more careful," both heightened monitoring for feedback and modification of movements are implied in a highly coupled way. When it became clear that the distended gallbladder would not afford grasping, all surgeons agreed that it was time to aspirate the gallbladder so that it could be grasped; evaluation of the gallbladder's graspability and recommended action to improve it were linked by every surgeon we interviewed. (This link implies monitoring and regulating of the situation but not of the self; hence most authors would not say that metacognition was involved.) Further, realizing that the anatomy was too obscured by inflammation to see structures and therefore assessing the risk of injury as being high led to suggestions for using techniques for better visualization and for mitigating the risk of injury (i.e., always moving from known to unknown structures).

Because we typically asked the surgeon interviewed to role-play as an attending surgeon, acting as the assistant to a resident operating under his or her supervision, stating that he or she would now take over the procedure was another form of regulation. This too illustrates the close relationship between monitoring and regulating, because taking over was typically done to ascertain better feedback about how tissues felt, hence providing more information with which to evaluate the situation. Taking over the procedure is a way surgeons can insert themselves more directly into the information loop rather than monitoring it from the assistant's position (the assistant retracts the gallbladder, providing tension on structures so that the operating surgeon can manipulate them).

Finally, at the most dramatic level of regulation, a surgeon can decide to convert, changing the entire approach to the operation. The following dialogue indicates how one resident surgeon described the benefits of opening:

SURGEON: You can still have an injury, but you have much more control doing it open.

INTERVIEWER: Control over fixing an injury?

SURGEON: Control over, yeah, you can get better exposure, you can get better retraction, you can feel things with your fingers that you can't feel with the instruments. You can use different instruments. A lot of times, it's much more technically demanding doing the cholangiogram laparoscopically, because you don't have as fine a feel through the catheter, and a lot of times it's easier to do a cholangiogram open technique than closed.

In this passage the resident focuses on control, which is a particularly appropriate way to describe the benefits of opening in light of a monitoring/regulating view. Opening allows a more accurate assessment of the situation, through better exposure and retraction and through feel, as well as greater ease in doing a cholangiogram. All of these things mitigate the risk of injury, because injuries often follow from incomplete (assessment of) information.

A sketch of Rasmussen's decision ladder (Rasmussen, Pejtersen, & Goodstein, 1994) has been included in Figure 1.5 to make the point that, depending upon one's definition of the *system state* node, all of the monitoring and regulating activities just described could be mapped onto this model. The left side and upper portion (predicting consequences in light of goals) of the decision ladder show information processing activities and states related to monitoring. The right side of the ladder depicts various stages in selecting, planning, and executing actions, which correspond to regulation. Shunts across the ladder show the adaptive and cyclical nature of these processes. Thus, monitoring and regulation of the situation and the self could just as easily be depicted in the flexible way that the decision ladder allows characterization of skill-, rule-, and knowledge-based cognitive control (Rasmussen, 1983).

Another way to view monitoring and regulation activities can be found in control theory. Carver and Scheier (1981) have developed a control-theoretic approach to human self-regulatory behavior that has gained a prominent position in the work motivation literature. In their model, it is assumed that self-regulation requires an individual to focus attention on his or her own behavior and that comparison between a goal (or behavioral standard) and current performance initiates controlling, or self-regulatory, processes to correct any discrepancy that might exist. This process in humans is likened to a negative feedback loop control system such as a thermostat, where the discrepancy between current temperature and the set point initiates a control action to reduce the discrepancy. However, surgeons use prediction and anticipation to project whether a course of action will lead to goal accomplishment or will result in deviation from the goal. Such feedforward actions are not accounted for in the negative feedback loop model that Carver and

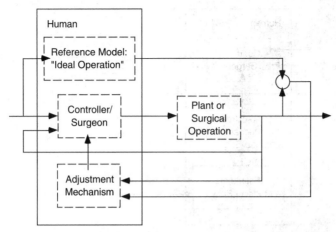

Figure 1.6 The model-reference style of adaptive control includes expectations for a *normal* or *ideal* surgery as a reference against which progress is monitored. Deviations from these expectations (surprises) result in adjustments to the mode of operation.

Scheier propose, but they should be incorporated in a control-theoretic model of monitoring and regulation.

Adaptive control models seem particularly well suited as an analogy for processes of monitoring and regulation. These models include the basic negative feedback loop just described, but they add other loops in which the control strategy is adapted according to how the system state is assessed (e.g., see Slotine & Li, 1991). Two general styles of adaptive control, the model-reference method and the self-tuning method, are illustrated in Figures 1.6 and 1.7. Model-reference control, as represented by Figure 1.6, can be interpreted for surgery in terms of an *ideal operation* to which a surgeon (the controller) refers and compares the current situation. The *plant* in this figure is the surgical operation. As a surgeon realizes through monitoring activity that the reference model is not being met, that is, realizes that vision is too obscured by inflammation and bleeding to continue safely, adaptation adjusts the approach to bring the situation in line with the reference model. This adjustment for surgery could include any of the regulatory actions listed in the right oval of Figure 1.5, ranging from being careful to opening.

Adaptive control systems can also be designed with a self-tuning mechanism, as shown in Figure 1.7. Self-tuning involves an *estimator*, which in surgery can be considered a model of the patient. The estimator continuously monitors and estimates the *plant parameters*, or the patient's state, based on prior interaction with the patient (or input and

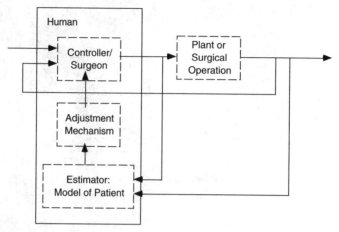

Figure 1.7 The self-tuning regulator style of adaptive control couples the dual goals of assessment and performance. The *estimator* loop represents an ongoing evaluation of the situation that results in adjustments to the performance mode in response to changing assessments of the situation.

output of the plant). This estimate of the patient's state modifies the control actions that follow, which yield a new estimate, and the process continues indefinitely. For example, attempting and failing to grasp a tense, distended gallbladder changes the assessment of the affordances of the situation and influences further control activities accordingly. Evidence for both an internal reference (normative expectations about how the surgery ought to proceed) and an internal model of the patient (expectations about the implications of age or disease state) are contained in the verbalizations of surgeons we interviewed.

In relation to considerations of the separability of object-level and meta-level cognition it is important to note that the two loops, the negative feedback loop and the adaptation loop, are not separable in observable activity. The first loop, which is the inside loop from the plant to the controller in both Figure 1.6 and Figure 1.7, is the error signal with regard to the goal. The second loop, the adaptation loop, causes a modification of control *strategies* in response to the observed system characteristics. In one sense, the first loop could be called cognition and the second loop metacognition. But the multiple loops are intertwined in actual activity.

The boxes in Figures 1.6 and 1.7 are dashed to emphasize that these are not "substances" in the head. These boxes represent constructs that may be useful to the analyst in thinking about the dynamic, but this distinction is a convenience for scientific dialogue and not a fact of the system. There is a single dynamic that spans human and environment. That is, every perception, decision, or action is influenced by every box (including the plant). Behavior is a dynamic over the human/environment/work system. Constructs like competence and expertise represent global properties of the stability of this dynamic. It is important to appreciate that there may be many stable (competent) solutions over this dynamic. One surgeon may achieve stability by opening to compensate for inexperience with the constraints of the laparoscopic procedure. Another surgeon may maintain stability within the restrictions of the laparoscopic procedure. On the other hand, there are many paths to instability – poorly calibrated expectations about surgery, an inaccurate assessment of the patient's state, or clumsiness in manipulating the instruments.

The key to stability (competence) will not be found within any of the boxes or ovals in the diagrams. It is an emergent property of the dynamic – a dynamic that is often significantly altered when phenomena like surgical decision making are translated into narrow laboratory paradigms or into component models of cognitive processes. Thus, in our attempts to understand competence, field studies and naturalistic observations will play a critical role in defining the problem. For now, a top-down, holistic approach to the phenomenon must lead. If we are clever and careful observers, we may eventually generate some interesting hypotheses and we may discover how to move this question into the laboratory so that we can bring the technology of experimentation to bear on these hypotheses.

In sum, this work has helped us to appreciate the rich coupling of cognitive processes that determine the dynamics of performance in a complex work domain like surgery. This work has helped us to appreciate that constructs like metacognition reflect dimensions of the dynamic but not of distinct processes. Further, evaluative constructs like competence seem to reflect global properties of the dynamic. This dynamic reflects relations over the capabilities of the perception–action system and the demands of the work situation. Thus, competent surgeons must be able to appreciate the situation relative to their specific limitations in order to navigate within the safe field of operation.

References

Baker, L., & Brown, A. L. (1984). Metacognitive skills and reading. In P. D. Pearson (Ed.), *Handbook of reading research* (pp. 353–394). New York: Longman.

Brown, A. L. (1978). Knowing when, where, and how to remember: A problem of metacognition. In R. Glaser (Ed.), *Advances in instructional psychology* (Vol. 1, pp. 77–165). Hillsdale, NJ: Erlbaum.

Carver, C. S., & Scheier, M. F. (1981). *Attention and self-regulation: A control-theory approach to human behavior.* New York: Springer-Verlaag.

Cohen, M., Freeman, J., & Wolf, S. (1996). Metarecognition in time-stressed decision making: Recognizing, critiquing, and correcting. *Human Factors, 38,* 206–219.

Cuschieri, A. (1995). Whither minimal access surgery: Tribulations and expectations. *The American Journal of Surgery, 169,* 9–19.

Flavell, J. H., & Wellman, H. M. (1977). Metamemory. In R. V. Kail, Jr., & J. W. Hagen (Eds.), *Perspectives on the development of memory and cognition* (pp. 3–33). Hillsdale, NJ: Erlbaum.

Gaster, B. (1993). The learning curve. *Journal of the American Medical Association, 270*(11), 1280.

Gibson, J. J. (1979/1986). *The ecological approach to visual perception.* Boston: Houghton Mifflin.

Gibson, J. J., & Crooks, L. (1938). A theoretical field analysis of automobile driving. *American Journal of Psychology, 51,* 453–471.

Gott, S. P., LaJoie, S. P., & Lesgold, A. (1991). Problem solving in technical domains: How mental models and metacognition affect performance. In R. F. Dillon & J. W. Pellegrino (Eds.), *Instruction: Theoretical and applied perspectives* (pp. 107–117). New York: Praeger.

Greene, F. L. (1995). Minimal access surgery and the "golden period" for conversion. *Surgical Endoscopy, 9,* 11.

Klein, G. A. (1989). Recognition-primed decisions. In W. B. Rouse (Ed.), *Advances in man-machine systems research* (Vol. 5, pp. 47–92). Greenwich, CT: JAI Press.

Klein, G. A., Calderwood, R., & McGregor, D. (1989). Critical decision method for eliciting knowledge. *IEEE Systems, Man, and Cybernetics, 19,* 462–472.

McGuinness, C. (1990). Talking about thinking: The role of metacognition in teaching thinking. In K. J. Gilhooly, M. T. G. Keane, R. H. Logie, & G. Erdos (Eds.), *Lines of thinking: Reflections on the psychology of thought* (Vol. 2, pp. 301–312). New York: Wiley.

Munson, J. L., & Sanders, L. E. (1994). Cholecystectomy: Open cholecystectomy revisited. *Surgical Clinics of North America, 74,* 741–754.

Nelson, T. O., & Narens, L. (1994). Why investigate metacognition? In J. Metcalf & A. P. Shimamura (Eds.), *Metacognition* (pp. 1–25). Cambridge, MA: MIT Press.

Rasmussen, J. (1983). Skills, rules, and knowledge: Signals, signs, and symbols, and other distinctions in human performance models. *IEEE Transactions on Systems, Man, and Cybernetics, SMC-13,* 257–266.

Rasmussen, J., Pejtersen, A. M., & Goodstein, L. P. (1994). *Cognitive systems engineering.* New York: Wiley.

Sanderson, P. M., Scott, J. P. P., Johnston, P., Mainzer, J., Watanabe, L. M., & James, J. M. (1994). MacSHAPA and the enterprise of exploratory sequential data analysis (ESDA). *International Journal of Human Computer Studies, 41,* 633–668.

Satava, R. M. (1993). Surgery 2001: A technologic framework for the future. *Surgical Endoscopy, 7*, 111–113.

Schrenk, P., & Woisetschlager, W. (1995). Laparoscopic cholecystectomy: Cause of conversions in 1,300 patients and analysis of risk factors. *Surgical Endoscopy, 9*, 25–28.

Slotine, J. J. E., & Li, W. (1991). *Applied nonlinear control.* Englewood Cliffs, NJ: Prentice Hall.

Southern Surgeons' Club (1991). A prospective analysis of 1,518 laparoscopic cholecystectomies. *New England Journal of Medicine, 324*, 1073–1078.

Stewart, L., & Way, L. W. (1995). Bile duct injuries during laparoscopic cholecystectomy. *Archives of Surgery, 130*, 1123–1128.

Way, L. W. (1992). Bile duct injury during laparoscopic cholecystectomy. *Annals of Surgery, 119*, 195.

2   Competence in Weather Forecasting

Rebecca M. Pliske, Beth Crandall, and Gary Klein

In recent years technological innovation has dramatically transformed the tools available to weather forecasters. Today's forecasters often find themselves overwhelmed by the sheer volume of computer products and displays that are now available (e.g., radar images, satellite pictures, computer-generated models). In this chapter, we describe a study we completed with weather forecasters that examined the development of competent performance in this context.

Weather forecasters have been studied for many years by both judgment and decision researchers and cognitive science researchers. Although a review of all this work is beyond the scope of this chapter, before describing our own research we briefly summarize some of the previous research conducted with weather forecasters. According to Stewart and Lusk (1994), the performance of a forecaster will depend on three factors: the environment about which the forecasts are being made (how predictable is it?), the information system that brings data about the environment to the forecaster (how reliable is the information provided?), and the forecaster's cognitive system (the forecaster's perceptual and judgmental processes). They point out that some weather phenomena are much more predictable than others (e.g., tomorrow's high temperature versus the size of the hailstones that will be produced by an approaching severe storm) and that some sources of information are more reliable than others (e.g., human observers are more

This research was supported by a contract from Armstrong Research Laboratory, Brooks Air Force Base, Texas. It was sponsored by the Air Weather Service, Scott Air Force Base, Illinois. We thank Anna Rowe and Carol Weaver for their help in obtaining the cooperation of the participants for this project. We also thank David Klinger, Robert Hutton, and Betsy Knight for their help in data collection and analysis.

reliable than electronic sensors for describing cloud cover). Stewart and his colleagues (Stewart, Heideman, Moninger, & Reagan-Cirincione, 1992) have also shown that forecasters use only a subset of the available information, and as the amount of information used increases, so does the unreliability of the forecasts.

Other research with forecasters described in the judgment literature has focused on *calibration*, which is defined as the extent to which decision makers' confidence matches their accuracy when making a set of judgments. Although many laypeople might disagree, judgment researchers have demonstrated that weather forecasters are well calibrated (Murphy & Winkler, 1977). For example, if a forecaster predicts a 60% chance of rain for a city, then rain is typically reported about 60% of the time.

Cognitive scientists have also studied weather forecasters. For example, Hoffman (1991) conducted interviews with 10 meteorologists in order to develop recommendations for the design of expert systems to support weather forecasters. Hoffman concluded that forecasters develop initial mental models based on the information presented to them on their various displays. These initial mental models imply various hypotheses, which the meteorologists then proceed to test. The particular type of information sought out by a particular meteorologist depends on the weather scenario for a given day.

The previous research conducted with weather forecasters gave us a starting point for our work with weather forecasters. We were funded by the U.S. Air Force (USAF) to conduct a cognitive task analysis of weather forecasters in order to provide recommendations on how to improve forecasting performance. Cognitive task analysis attempts to describe the cognitive activities that underlie an experienced person's job or task performance. In the past decade, the USAF has made an enormous investment in the new technologies available to support weather forecasting in an attempt to offset the effects of reductions in senior-level personnel. Unfortunately, weather forecasting performance has declined rather than improved since the introduction of many of these new technologies.

Our USAF sponsors were concerned that forecasters may have become overly reliant on computer models when developing their forecasts. These models are meant to be only one of many sources of information considered by the forecaster. A similar finding, called the *automation bias*, has been documented in other high-tech domains (Mosier & Skitka, 1996; Mosier, Skitka, & Heers, 1996). Mosier and her colleagues have found that some pilot errors result from overreliance on automated systems.

The majority of USAF weather personnel work in base weather stations that are equipped with all the latest technology available to support weather forecasters (e.g., Doppler radar, satellite imagery, and state-of-the-art decision support systems). These forecasters are referred to as *in-garrison forecasters*, and their job is to provide weather information to support air operations. Other USAF weather personnel work on cadre weather teams that are dedicated to supporting operational U.S. Army units (artillery, tanks, etc.), Special Operation units, and Army Ranger units. These forecasters work solely with tactical weather equipment and are referred to as *tactical forecasters*. We studied both types of forecasters for this project, which is described in detail in Pliske et al. (1997). In this chapter, we describe the results of our research with in-garrison forecasters and with National Weather Service (NWS) forecasters.

This research was guided by the Naturalistic Decision Making (NDM) theoretical perspective, which studies how people use their experience to make decisions in field settings. The NDM perspective investigates the strategies people use in performing complex, ill-structured, and high-stakes tasks under time pressure and uncertainty, and in the context of team and organizational constraints (Klein, Orasanu, Calderwood, & Zsambok, 1993; Zsambok & Klein, 1997). In many dynamic, uncertain, and fast-paced environments, there is no single right way to make decisions. Thus, NDM researchers typically study experts to define quality decision making and describe good decision-making processes. Researchers using the NDM framework have examined expert performance with a wide variety of professionals such as firefighters (Klein, Calderwood, & Clinton-Cirocco, 1986), critical care nurses (Crandall & Getchell-Reiter, 1993), weapons directors (Klinger et al., 1993), anti–air warfare command and control officers (Kaempf, Klein, Thordsen, & Wolf, 1996), pilots (Orasanu & Fischer, 1997), and electronic warfare officers (Randel, Pugh, & Reed, 1996). By studying the cognitive aspects of expert performance in these domains, NDM researchers have been able to make recommendations on how to improve training and system support to facilitate the performance of nonexperts.

When we began to study the weather forecasting domain, we were surprised to discover that it was very difficult to identify true experts due to the lack of operationally defined criteria for optimal performance. Prior to conducting our study, we believed that determining the accuracy of a weather forecast would be very straightforward (i.e., was the forecast correct or not?). However, we learned that validating the accuracy of a forecast is not as simple as it seems. For example, a forecaster may forecast rain in a certain city; if it rains in only half of the city, was the forecaster right or wrong? Furthermore, we learned that forecasters are not judged, by their peers or supervisors, to have made a bad forecast as long as their rationale for the forecast was sound. There is a widely shared belief that the weather is unpredictable given our current knowledge of the atmosphere and current technology. Therefore, a given forecast can be inaccurate, but the forecaster is still considered to have been correct in his or her prediction. Because the weather forecasting domain lacks clear criteria for defining optimal performance, we believe it fits the definition of competency-based performance as described by Smith, Shanteau, and Johnson (this volume).

We started our search for expert weather forecasters by interviewing forecasters with many years of experience. We quickly learned that expertise in weather forecasting is not purely a function of years on the job. This was not a surprise. In other domains we have studied, the opportunity for the decision makers to experience many different scenarios and situations is often a more important determinant of expertise than the number of years they have held their current positions. For example, an urban firefighter may attend several calls a day and become an expert in only a few years, whereas a volunteer rural firefighter may only attend one call a week and may never develop a high level of expertise.

Because there was no objective criterion for identifying true experts in the weather forecasting domain and because we could not equate years of forecasting experience to expertise, we developed a description of expertise in this domain based on the results of our own observations and interviews with weather forecasters. In the following sections, we describe the methods we used to collect and analyze our data and the conclusions we drew. We conclude with a discussion of the importance of metacognitive skills in the development of forecasting expertise.

Methods

Sample Description

Our research team interviewed USAF weather forecasters stationed in Ohio, Florida, Alabama, Texas, and Colorado. We conducted a total of 22 in-depth interviews with USAF in-garrison weather forecasters.

Our sample included 5 civilians (all of whom had previous active duty experience in the Air Force), 1 forecaster who was currently serving in the Air Force Reserves, and 16 active duty enlisted personnel. The number of years of experience as a forecaster varied from 4 months to 21 years, with a median of 11 years.

In order to gain a broader perspective on the weather forecasting domain, we interviewed two NWS forecasters at an NWS office in the Midwest, and we interviewed 13 forecasters who had worked as part of the 1996 Olympic weather support forecasting team. The number of years of forecasting experience reported by the NWS forecasters ranged from 3 to 25, with a median of 7 years. Several NWS participants came from forecasting jobs that involved producing regional aviation forecasts or national forecasts for severe storms, hurricanes, or heavy precipitation. Others came from NWS forecasting offices in California, Florida, Georgia, Texas, Arizona, and Alabama.

Procedure

We used a semistructured interview procedure that included two knowledge elicitation methods: the critical decision method (CDM) and the knowledge audit. The CDM uses an event-based approach and is organized around an account of a specific incident. Interviewees are asked to describe an incident in which their expertise made a difference. For the weather forecasting domain, we found that a useful opening query was to ask forecasters to describe a time when they made a forecast and other people thought they were wrong, but it turned out that they were right. Once a relevant incident had been described by the interviewee, the interviewer led the interviewee back over the incident to solicit specific information. Elicited information included the presence or absence of salient cues and the nature of those cues, assessment of the situation and the basis for that assessment, expectations about how the situation might evolve, goals considered, and options evaluated and chosen. For a more complete description of the CDM, see Hoffman, Crandall, and Shadbolt (1998).

The knowledge audit includes a series of questions (or probes) that ask interviewees to provide specific examples of expertise in a domain with which they are familiar. This method is typically used with interviewees who have a high level of expertise in the domain. However, it can also be used with nonexperts to provide concrete, domain-relevant examples that reflect a wide range of proficiency. The knowledge audit elicitation technique was developed from the literature on expert–novice differences (Chi, Feltovich, & Glaser, 1981; Dreyfus, 1972; Dreyfus & Dreyfus, 1986; Klein & Hoffman, 1993; Shanteau, 1988). The set of knowledge audit probes was designed to help subject matter experts articulate their expertise. Each probe addresses an area identified in the literature as representing key areas of distinction between the performance of experts versus that of novices. These areas include diagnosing and predicting, situation awareness, perceptual skills, developing and knowing when to apply tricks of the trade, improvising, metacognitive skills, recognizing anomalies, and compensating for equipment limitations. For a more complete description of the knowledge audit method see Militello and Hutton (1998). An example of the types of probe used for this study is as follows:

Equipment can sometimes mislead. Novices usually believe whatever the equipment tells them; they do not know when to be skeptical. Have there been times when the equipment pointed in one direction but your own judgment told you to do something else? Were there times when you had to rely on experience to avoid being led astray by the equipment?

Interview Process

Interviews took place in private offices or conference rooms, depending on what was available at the different locations. Interviewees were told that the content of the interviews would be confidential. We requested permission to audiotape the interviews for subsequent transcription for verification of our notes. All but one of the forecasters agreed to this procedure. For most of the interviews, two researchers were present; for a few of the interviews, three researchers attended. Interviews lasted for 1 to 2 hours. Due to time constraints, the interviews conducted with the Olympic weather forecasters were conducted in groups of three to four forecasters, whereas all the other interviews were conducted with individual forecasters.

In addition to conducting in-depth interviews, researchers observed the forecaster's work environment and made note of the types of equipment available, the number of personnel on duty, the types of customer requests for weather information, and other relevant incidents. Researchers watched forecasters carry out their duties during routine work shifts and talked briefly with the forecasters on duty about what they were doing.

Results and Discussion

Data Summary

Analyses were based on notes of interview and observation sessions. Typically, one researcher prepared a detailed summary of the interview content. A second researcher, who had also been present for the interview, reviewed the summary and made additions or revisions. We transcribed sections of interviews that contained critical incidents or clear descriptions of the forecasting process. The interview notes and transcripts were systematically reviewed for specific types of information relevant to our goal of developing a better understanding of the knowledge and skills underlying expert weather forecasters. For example, we made lists of all the comments related to good versus bad forecaster characteristics, examples of information overload, the types of information forecasters used, and so on. In addition, we conducted the two analyses described in this section.

Sorting Forecasters into Similar Categories. We used a card-sorting process to determine if we could identify different types of USAF forecasters. Each of the 22 in-garrison forecasters' names were written on a file card.[1] Working as a group, the four researchers who had interviewed these forecasters sorted the cards into categories of individuals who were similar to each other. Once all four researchers agreed that the forecasters within each category were similar to each other and different from those in the other categories, we identified the common elements that defined each category. This sort resulted in a set of five forecaster groups and a sixth group of forecasters who could not be reliably classified into any of the other five groups. Due to the subjective nature of these classifications, we decided that it was preferable not to categorize forecasters into any category unless all four researchers were confident of the classification. The final step in the categorization task was to develop a definition for each category and a label that captured the central meaning of the category. We agreed

---

[1] This analysis was done before we conducted the in-depth interviews with the tactical forecasters, so they were not included. The NWS forecasters were not included because most of these interviews were conducted with small groups and did not elicit sufficient detail on individual forecasters' processes. However, what we learned from these interviews with "true" expert forecasters undoubtedly had an impact on how we sorted the USAF forecasters into categories for this analysis.

on the following labels for defining the five categories of forecasters: Intuitive-based Scientists, Rule-based Scientists, Procedure-based Observers, Procedure-based Mechanics, and Disengaged Forecasters. Attributes and forecasting processes that characterize each group will now be described.

We called one group of forecasters Intuitive-based Scientists. These forecasters seemed to love the weather at some basic affective level. They could talk in vivid detail about past weather events. Their mental representations of the weather were highly visual, at times even tactile in nature. For example, these forecasters recalled incidents in which they described feeling the amount of humidity in the air. Their descriptions of the weather forecasting process included rich visual imagery and the use of dynamic mental models and simulations that allowed them to mentally construct weather systems and "observe" changes in these systems over time. These forecasters evidenced high-level skills for pattern recognition and flexible use of various sources of information as they attempted to solve the problem of the day. Although these forecasters seemed to have a highly developed intuitive understanding of weather dynamics, they did not seem to think in terms of weather rules. Only two of the USAF forecasters included in our sort fell into this category; they had 11 and 15 years of forecasting experience.

A second group of forecasters we labeled the Rule-based Scientists. These forecasters were characterized by an extensive knowledge base of meteorological rules. They used these rules to construct a complete understanding of the current weather situation. They knew how to use a wide variety of tools to obtain the information they needed. They were able to detect patterns of cues presented on a variety of information sources (satellite, radar, etc.) and integrate this information into a useful mental representation. These forecasters seemed to have a good sense of the physical dynamics of various weather systems. Their self-reports of the forecasting process reflected an analytic reasoning style characterized by use of critical thinking and reasoning skills. These forecasters typically had experience forecasting at a variety of geographic locations, and this seems to have contributed substantially to their development of expertise. Four of the USAF forecasters included in our sort fell into this category; they had between 12 and 21 years of experience.

We labeled another group of forecasters Procedure-based Observers. They approached the weather forecasting task as a rule-based, procedural task. Unlike the Rule-based Scientists, however, the forecasters in this group could not seem to use their rule-based knowledge to construct a detailed understanding of the current weather situation. This group was also characterized by their love of the weather and their keen observation skills. Their verbal reports contained occasional glimmers of the higher-level understanding that characterized the Rule-based Scientist and Intuitive-based Scientist groups, but this higher level of understanding disintegrated with further probing by the interviewer. Much of their knowledge base was limited to the types of weather patterns they had observed at a specific location. They seemed to lack the understanding of weather as a global system that characterized both of the scientist groups previously described. Three of the USAF forecasters included in our sort fell into this category. This group of forecasters primarily included younger forecasters with relatively few years of forecasting experience (2–8 years). It is our belief that with more experience and training opportunities, they would develop into weather scientists.

We also identified a group of forecasters whom we called Procedure-based Mechanics. Their approach to the weather forecasting task was to complete a relatively fixed set of procedures. These forecasters had a limited knowledge base of meteorological rules. They appeared to look at the same sources of information, in the same sequence, every day. (We interviewed forecasters only during the summer months, but we believe that this group of forecasters varied their standard set of procedures according to the season of the year.) When asked to describe the thinking behind their weather forecasting process, these forecasters got to a point where they verbally faded out, wandering to the end of a sentence and just stopping. We considered these forecasters to be "locally proficient" because they knew enough to produce a reasonable forecast and give an acceptable pilot briefing, but they did not appear to be motivated to improve their forecasting skill. Three of the USAF forecasters included in our sort fell into this category; they had between 5 and 11 years of forecasting experience.

A fifth category we described as Disengaged. These forecasters had a very limited knowledge base of meteorological rules specific to their current location. Our perception was that they could use these rules to produce a marginal forecast. They did not like being weather forecasters, and they did not seem to like to think about the weather. One of the forecasters in this group had only a few months of forecasting experience, but the others had sufficient experience to have developed a more advanced level of expertise (2–12 years). Four of the USAF forecasters included in our sort fell into this category.

Levels of Expertise

After completing our descriptions of the five categories of forecasters, we were struck by the similarity of the ordering of our forecaster categories to the five levels of expertise described by Dreyfus and Dreyfus (1986). Their model claims that novices initially make decisions and take action by learning a set of rules. As they gain competency, they compile these rules into more and more comprehensive and abstract rules that facilitate more efficient actions. However, Dreyfus and Dreyfus claim that there is a qualitative difference that separates individuals performing at the highest level of competency from nonexperts who have task experience. Experts do not simply rely on more highly developed rules or proceduralized knowledge; they possess a qualitatively different type of knowledge representation.

Dreyfus and Dreyfus have described the development of expertise as proceeding through the five levels described in Table 2.1. The forecasters whom we labeled Intuitive-based Scientists were most similar to the *expert* level described by Dreyfus and Dreyfus. These individuals had an intuitive grasp of the current situation, and their performance was characterized as fluid, flexible, and highly proficient. Dreyfus and Dreyfus label the next level of expertise *proficient,* and this category corresponds to the category of forecasters we labeled Rule-based Scientists. These individuals formed a holistic representation of the situation, had keen perceptual skills, and had a large experience base that they used to determine the typicality of the present situation. Although these individuals were very flexible, they did not rely on their intuition, but instead used their rule-based knowledge of meteorology. Dreyfus and Dreyfus label the next level of expertise as *competent,* and this label relates to the categories of forecasters we called Procedure-based Observers and Procedure-based Mechanics. These individuals were able to perform well given a limited range of situations, but they lacked the flexibility and knowledge that would allow them to perform well in a wider variety of situations. The next level of expertise is labeled as *advanced beginner* by Dreyfus and Dreyfus, and this level corresponds in some ways to the category of forecasters we called Disengaged. These individuals were able to recognize recurring patterns of features in their environment and operate using general procedures. The *novice* category described by Dreyfus and Dreyfus does not seem to relate directly to any of the forecaster categories we described. This is probably due to the fact that we interviewed only one forecaster who had less than 2 years of forecasting experience.

Table 2.1. *Levels of Expertise*

Novice

Beginners have had little experience in the situation in which they are expected to perform. Their initial learning about the situation is in terms of objective, measurable attributes. These attributes can be recognized without situational experiences because novices are very limited in their understanding; their behavior is limited and inflexible.

Advanced Beginner

Advanced beginners have coped with enough real situations to recognize recurring, meaningful situational components. At this level, understanding the aspects of the situation is limited to global characteristics that reflect prior experience in actual situations. Advanced beginners need help setting priorities, because they operate on general guidelines and are only beginning to perceive recurrent, meaningful patterns.

Competent

Performers at a competent or journeyman's level can see their actions in terms of long-range goals or plans. They are able to formulate, evaluate, and modify goals and plans. These plans are generated in terms of the current and future aspects that are most important. The competent performer lacks the speed and flexibility that emerges at higher levels of expertise, but has a sense of mastery and the ability to cope with a variety of situations.

Proficient

Proficient performers perceive situations as wholes rather than in terms of components. Their performance is rule-based and aided by well-developed perceptual skills. Proficient performers have learned what typical events to expect in a given situation and how to modify plans in accord with these events. They also recognize when the expected typical picture does not materialize and modify their plans and goals accordingly.

Expert

Expert performers no longer rely on analytic principles (rules, guidelines) to develop their understanding of the situation to select an appropriate action. The expert, with an enormous background of experience, has an intuitive grasp of each situation and focuses on the accurate region of the problem without consideration of a large range of irrelevant, alternative diagnoses and solutions. Expert performers are no longer aware of features and rules, and their performance becomes fluid, flexible, and highly proficient.

Source: Adapted from Dreyfus and Dreyfus (1986).

Content Analysis

In order to examine the data for the cognitive activities involved in the forecasting process, we generated a list of cognitive activities that had been described in the interviews. Two researchers then reviewed the notes from the 22 interviews with in-garrison forecasters to identify which of these cognitive activities occurred with sufficient frequency to allow us to code these activities reliably across the different forecasters. The following activities, which are defined later, were identified for subsequent analysis: noticing patterns, seeking information, meaning making, use of visual mental representations, and metacognitive processes. The initial review of the interview notes also identified five interviews with in-garrison forecasters that seemed to lack sufficient detail for the content analysis. The participants in these five interviews were not currently involved in producing forecasts because they had been promoted to management positions, and they did not describe their forecasting process in a very detailed manner.

The coding of the cognitive activities was carried out by a pair of coders as follows. Working with interview notes and preselected portions of transcripts from interviews with 17 forecasters, one coder made an initial pass through the protocol data, highlighting any portion of the data that contained information about self-reported cognitive activity. No attempt was made at this point to determine the nature of the cognitive activity, just that it occurred. Working with an initial set of five protocols, two coders worked independently to evaluate the highlighted portions of the protocols, assigning codes to any cognitive activity category that appeared to apply. The two coders then compared category codings, discussed disagreements, and refined the category definitions. After the practice coding was completed, a second set of five protocols was coded using this same process. The two coders agreed on 69% of the codes; differences were resolved by consensus. The remaining data were divided between the two coders to be coded separately.

The results of the content coding are summarized in Table 2.2. Note that the numbers shown in this table are the average number of cognitive activities coded for a particular cognitive activity for each skill level, collapsed across individual forecasters. We used a coding scheme that allowed an individual forecaster to receive more than one code per category if the forecaster described multiple instances of those cognitive activities during the interview. In order to develop the skill level classification used for this analysis, a second category sort was conducted.

Table 2.2. *Mean Number of Cognitive Activities by Forecast Skill Level*

Skill Level	Cognitive Skill					
	Noticing Patterns	Seeking Information	Meaning Making	Visual Mental Representation	Metacognitive Processes	Total
Highest (N = 5)	3.8	3.8	5.0	1.2	1.4	15.2
Medium (N = 6)	3.5	2.7	2.8	1.2	1.2	12.6
Lowest (N = 6)	1.5	3.0	1.5	.2	.8	7.5
TOTAL (N = 17)	8.8	9.5	9.3	2.6	3.4	35.3

Whereas the sort described previously was based on similarity in forecasting style, this sort was based on the researchers' subjective judgments of skill level. An initial sort produced six levels of forecasting skill, which were then combined to produce three categories of skill level due to the small number of forecasters within each category.[2]

Several general trends can be seen in Table 2.2. First, the forecasters at the higher skill levels (highest: $M = 15.2$; medium: $M = 12.6$) reported more frequent use of all of the cognitive elements than the forecasters in the lowest skill category ($M = 7.5$). Second, forecasters at all skill levels were more likely to describe the cognitive skills of Noticing Patterns ($M = 8.8$), Seeking Information ($M = 9.5$), and Meaning Making ($M = 9.3$) than they were to describe the use of Visual Mental Representations ($M = 2.6$) or Metacognitive Skills ($M = 3.4$). More important than the observed quantitative trends are the qualitative differences observed for these cognitive activities for forecasters of the different skill levels. We now describe these differences.

[2] Although the two sorts focused on different criteria (forecasting style versus forecasting skill level), the results were very similar. All but one of the forecasters classified in the Scientist categories were categorized as having a high skill level (the exception was categorized as having a medium skill level). The forecasters classified in the Disengaged category were categorized as having low forecasting skill, and the remaining forecasters were all categorized as having a medium skill level. The results of the two sorts cannot be considered independent analyses because the same researchers conducted both sorts and the results of the first sort may have influenced the results of the second sort. We believed both sorts were necessary because it was theoretically possible that forecasting style would not map directly onto forecasting skill level.

Noticing Patterns. This category included instances in which the fore-casters described an awareness of typical co-occurrences, deviations, and/or patterns in the weather information available to them. All but two of the forecasters (both from the lowest skill category) described some cognitive activity that we coded as noticing. The forecasters at the medium and highest skill levels described about twice as many instances of noticing as did forecasters at the lowest skill level. When we exam-ined the content of the forecasters' comments for this category, we saw a great deal of similarity across the different skill levels. All of the groups talked about the importance of local effects, their knowledge of typical deviations caused by local terrain features, and seasonal variations at their particular location.

The nature of the subtle cues and patterns varied according to skill level. Many of the cues discussed by the most skilled forecasters could not be listed in a catalog. They include inconsistencies (which can only be spotted from a coherent sense of the overall pattern). They include violations of expectancies in which something happened that was not anticipated or something that was supposed to happen did not (both of which require a comprehensive mental simulation). They include inter-esting places on the map (which are interesting only in the context of the overall weather pattern). They include the ease with which inconsisten-cies are explained away, and how this explanation makes other facets of the weather settle into place or build up strain that leads to a suspicion that the obvious forecast may not be holding. They include accelera-tion cues – indicators showing rapid change that can signal dynamic shifts (which can only be spotted if these indicators are being studied over time). They include areas of instability that are often smoothed by computer graphics and can indicate turning points in the weather pat-tern (which can only be spotted by hand plotting the appropriate data once the forecaster knows what these are). For less skilled forecasters, their attention is on the centers of the masses (e.g., high-pressure areas) as they move. For the competent forecasters, their attention is on the edges, looking for areas of instability.

Seeking Information. This category included instances in which the fore-caster described the collection of information to produce a forecast. All but one of the forecasters (from the lowest skill category) described some cognitive activity that we coded as Seeking Information. Thus, it ap-pears that almost all forecasters are involved in data-seeking/gathering activities as part of their forecasting process. The one forecaster who did not report any cognitive activity that we coded as Seeking Information claimed that "he sometimes can skip analyzing the charts" while formulating his forecast. Even though the rest of the forecasters we interviewed all described actively seeking out weather information, the types of data they sought and how they used these data varied across the skill levels.

Forecasters at the highest skill level drew on a wider variety of technologies than forecasters at the lower skill levels. Their data-gathering strategies were fluid and flexible, guided by their sense of what was important for today's problem. The most highly skilled forecasters shared an information-seeking strategy in which they continuously shifted their perspectives. For example, these forecasters reported shifting their perspective from examining the satellite imagery down through the cloud layers and then examining the local surface observations and relating this information back to the satellite image. They were also keenly aware of the need to adjust observations and other products (e.g., radar, satellite images) in accord with the amount of time that has passed since these data were gathered and to consider the timing and location of data sources in order to recalibrate and adjust their understanding of what was going on. The most highly skilled forecasters considered computer models as an important source of data but not as the only source. They tended to examine *subelements* of the computer models for particular types of data they needed (such as wind speeds); they did not talk about the models in general terms of being "right" or "wrong."

Forecasters categorized as having a medium level of skill tended to rely heavily on the continuity principle. They placed a great deal of emphasis on looking upstream to obtain data. Their information seeking focused on trying to determine how fast the approaching weather pattern was moving toward them. It also appeared to be much more proceduralized; they typically followed the same steps every day (although these steps varied among the different forecasters). They placed greater emphasis on computer models than did the more highly skilled forecasters, and they referred to the models as intact representations rather than referring to subelements of the models. Many of the forecasters in the medium skill level category focused their information-seeking activity on determining whether or not "the model is right today."

Forecasters in the lowest skill category described their information seeking as highly proceduralized and static. There was no evidence that their strategies varied in accord with local effects or weather events of the particular day. Some of these forecasters described a very limited data-gathering strategy that involved few data points and few data sources; other forecasters in this category described data-gathering strategies that involved looking at everything, although they did not attempt to link these data together in a meaningful way.

It appears that the information seeking of the more skilled forecasters was structured around their ability to detect problems and to identify the problem of the day (e.g., will this front move east or southeast?). The problem of the day was the instability or complication that required close attention, particularly if it could have major implications for severe weather. The problem of the day anchored their situation awareness. In addition, the act of information seeking seemed to provide ownership of the data, particularly if it required some sort of hand plotting.

Meaning Making. This category referred to a process by which forecasters organized or explained the information they had previously gathered in an attempt to make sense of it. All of the forecasters described some cognitive activity that we coded as Meaning Making, but the more highly skilled forecasters ($M = 5.0$) reported more incidents of meaning making than did the medium-skill ($M = 2.8$) and lower-skill forecasters ($M = 1.5$). An examination of the protocols indicated that the most highly skilled forecasters were more likely to describe the forecasting process in terms of causal reasoning than were forecasters in the other skill categories. All five of the forecasters in the highest skill category reported trying to understand the causal connections among various data elements and trying to construct an understanding of weather events. Their attempts to make meaning of the data involved using multiple weather events and multiple potential causes of these events; they anticipated interactions among complex sets of factors.

In contrast, the forecasters in the medium-skill category rarely talked about trying to determine the causes of the weather. Only two of the six forecasters in this group talked about causal connections. Most of this group's efforts at meaning making focused on determining how quickly the weather would change rather than trying to figure out how complex weather systems were likely to develop across the Earth's surface. Although all of the forecasters in the lowest skill category described some cognitive activity coded as Meaning Making, in general these remarks reflected very little depth of understanding of meteorology. For example, one forecaster's comment that "If the K Index is in the thirties, then there is a chance of thunderstorms" was coded as Meaning Making because the forecaster was going beyond Seeking Information and was making sense of the data. However, this remark does not reflect an in-depth understanding of the forces of the atmosphere; it is simply a rule that the forecaster had memorized.

We concluded that the skilled forecasters were not building up meaning from basic data elements. Rather, the act of interpretation also determined what counted as data. These forecasters have no standard "grain" for analyzing events. One forecaster described a case where he believed there was a second front. However, the computer-generated picture was plotted at the 500 millibar grain. Therefore, he hand plotted the data at the 200 millibar grain for the area he believed was critical, and he found the evidence for the second front. He would not have wanted an entire map at the 200 millibar grain.

Visual Mental Representation. This category included instances in which forecasters described the use of visual mental representations when they discussed their forecasting processes. If forecasters reported making a "picture" in their minds as they tried to understand the weather, we coded their representation as Visual Mental Representation. For example, one forecaster described his use of visual mental representation when he stated that he "needs to build a big picture of the atmosphere. The atmosphere is fluid; like a rock in the pond, there are ripple effects." Another forecaster described how he forms a picture of the weather: "I stack the upper levels of the atmosphere over the surface features and think about how these features will change the surface features and when these changes will occur."

Four of the five forecasters in the highest skill group reported using a visual mental representation, while the other highly skilled forecaster specifically stated that he did not form a visual representation of the weather. All but one of the forecasters in the medium-skill group described the use of visual mental representation; however, only one of the forecasters in the lowest skill group reported using a visual representation, and three of these forecasters failed to describe any type of mental representation.

Although there was no difference between the highly skilled and the medium-skilled forecasters in terms of the frequency with which they reported using visual mental models, an examination of their protocols indicated a qualitative difference in many of the instances that were reported. In general, the descriptions of the visual representations used by the highly skilled forecasters included more use of vivid visual imagery. Their protocols were more likely to describe three-dimensional, dynamic representations, whereas the medium-skilled group were more likely to describe more static images. For example, one highly skilled forecaster stated that "The central analysis smoothes the fronts, how consistent they are, and how smoothly they move. In reality, the fronts wiggle as they move across the land. And it's at those whorls and wiggles that weather happens." In contrast, only one medium-skilled forecaster stated that he pictures in his mind "what's happening at each of the [atmospheric] levels and then he begins to stack the features on top of one another."

The type of visual imagery reported by the forecasters focused on three aspects of the weather. Some forecasters reported visualizing the atmosphere as a fluid and picturing atmospheric dynamics within that fluid space. Others reported visualizing the interface between the atmosphere and the surface of the earth (land and water). Forecasters also reported visualizing the dynamics of the weather systems as they move across the Earth's surface. It appears that these forecasters used visual imagery and mental simulations to explore weather phenomena that they could not experience in any direct physical way.

Metacognitive Processes. This category included instances in which forecasters described cognitive activities that were self-reflective. Approximately two-thirds of the forecasters described some cognitive activity that we coded as Metacognitive. Although there were no quantitative differences across the different categories of skill level, there were several interesting qualitative differences that we found in the protocols.

Protocol data from more highly skilled forecasters suggested that they consciously managed their cognitive approach to the forecasting task, thought about what worked best, and were capable of stepping away from their own cognitive processes and evaluating them. Several comments indicated strongly held opinions about the interplay between current weather technology and information management tasks. The more highly skilled forecasters indicated that data overload makes their job more difficult and that they had to develop methods for managing the information stream. For example, one forecaster said, "You have to analyze what you have and what you don't have. Then you have to figure out how you can fill in what you don't have."

The more highly skilled forecasters stated that from their point of view, current technology has made some of the cognitive elements of their job more difficult. They identified the "big picture" as being important but not well supported by current technology. One forecaster noted that he used to generate multiple observations over space and time. Because they were on paper, he could look across localities and time to get a sense of emerging patterns. He said:

> Now, you can get this data, but in single elements and separated by screens and menus. It's there, but not in front of you. The forecaster has to go and get the data, know how to put the big picture together, and hold various elements of it in his head. They have the detail but none of the big view. They have the data but have lost the ability to process and represent it.

Forecasters from the medium-level skill category also expressed an awareness of the importance of data management strategies, particularly in situations where time was short or data conflicted. How to set priorities for additional data seeking was noted as being an important skill. These types of comments were not found in the protocols of the lower-skilled forecasters.

Olympic Forecasters

The results of the analyses just summarized increased our understanding of the characteristics of competent performers in the weather forecasting domain. However, because there were very few highly skilled USAF forecasters in our sample, we believed we needed to talk to some "true experts" before we could make our recommendations to the USAF. We learned that a team of expert NWS forecasters had been assembled to predict the weather for the 1996 Olympic games in Atlanta, and we arranged to conduct small-group interviews with most of these forecasters. Because these interviews were conducted in small groups, we did not obtain sufficiently detailed information on individual forecasters to allow us to include their data in the analyses described previously. However, the interviews we conducted with the Olympic forecasters influenced our thinking, so we provide a brief description of what we learned before presenting our conclusions.

The task of the Olympic forecasters was actually much more similar to the forecasting task faced by USAF forecasters, who have to make very specific predictions and warnings for an airfield, than the task faced by most NWS forecasters, who typically forecast by region and issue countywide warnings. For the Olympic Games, very specific warnings had to be issued for the different venues for different sporting events (e.g., dew warnings for cycling events, wind warnings for divers). Like the USAF forecasters we interviewed, each of these forecasters seemed to have his or her own approach to the forecasting process. One forecaster described his process as follows: First, he looks at current observations (the surface data, the upper air, radar, and satellite images); then he looks back to see what was happening earlier in time to figure out what caused the current situation; then he tries to figure out what sequence of events will occur given the current situation; and only then does he look at the computer models. At this point, he tries to reconcile differences between his prediction and the computer models.

When asked to talk about the forecasting process, several Olympic forecasters mentioned that they used a *pattern recognition* process. In addition, almost all of them described their use of visual mental models in the forecasting process. Some forecasters described two-dimensional visual models that looked like the weather maps shown on TV, which have areas of high pressure and low pressure, with fronts marked. Other forecasters described four-dimensional (including time) models that allow them to construct an understanding of the weather over their geographic area of interest. For example, one forecaster described his visual model as follows:

> Then you get a picture in your mind and you can say "Okay, well, they've [thunderstorms] already developed in this area, and they're going to move in this direction over time, and that's going to have an effect on the clouds coming into Nashville, or which way the wind's coming from, or have an effect on temperatures." In my mind, I watch the problem whether it's going to evolve throughout the day.

Several of the Olympic forecasters mentioned that they suffered from information overload given all the new technology available to them. For example, one forecaster said, "Now, when you sit down on a shift, there is too much information. You cannot look at it all. You literally have to decide what you want to look at, what you think you need to look at, and use that information. There's too much data now."

Although we had only a limited amount of time to spend with these forecasters, most of them impressed us as true experts according to the levels of expertise described in Table 2.1. These forecasters all talked about identifying the "problem of the day" in order to focus their information-gathering activities. They seemed to have a fluid, flexible style that allowed them to quickly get up to speed in a new environment.

Characteristics of Competent Weather Forecasters

After analyzing the information we collected by conducting observations and interviews with USAF and NWS forecasters, we concluded that the following characteristics differentiate competent forecasters from noncompetent forecasters. Competent forecasters are characterized as follows:

- They typically identify a specific weather problem of the day, which serves as an anchor for information seeking and interpretation.
- They form their mental model prior to seeing computerized forecasts.
- They look at the weather situation using a larger (more global) perspective and can switch easily between a global and a local perspective.
- They are flexible in their use of various tools and procedures.
- They have a mental representation that incorporates the dynamic causes underlying the current weather situation.
- They can use their mental representation to quickly provide whatever weather information they are asked for (a forecast, a pilot briefing).

In contrast, forecasters who do not display competency are characterized as follows:

- They rely too much on computer models.
- They use a fixed set of procedures to produce their forecast.
- They have a narrow focus and do not attempt to understand the relevant larger-scale weather features.
- They are reactive and end up "chasing the obs."[3]

The Development of Forecasting Expertise

After we identified the characteristics of competent weather forecasters, we reviewed our data to determine what factors contribute to the

---

[3] *Chasing the obs* refers to a practice used by some forecasters in which they amend their current forecast only after the current observations prove the forecast to be wrong. For example, rather than predicting that winds may exceed the minimum required to issue a warning, the forecaster waits until the winds observed are over the minimum and then issues the warning.

development of forecasting expertise. We identified the following three factors as being important: formal training opportunities, on-the-job training opportunities, and opportunities for feedback on specific forecasts. We discuss each of these in turn.

Formal Training. A major difference between the USAF and NWS forecasters we interviewed was the amount of formal training they received in meteorology. NWS forecasters must have completed a bachelor's-level degree in meteorology before they can serve as intern forecasters in the NWS. In contrast, enlisted personnel in the USAF receive a total of 35 weeks of formal classroom training to prepare them to act as forecasters. It was clear to us that more extensive training in meteorology contributes significantly to a forecaster's ability to develop a detailed understanding of the current weather situation. In addition to obtaining an extensive knowledge base of the science of meteorology, forecasters who have completed college are more likely to have had practice using critical thinking skills to solve abstract problems and to have developed and practiced their formal communication skills.

On-the-Job Training. Many of the more highly skilled USAF forecasters we interviewed commented that they were fortunate to have had a mentor early in their career. That is, they were stationed at a location in which a senior-level person (an officer, senior enlisted person, or civilian) guided their on-the-job forecaster training. No matter how much formal scientific training forecasters receive prior to their first assignment, they need an extended period of on-the-job training in their new location. Based on our observations at USAF weather stations, it appears that there is no standard practice regarding on-the-job training. There are also very few senior-level people who have the expertise to share. In contrast, the NWS requires forecasters to serve as intern forecasters for at least 2 years before they issue forecasts on their own.

Feedback Opportunities. A fundamental law in the psychology of learning is that learners must have feedback on their performance if they are to improve their skills. Based on our observations and interviews at USAF weather stations, there is little opportunity for individual forecasters to obtain timely feedback on the accuracy of their forecasts, and there is even less opportunity to get feedback on the effectiveness of their forecasting process. This second point is an important distinction because it is possible for the forecaster to have done everything "right" but still to have produced an inaccurate forecast; conversely, the forecaster may have done everything "wrong" and still not "busted" the forecast. If forecasters are highly motivated, they can attempt to get feedback on their forecast by checking pilots' reports or examining observations from the period for which they produced their forecast. However, this did not occur routinely in the stations we visited.

When we visited the Olympic Weather Support Office, we were surprised to learn how little formal training the forecasters were given to learn how to use new technology to make precise predictions in an unfamiliar geographic region. How did they get up to speed so quickly? They were brought to Peachtree City, Georgia, about 12 months prior to the Olympics for 2 weeks of training. They had an additional 2 weeks of training immediately before the beginning of the Olympics that included site visits to the various locations for which they would be making forecasts. The site visits allowed them to identify local terrain features that might affect their forecasts. Two additional factors were also identified as being critical to their rapid learning. First, the forecasters got timely and detailed feedback on their forecasts for 2 weeks before they had to produce real forecasts. They developed forecasts each day for the specific venues but did not disseminate this information. They were able to get detailed feedback on the correctness of these predictions based on observations taken at each location. Second, because they worked in teams of four to nine forecasters per shift, they learned from critiques of each other's forecasts.

To summarize, we concluded that there are a number of factors that may work against the development of high levels of skill among USAF forecasters. We believe that abbreviated schoolhouse training, uneven on-the-job training programs, and feedback opportunities that are rare or missing altogether may all contribute to the extreme variability in skill levels we found among USAF forecasters. An additional factor that appears to bear directly on forecasters' performance is the type of technology made available to them. For a detailed discussion of the impact of technology on USAF weather forecaster performance, see Pliske et al. (1997). In brief, we concluded that USAF forecasters have become overly reliant on technology and insufficiently reflective and self-regulated. USAF forecasters have access to computer models developed by the NWS that allow them to produce a good enough forecast most of the time. They have advanced radar systems that alert them to times when they need to issue warnings. These technologies allow USAF forecasters to produce forecasts in the absence of a well-developed understanding of basic principles of meteorology, or even of the technology itself. An important consequence of this overreliance on technology is that USAF forecasters are unable to function when that technological support is missing, as commonly occurs in tactical settings and frequently occurs at base weather stations when their technological tools malfunction.

Conclusions

This chapter has described an exploratory investigation of the decision making of weather forecasters. We relied on qualitative data to form conclusions and hypotheses about the nature of competence in this domain. If we had used more rigorous methods, such as presenting a standardized weather scenario, we might have been able to conduct more objective analyses and obtained cleaner findings. We considered using standardized scenarios, but we rejected that strategy for two reasons. The first reason was a practical concern; our USAF sponsor needed this research project to be completed within 7 months. This constraint did not allow sufficient time for the enormous effort that would have been involved in assembling and pilot testing realistic scenario packages, including all of the different maps and readings from the large variety of available instruments. The second reason had to do with issues of representativeness and generalizability. Our initial interviews clearly indicated that the types of information utilized by particular forecasters varied greatly, depending on the nature of the weather problem, which in turn was strongly affected by their geographic location. We were told to make recommendations relevant to all USAF forecasters and not to focus on a specific weather problem (e.g., severe storms) or limit our study to a specific geographic region. We were concerned that if we focused our efforts on documenting the skills and knowledge underlying forecasts developed for one or two specific weather scenarios, the resulting recommendations would not address the most significant training and system design needs currently facing USAF forecasters.

Consequently, we chose to use actual incidents, and to accept the vagaries of the forecasters' memories and the lack of standardization across participants. This strategy allowed us to gain a broad understanding of what characterizes competence in the weather forecasting domain. We were then able to provide our sponsor with general recommendations for changes in current training programs and with specific recommendations about the types of future research that needs to be done in order to redesign the technological tools provided to USAF forecasters.

With our approach, we learned that there were no standard information-seeking strategies used by weather forecasters, but that the skilled performers could flexibly adapt their information seeking to their interpretation of the problem of the day. We learned about the importance of constructing an explanatory causal model and found that unskilled personnel can generate (mediocre) forecasts without having a causal model in mind. We learned how important ownership was for them – forming their own interpretation prior to seeing the forecast of another person or of a computer program.

In contrast to the earlier research on weather forecasters, which focused exclusively on highly skilled forecasters, our research examined forecasters with a wide variety of skill levels. This provided us with an opportunity to explore the characteristics of competent performance. Shanteau (1989) describes a theory of expert competence that assumes that competence depends on five components: the decision maker's competence in the domain in question, psychological traits of the decision maker, the cognitive skills of the decision maker, the strategies used by the decision maker, and the characteristics of the decision-making task. Shanteau goes on to describe the characteristics of tasks that should lead to good versus poor performance by experts. We would argue that the weather forecasting task has characteristics that could promote both good and poor performance. In some ways, forecasting the weather at a particular airfield is a highly repetitive task. A USAF forecaster has to predict ceiling and visibility for his or her airfield at least every 4 hours during a 12-hour shift. Furthermore, feedback can be made available to the forecaster (e.g., did the predicted visibility occur?). On the other hand, one of the important features of tasks that Shanteau claims leads to poor performance is the nature of the stimuli involved: Are they static or dynamic? In most cases, the stimuli in the weather forecasting task are highly dynamic: The atmosphere is constantly changing, sometimes in unpredictable ways. The dynamic nature of the weather forecasting task could hinder the development of competency.

One of the key observations we made in this research project was that USAF forecasters were operating with virtually no feedback on their performance. Although in most situations this information could be made readily accessible to these forecasters, it typically was not. The only time many of the forecasters we interviewed received feedback on their forecasts was when they had failed to issue a critical warning when appropriate. These feedback sessions were viewed more as a type of punishment than as a learning opportunity. Without the opportunity to learn from their experience, most of these forecasters seemed destined to stay at fairly low levels of proficiency rather than develop into competent performers.

The importance of feedback has been discussed extensively by researchers who have studied the development of expertise (Ericsson, 1996). For example, Ericsson, Krampe, and Tesch-Romer (1993) reviewed laboratory studies of learning and skill acquisition in order to identify training activities related to the development of expertise. They concluded that the most effective learning results from deliberate practice that involves a well-defined task at an appropriate level of difficulty, informative feedback, and opportunities for correcting errors. Repeated trials without informative feedback and without opportunities for correcting errors will not result in improved performance.

Glaser (1996) also discusses the necessary conditions for the development of expertise. He describes the importance of self-regulation in deliberate practice. According to Glaser, individual performers must eventually develop the ability to structure their own learning situations and provide their own performance feedback. Our results generally support his claim. As discussed previously in this chapter, the more highly skilled weather forecasters in our sample were more likely to report using metacognitive strategies in their forecasting process that involved the evaluation of their own forecasting processes. These forecasters were also more likely to report seeking out feedback on the correctness of their forecasts. Metacognition-self is a critical part of their expertise.

In addition to describing metacognitive activity involving self-monitoring, forecasters in our study also described metacognitive activity reflecting their ability to handle the high degree of uncertainty that is inherent in the forecasting task. Several of the forecasters from the medium-level skill group indicated that they had difficulty handling the uncertainty in the forecasting task. Although several forecasters mentioned their tendency to second-guess themselves, there was no clear consensus on whether second-guessing was a positive strategy. On the one hand, these forecasters appeared to recognize that seeking verification or disconfirmation of their forecasts can be an important check. For example, one forecaster noted that "You have to be willing to second-guess yourself. . . . [Novices] need to have checkpoints for their forecasts so they can revise, check, and verify." But another forecaster acknowledged that second-guessing often led him astray. "My first belief or forecast reasoning is usually correct. It's when I begin to second-guess myself that I miss them." We do not know what accounts for this variation in viewpoint across forecasters from the medium-level skill category, but we note that it was absent from the more highly skilled group, who did not mention second-guessing at all. Furthermore, we found no evidence that lower-level skill forecasters experience difficulty dealing with uncertainty, perhaps because their approach to forecasting avoids the issue altogether. Several forecasters in this group mentioned seeking disconfirming information or generating alternate scenarios. For example, "[We] have to be flexible, let [our] imaginations wander over different potential, hypothetical scenarios so that [we] can think of what might or could happen." But none of these forecasters offered information about how they handle situations when disconfirming information or puzzling scenarios occur. Perhaps most striking in the protocol data from the lower-skilled forecasters was the evidence of a "quick size-up" strategy, which allowed them to move quickly from initial diagnosis to forecast. They were more likely to skim the surface of the information stream, go with their first impression, and be satisfied with it. For example, one of these forecasters asserted, "[I] really trust [my] first impression of the weather and don't really try to figure out where I might be wrong."

How weather forecasters at various skill levels deal with uncertainty is an important topic for future research. In addition, research using more scientifically rigorous methods is needed to validate and extend the results of this exploratory study. However, based on our findings, we were able to make a number of recommendations to the USAF as to how they could improve their weather forecasting performance. Many of these recommendations addressed training issues, whereas others addressed needed changes to the existing interfaces for the technical tools currently used by USAF forecasters. Our USAF sponsors are currently using our findings as they attempt to reengineer Air Force Weather.

References

Chi, M. T. H., Feltovich, P. J., & Glaser, R. (1981). Categorization and representation of physics problems by experts and novices. *Cognitive Science*, 5, 121–152.

Crandall, B., & Getchell-Reiter, K. (1993). Critical decision method: A technique for eliciting concrete assessment indicators from the intuition of NICU nurses. *Advances in Nursing Sciences*, 16(1), 42–51.

Dreyfus, H. L. (1972). *What computers can't do: A critique of artificial reason*. New York: Harper & Row.

Dreyfus, H. L., & Dreyfus, S. E. (1986). *Mind over machine: The power of human intuitive expertise in the era of the computer*. New York: Free Press.

Ericsson, K. A. (Ed.). (1996). *The road to excellence*. Mahwah, NJ: Erlbaum.

Ericsson, K. A., Krampe, R. T., & Tesch-Römer, C. (1993). The role of deliberate practice in the acquisition of expert performance. *Psychological Review, 100*(3), 363–406.

Glaser, R. (1996). Changing the agency for learning: Acquiring expert performance. In K. A. Ericsson (Ed.), *The road to excellence* (pp. 303–311). Mahwah, NJ: Erlbaum.

Hoffman, R. R. (1991). Human factors psychology in the support of forecasting: The design of advanced meteorological workstations. *Weather and Forecasting, 6*, 98–110.

Hoffman, R. R., Crandall, B. W., & Shadbolt, N. R. (1998). A case study in cognitive task analysis methodology: The Critical Decision Method for the elicitation of expert knowledge. *Human Factors, 40*, 254–276.

Kaempf, G. L., Klein, G. A., Thordsen, M. L., & Wolf, S. (1996). Decision making in complex command-and-control environments. *Human Factors, 38*(2), 220–231.

Klein, G. A., Calderwood, R., & Clinton-Cirocco, A. (1986). Rapid decision making on the fireground. *Proceedings of the Human Factors Society 30th Annual Meeting, 1*, 576–580.

Klein, G. A., & Hoffman, R. (1993). Seeing the invisible: Perceptual/cognitive aspects of expertise. In M. Rabinowitz (Ed.), *Cognitive science foundations of instruction* (pp. 203–226). Hillsdale, NJ: Erlbaum.

Klein, G. A., Orasanu, J., Calderwood, R., & Zsambok, C. E. (Eds.). (1993). *Decision making in action: Models and methods*. Norwood, NJ: Ablex.

Klinger, D. W., Andriole, S. J., Militello, L. G., Adelman, L., Klein, G., & Gomes, M. E. (1993). *Designing for performance: A cognitive systems engineering approach to modifying an* AWACS *human–computer interfac*e (AL/CF-TR-1993-0093 for the Department of the Air Force, Armstrong Laboratory, Air Force Materiel Command, Wright-Patterson AFB, OH). Yellow Springs, OH: Klein Associates, Inc.

Militello, L. G., & Hutton, R. J. B. (1998). Applied Cognitive Task Analysis (ACTA): A practitioner's toolkit for understanding cognitive task demands. *Ergonomics, 42*(11), 1618–1641.

Mosier, K. L., & Skitka, L. J. (1996). Human decision makers and automated decision aids: Made for each other? In R. Parasuraman & M. Mouloua (Eds.), *Automation and human performance: Theory and applications* (pp. 201–220). Mahwah, NJ: Erlbaum.

Mosier, K. L., Skitka, L. J., & Heers, S. T. (1996). Automation bias, accountability, and verification behaviors. *Proceedings of the Human Factors and Ergonomics Society 40th Annual Meeting* (pp. 204–208).

Murphy, A. H., & Winkler, R. L. (1977) Can weather forecasters formulate reliable forecasts of precipitation and temperature? *National Weather Digest, 2*, 2–9.

Orasanu, J., & Fischer, U. (1997). Finding decisions in natural environments: The view from the cockpit. In C. Zsambok & G. Klein (Eds.), *Naturalistic decision making* (pp. 343–358). Mahwah, NJ: Erlbaum.

Pliske, R., Klinger, D., Hutton, R., Crandall, B., Knight, B., & Klein, G. (1997). *Understanding skilled weather forecasting: Implications for training and the design of forecasting tools* (Technical Report No. 1L/HR-CR-1997-0003 for

Armstrong Laboratory: Brooks AFB, TX). Fairborn, OH: Klein Associates, Inc.

Randel, J. M., Pugh, H. L., & Reed, S. K. (1996). Methods for analyzing cognitive skills for a technical task. *International Journal of Human-Computer Studies, 45,* 579–597.

Shanteau, J. (1988). Psychological characteristics and strategies of expert decision makers. *Acta Psychologica, 68,* 203–215.

Shanteau, J. (1989) Competence in experts: The role of task characteristics. *Organizational Behavior and Human Decision Processes, 53,* 252–266.

Stewart, T. R., Heideman, K. F., Moninger, W. R., & Reagan-Cirincione, P. (1992). Effects of improved information on the components of skill in weather forecasting. *Organizational Behavior and Human Decision Processes, 53,* 107–134.

Stewart, T. R., & Lusk, C. M. (1994). Seven components of judgmental forecasting skill: Implications for research and the improvement of forecasts. *Journal of Forecasting, 13,* 579–599.

Zsambok, C. E., & Klein, G. (Eds.). (1997). *Naturalistic decision making.* Mahwah, NJ: Erlbaum.

Part II

Metacognition-Others

3   Managing Risk in Social Exchange

Stefano Grazioli, Kip Smith, and Paul Johnson

In this chapter we present an analysis of decision making to manage risk in environments characterized by social exchange. We take a pragmatic approach, defining risk as the potential for loss and social exchange as an interaction where two or more agents define the outcomes (costs and benefits) for each other. We propose an information processing model of decision making to manage risk in such environments. The critical steps in the model are (1) ascribing beliefs and goals to the other agent(s) and (2) modifying behavior to reflect the ascription. We use the model to investigate the decision making of professionals who manage risk in two different environments characterized by social exchange: spot currency trading (banking) and second partner review of financial statements (auditing). We argue that ascription is an important component of competent decision making in both domains. The spot currency market is a dynamic environment that places a premium on real-time decision making. Traders ascribe beliefs to the market in order to anticipate the direction of prices. Financial statements auditing is characterized by the potential for opportunistic manipulation of information by its provider (management). Auditors ascribe intentions to management in order to detect these manipulations. To evaluate the role of ascription in risky social exchange, we (1) conducted experiments with professional subjects, (2) built two production systems, one for each domain, that implement the ascription process and emulate the behavior of the subjects in our experiments, (3) excised the ascription process from the systems to create a pair of alternative systems, and (4) compared the systems' and subjects' performance. The comparison demonstrates that ascription of beliefs and goals to others is a major determinant of success in managing risk in social exchange. This thinking about others' thinking is the crux of metacognition-others.

Risk in Social Exchange

During the past several years, we have been investigating decision making in two managerial domains: spot currency trading and second partner review of financial statements. Currency traders are bankers who manage the risk associated with exchanging currencies in markets characterized by fluctuating prices. These price fluctuations depend largely on the aggregate behavior of the other traders who participate in each market. Second partner reviewers are auditors who manage the risk associated with providing assurance that financial information used as a basis for decision making is reliable. The risk in this instance is that a client company intentionally manipulates its financial statements for the purpose of favorably affecting the behavior of the users of that information. For all their differences, these two domains share a defining characteristic: They both require agents to manage forms of risk that are dependent on the behavior of others.

We depart from more traditional accounts that equate risk with probability (e.g., Keynes, 1921; von Neumann & Morgenstern, 1944) and take a more pragmatic approach to define risk as the potential for loss (March & Shapira, 1987; Schoemaker, 1993; Shapira, 1995; Yates & Stone, 1992). Loss is generally defined as a negative change in an agent's economic position. Risk, being the opportunity for loss, does not necessarily generate a loss. Loss is the realization of risk. Risk is present whenever you stand to lose. Serious risk is present whenever you stand to lose a lot.

Social exchanges are situations where two agents interact to define outcomes – that is, costs and benefits – for each other (Cosmides, 1985; Cosmides & Tooby, 1992, 1995). As a result, one agent's action may negatively affect the other's outcome. Such a possibility for loss implies that risk is an inherent characteristic of social exchange. The possibility of losing millions of dollars in the blink of an eye by holding the wrong position in the foreign currency markets is an example of risk in social exchange. The potential for a lawsuit and loss of professional prestige that arises from failure to detect a financial fraud is another.

We argue that managing situations where others, acting alone or in concert with your behavior, provide the opportunity for loss is a critical aspect of decision making. Although domain knowledge is clearly necessary for most decision-making situations in the world, an additional kind of knowledge is necessary to support competence at decision making characterized by risks posed by others. This addition – the process of ascription – provides the margin for success. Our claim is that skilled decision making about social exchange risk is rooted in the process of thinking about the intentions of the others involved in the exchange (Clark, 1987; Dennett, 1987; Thagard, 1992), and that ascription of goals and/or beliefs to others is the key to detecting and managing the risks that others may pose.

The plan for this chapter is as follows. We begin with a discussion of two conditions that enable the actions of others to originate risk. The first condition – interacting with a large number of other agents in a dynamic environment – is exemplified by trading in the spot currency markets. The second condition – asymmetric distribution of information under conflict of interest – is exemplified by second partner review. A discussion of why these tasks are difficult sets the stage for a theory of assessing risk posed by others.

The theory focuses on the process of ascription as the key for competent decision making in social exchange. We illustrate this concept with data from experiments with experienced currency traders and auditors, as well as with a description of two information processing models of competent decision making, one for each domain. Both models are based on empirical data and contain procedures to ascribe goals and beliefs to others.

The theory is evaluated by means of parallel experiments with the two models. We ablate the process of ascription from the models and contrast the behavior of the original and modified models with the behavior of skilled decision makers. The results from the comparison are the basis for evaluating the argument that the process of ascription is a key component of competence in both domains.

Dynamic Interaction with Numerous Agents

Markets are dynamic arenas for exchange populated by a large number of interacting agents. For one agent to buy, another must sell. The exchange provides the possibility for loss on both sides of the transaction. By participating in a market, an agent allows the actions of others to define risk. The market agent realizes risk – takes a loss – only by taking action, that is, by making a trade with another.

Trading in the *spot currency markets* illustrates the risk posed by interacting with a large number of other agents in a dynamic environment. Spot markets are electronic arenas for the exchange of currencies for immediate (within 3 working days) delivery. There is one spot market per foreign currency. The word *market* refers both to the arena for exchange and to the network of traders actively trading.

The currency trader is a banker. Banks participate in the market in order to hold foreign currencies and to provide the service of exchanging currencies for customers. The trader's job is to manage the risk posed to the bank by participating in the currency markets. Because a currency is essentially worthless except in its country of issue and in the international markets, a foreign currency is a risky asset that is subject to the vagaries of international events. Traders refer to the asset they manage as a *position*. Position size is typically on the order of millions of dollars.

Unlike the futures markets for commodities, where trading is conducted in a *pit* (e.g., the Chicago Board of Trade), there is no face-to-face action in currency trading. Currency markets are electronic markets or *cybermarkets* (Kurtzman, 1993); they exist only in a web of specialized information systems. All information arrives at the trading desk across worldwide communications networks provided by wire services (e.g., Reuters, Bridge) or by telephone.

The trader samples five types of information: (1) an *overnight report*, a synopsis of global events prepared by the bank, (2) the prices currently showing in the market, that is, the exchange rates, (3) headlines from around the world, (4) the size and breakeven rates of his or her positions, and (5) the behavior of trading partners. Traders everywhere receive at approximately the same time essentially identical information about exchange rates and headlines. The only exceptions to the universality of information are the private data about positions and the in-house research done to support the trading function.

The currency markets are largely unregulated. Traders rely on the integrity of their trading partners and their bank. Both parties to a trade assume that the other's word is good. Each understands that the other is unwilling to assume unwarranted losses. Each anticipates that the other will quote rates close to the prices showing on his or her monitor. This mutual knowledge and the respect it engenders are built upon the scores of trades the trader makes each day. The countless iteration of one-on-one social exchanges supports cooperation and punishes deception (Holland, 1975/1992). Prices are the product of the cumulative interaction of this network of traders engaged in social exchanges. Fluctuations in prices reflect the fluid consensus of the network.

Traders make money by holding positions that most others in the market want. The value of these positions increases as the exchange rates change. Traders lose money by holding positions that no one else wants. The need to predict exchange-rate fluctuations creates the need to understand and anticipate others' behavior. This need constrains the knowledge the trader brings to the task: The spot currency trader needs to know how to understand and anticipate the behavior of the market, that is, to understand and anticipate the behavior of a network of traders. Although all traders pursue their own self-interests, they cannot afford to forget that other traders know them as well as they know the others. Survival in the spot currency markets depends on one's ability to understand what the market wants.

Asymmetry of Information Under Conflict of Interest

Asymmetry of information is the second condition that engenders risk in social exchange. Information is asymmetrically distributed when somebody possesses information that others cannot readily access. The asymmetry makes those in need of information vulnerable to opportunistic behavior. When an agent relies on asymmetrically distributed information to make a decision, the provider of such information may opt to manipulate it for the purpose of steering the decision process toward a desired, favorable outcome.

From the perspective of the information user, risk is the possibility that the information used to make a decision has been manipulated by its provider. The realization of risk, that is, the actual occurrence of a successful manipulation, produces a loss because the decision is made on the basis of tainted information. The decision outcome is not what the decision maker would have selected without the manipulation.

Second partner review is an auditing task that exemplifies the risk posed by asymmetric distribution of information between the management of a company and the public of individuals who make decisions based on the financial statements issued by the company. Because many of these decisions (e.g., investing in the company's securities or granting it a loan) have serious consequences for the company's well-being, management is motivated to manipulate the reported financial information to influence the behavior of these decision makers (Johnson, Grazioli, & Jamal, 1993).

Independent auditors have the general goal of verifying that financial statements issued by companies adhere to a set of principles (called the *generally accepted accounting principles*) that define how to fairly portray a company's economic condition. The task of interest here – second partner review – is a quality control procedure performed by a partner in an accounting firm at the end of the audit of a client. The second partner does not direct the audit. The objective of the review is to validate the conclusion (called an audit *opinion*) that has been reached by the partner in charge of the client audit.

Several different opinions are possible. An *unqualified* opinion means that the auditor believes that the financial statements issued by a client company are fair. An *adverse* opinion means that the auditor believes that there are substantial departures from a fair portrayal of the economic conditions of the company. Because the public and other users of the financial statements largely rely on the auditors' professional judgment, it is paramount for management to obtain an unqualified opinion.

When management successfully manipulates a company's financial statements, both the public and the auditors stand to lose. The users of the financial statements lose financial resources because decisions are made on the basis of deceptive information. When (and if) the manipulation is uncovered, the auditor loses professional reputation and may become the target of the stakeholders' lawsuits (Albrecht, Wernz, & Williams, 1995). To avoid these losses, the auditor needs to manage the risk that the financial officers of the company have manipulated financial information. Activities designed to detect manipulations of information, such as the second partner review, are a means to manage this risk.

For the auditor, thinking about the thinking of other agents involved in the communication of financial information is a determinant of detection success (Grazioli, 1997; Johnson et al., 1993). To do this, the auditor needs to understand management's possible goals and the possible manipulations that can be used to achieve them.

Why Is Managing Risk in Social Exchange Difficult?

Agents in social exchange, including traders and auditors, are faced with the problem of managing the potential for loss posed by interaction with others. Solving this ill-defined problem is difficult. If it were easy to manage risk in social exchange, confidence men (and lawyers) would be out of work.

Shanteau's (1992) theory of expert competence suggests why this problem is difficult to solve, even in settings where problem solvers enjoy high motivation, resources, and training. Shanteau enumerates several task characteristics that are expected to make a task intrinsically difficult and that are associated with correspondingly poor levels of "expert" performance. Six of these characteristics are relevant to the management of risk in social exchange and would be expected to lead to poor performance in the tasks we address:

- dynamic (changeable) stimuli
- unique tasks
- decisions about behavior
- experts' disagreement on stimuli
- subjective analysis only
- unavailability of feedback

Dynamic stimuli and unique (low base-rate) tasks are sources of novelty. Novelty makes task performance difficult because the task cannot easily be seen as an instance of a familiar class of problems for which the solution is known. Decisions about behavior, disagreements on stimuli, and subjective analyses all lack objective standards. A lack of feedback or objective standards for comparison makes task performance problematic. Without feedback or standards, it is often difficult to define the solution or to judge its proximity.

Most of the six characteristics identified by Shanteau are likely to be present to some degree in trading and auditing settings. Dynamic stimuli in unique configurations, disagreements about stimuli, and decision making about behavior are salient in the spot markets. Decisions about behavior, disagreements about stimuli, lack of feedback, and subjective analysis are salient in detecting manipulations of financial information.

These considerations lead us to expect that few, if any, experts would emerge in the spot markets or in the detection of financial manipulations. Rather, we would expect the level of performance of experts to be relatively poor. This is, in fact, what we observe in the two settings. Available data on the currency markets (Smith, 1996) and fraud detection (Albrecht et al., 1995) show that it is difficult to beat the market systematically or to catch con artists.

By contrast, the same studies have also shown that there is a small number of individuals who seem to be relatively skillful at managing risk in social exchanges (Grazioli, 1997; Johnson, Grazioli, Jamal, & Zualkernan, 1992; Smith, 1996). In the next sections, we propose a theory and a model of the information processing behavior of those individuals who perform competently at the task of managing risk in social exchange.

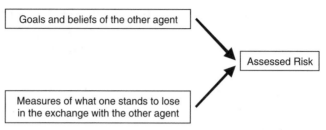

Figure 3.1 Risk assessment in social exchange.

Theory of Assessing Risk in Social Exchange

Drawing from early work by Einhorn and Hogarth (1986), we propose that an individual's assessment of risk in social exchange is influenced by two factors: an understanding of the other agent and a representation of what the individual stands to lose. The individual's representation of what might be lost in the exchange provides the scale for the process of risk assessment. The scale of risk is set high when the individual has a lot to lose. Understanding the other agent's goals and beliefs provides the information to be compared. Figure 3.1 illustrates the main components of risk assessment in social exchange.

We assume that risk assessment is done by taking what Daniel Dennett has called the *intentional stance*:

> Here is how it works: first you decide to treat the object whose behavior is to be predicted as a rational agent; then you figure out what beliefs that agent ought to have, given its place in the world and its purpose. Then you figure out what desires it ought to have, on the same considerations, and finally you predict that this rational agent will act to further its goals in the light of its beliefs. A little practical reasoning from the chosen set of beliefs and desires will in many – but not all – instances yield a decision about what the agent ought to do; that is what you predict the agent will do. (Dennett, 1987, p. 17)

The strategy takes two steps. First, the agent assigns to a *system* the goals and beliefs that the system "ought to have," given its environment and assuming that it is rational. The goals that a system ought to have are those that directly or instrumentally serve to further its needs and wants. Similarly, its beliefs are assumed to be those it ought to have about its environment: beliefs that match an objective observer's definition of truth.

In the second step, the agent predicts the system's behavior in the light of the assigned beliefs and goals, given the assumption that the system is rational (Newell, 1982). Taking the intentional stance works "because we are close enough approximations of optimal cognitive design" (Dennett, 1987). Its power consists in the reduction of the set of behaviors that it makes sense to expect.

In social environments, the system may be another agent (e.g., an audit client) or an aggregate agent (e.g., the market). Dennett's analysis suggests that agents involved in social exchange will treat the beliefs and goals of others as causes of their behavior. Attributing beliefs and goals to others vastly simplifies the task of understanding (predicting) their (future) behavior. Understanding and predicting the behavior of others enables the agent to invoke domain knowledge to anticipate losses and take actions that can counter (the effect of) actions taken by others.

Although Dennett is persuasive in arguing that taking the intentional stance is a powerful strategy for understanding and predicting the behaviors of others, he provides only limited detail about the processing that supports it. In what follows, we shall suppose that the process underlying the intentional stance is that of *ascription*. We define ascription as the generation of an inference of the goals and beliefs of an agent, given knowledge about this agent, cues to its behavior, and the environment in which it operates. Ascribing the behavior of others enables an agent to take action to manage the risk the others pose.

As a limitation, we recognize that the process of ascription described here is one of many decision processes required to manage risk in social exchange. Processing of task-specific domain knowledge is the usual focus of studies of expert performance (e.g., Ericsson & Smith, 1991; Peters, 1990). Our focus is on the process of ascription itself.

In the following section, we consider a general model of the ascription process derived from work in social psychology and cognition. We then proceed to test domain-specific models of competent decision making in social exchange that include ascription mechanisms.

Dispositional Attribution

Our model of ascription borrows from the work of Trope (1986; Trope, Cohen, & Maoz, 1988) and other social psychologists who wrote on attribution theory. Attribution theory deals with how the social perceiver uses information to arrive at a causal explanation for events. The theory examines how information is gathered and how this information is combined to form a causal judgment (Fiske & Taylor, 1991).

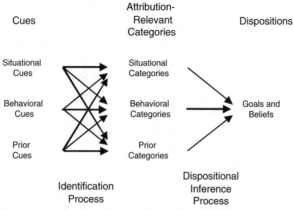

Figure 3.2 Ascription. (Adapted from Trope, 1986.)

Several models have been proposed to account for the attribution process (e.g., Heider, 1958; Jones & Harris, 1967; Kelley, 1971; Kruglanski, 1980). Reckers, Wong-On-Wing, and Krull (1992) have applied the theory of correspondent inferences (a variant of attribution theory) to analyze auditors' assessment of management's dispositions.

Trope has proposed a domain-independent two-stage model of dispositional (intentional) attribution. Because of its generality, we adopt Trope's model as a framework to describe the basic processes and representations that compose ascription in social exchange. Whereas for Trope a *disposition* may be an attitude, a motive, a personality trait, or an ability, we restrict the term to intentional states, specifically to the other agent's goals and beliefs. We also restrict our use of the term *Agent* to the individual doing the ascription. We use the term *Other* to refer to the target of the Agent's ascription process.

Figure 3.2 presents Trope's (1986) two-stage model of dispositional attribution. From left to right, the elements of the model are (1) the inputs to the ascription process – cues from the environment to the Other's dispositions, (2) the first stage of processing, called *identification*, (3) attribution-relevant categories, (4) the second stage of processing, called *dispositional inference*, and (5) the output of the ascription process – the Agent's attribution of the Other's goals and beliefs.

Trope distinguishes three types of cues: situational, behavioral, and prior. Situational cues are cues from the environment, such as economic forces or industry characteristics, that are assumed to be beyond the control of both the Agent and the Other and to which both are likely to respond. Behavioral cues are actions or events that are assumed to be controlled or influenced by the Other. Prior cues are past information about the Other.

Three parallel classes of constructs mediate the two stages of processing. These constructs are domain-relevant categories that the Agent believes either reveal or influence the Other's goals and beliefs. Together, these categories comprise the Agent's cognitive representation of how cues in the environment either drive or are driven by the Other's disposition. The categories provide meaning for the cues and provide contextual information for the subsequent identification of other incoming cues.

Two stages of processing link the cues to the categories and the categories to the dispositions. The first stage is *spontaneous* identification that associates cues with attribution-relevant categories. The process of identification maps cues into relevant categories (e.g., classifying a behavior as aggressive or secretive). According to Trope, identification is *instantaneous* and context driven:

> [G]iven that the identification process is highly practiced and closely related to the properties of the stimulus information, it is likely to be performed unconsciously and automatically.... (Trope, 1986, p. 241; see also Cosmides & Tooby, 1995)

The second stage of processing is *deliberate* dispositional inference that integrates the identified categories to assign a disposition to the Other (e.g., the intent to be an aggressive seller or to be deceitful). The assigned disposition is a domain-relevant goal or belief that the Other ought to have in light of the current situation.

Dispositional inference assesses the cumulative impact of the attribution-relevant categories. In Trope's words, inference is deliberate and driven by *causal schemata* that specify the procedures for arriving at an attribution of disposition to the Other. As Trope and others illustrate, the causal schemata are often relatively simple algorithmic expressions (Cheng & Holyoak, 1985; Cosmides, 1985). We suggest that appropriate inference procedures in social exchange are fully specified by each of the attribution-relevant categories, making their invocation relatively straightforward.

The original work by Trope is the analytical tool that we use to sharpen our understanding of how goals and beliefs are ascribed to Others in specific domains of human activity. We now apply Trope's framework first to spot currency trading and then to second partner review.

Ascription in Spot Currency Trading

Smith (1996) developed and tested an information processing model of risk management in spot currency trading in a series of experiments with professional traders as subjects. The first experiment informed the specification of a trading model. A computer implementation of the model (1) emulated both profitable and unprofitable trading by the traders in the first experiment and (2) predicted their behavior in the second experiment. Smith concluded from this work that the knowledge that supports traders' ability to anticipate the market is a component of trading competence. Here we employ an example from one trader's concurrent verbal report to illustrate how anticipating the market is an exemplar of Trope's general model of ascription.

Experimentation. The illustration requires a brief preface on the experiment that elicited it. Three professional spot currency traders from a mid-sized Twin Cities commercial bank agreed to participate in the experiment. The traders' task was to do their job: to monitor positions in two currencies, to make trades for their bank's customers, to generate profits for their bank, and to square up by the end of the trading day (e.g., 24:00 Greenwich Mean Time, GMT). During the experiment, the traders' thinking processes were captured by asking them to think aloud and by recording their verbalizations. The experiments were conducted in 1993 and 1994, before the introduction of the euro.

The experimental materials were eight scripted spot-market scenarios that compressed realistic world events into compelling trading days. The scenarios were scripted to challenge the traders and to elicit decision making that could be used to generate hypotheses about the organization of the traders' information processing. The scenarios had two parts, an *overnight report* and a simulated *trading day*. The overnight report portrayed the current global socioeconomic and political conditions that provide the context for the trading day. The trader began each session by reading a paper copy of the overnight report. During the trading day, prices in two currencies were continually updated on a price screen, headlines periodically scrolled across a news screen, and the "telephone" repeatedly rang with requests to quote prices. The trader was able at any time to toggle among screens and to initiate a trade.

A commercial PC-based foreign exchange training package (FXPlus, Chisholm-Roth, Ltd.) made it possible to script and present the trading days to participants. The training package simulates the Reuters trading desk. It has five alternate display screens: three information displays – prices, news, and position – and two trading screens – quoting and dealing. The trader toggled among the five screens to obtain different types of information and to make trades.

Example. The overnight report for the scenario excerpted here indicates that the U.S. Department of Commerce would release data on wholesale prices sometime during the day and that the market expected prices to rise by 0.4%. The excerpt begins during the trading day with the trader reading the headline about U.S. wholesale prices.

Session Time (GMT)

    News Screen

6:55   14:10 Washington, 17 May – US wholesale prices rose 0.6 pct in April, a slight increase over the 0.5 pct rise in March, Department of Commerce said.

    Transcript

6:58   "Wholesale prices up point six as expected. Wait, wholesale [scans overnight report] zero point four, so they're not going to like the dollar on that one

7:02   and I'm okay against Swiss; Let's get rid of some yen"

In Trope's terminology, this excerpt shows the trader using a situational cue (see Figure 3.2) and a prior cue to invoke a situational category and to ascribe a belief to the market: "they're not going to like the dollar on that one." The headline is the situational cue. The value the market was said to expect is the prior cue. The trader read the headline and interpreted it by comparing the value reported in the headline (0.6%) to the value the market was said to expect (0.4%). The standard for comparison is the situational category. The category for news about inflation indicates that an increase in inflation (e.g., actual minus prior, 0.6% − 0.4%) is bearish for the relevant currency. This standard for comparison prompted the trader to attribute a belief to the market given the news: "they're not going to like the dollar on that one."

The trader's decision making did not stop with the ascription. He moved on to use the ascribed belief to infer the direction in which the market would drive prices (down) and to assess the risk of holding his positions. The trader concluded that the anticipated selling would help his short U.S. dollar–Swiss franc position but hurt his long dollar–yen position, which provoked his decision to trade the dollar–yen. The

Figure 3.3 The instance of ascription seen in the trader's concurrent verbal report.

ascription of a disposition to the market – "they're not going to like the dollar on that one" – is the key step in the process of deciding how to manage the risk of holding these particular positions in the next few minutes.

Traders ascribe beliefs to the market in order to decide how to manage risk. Figure 3.3 places the instance of ascription seen in the excerpt within the context of our general model (Figure 3.2). The discussion that follows unpacks the components of the ascription process observed in spot currency trading.

Cues. Situational cues are headlines, rumors, and news stories. The spot markets live and die by fact and rumor. To meet the markets' thirst for news, the wire services relay headlines from around the world as soon as they are made. Some headlines appear at scheduled times. Foremost among scheduled news items are government releases of economic indicators like the wholesale price index (WPI) in the previous example.

Market activity tends to slow prior to the scheduled release of a key index or announcement. The Associated Press can be trusted to supply justification for a slowdown in the markets. For example:

Many dealers with mark holdings have moved to the sidelines ahead of Thursday's meeting of Germany's central bank. Members of the Bundesbank are not expected to take any specific action at the meeting, but dealers are concerned the German interest rates could eventually come down. (June 29, 1993)

Other headlines, like the dissolution of the Japanese Diet or the start of Operation Desert Storm, follow no schedule. Trading activity can be driven to a frenzy by unexpected events like the following:

Tuesday 18:00, London – BRITAIN WITHDRAWS FROM EMS
Prime Minister Major has announced that Britain has dropped out, at least
temporarily, of the European monetary system. He added "massive speculative flow has continued to disrupt the functioning of the exchange-rate
mechanism."

Often the market does not bother to distinguish between news and
rumor (false reports) about a topic (Kurtzman, 1993). The chief difference
is that the market tends to hold its belief a little longer when the report
is true.

Behavioral cues are the direction of prices. Prices are driven by the
consensus of market opinion. Price formation is the behavior traders
work to understand. In the example, the trader did not use a behavioral
cue.

Prior cues are the trader's preexisting expectations for the direction of
prices. In the example, the prior was provided to the trader in the form
of an overnight report. Banks prepare overnight reports every night to
help their traders to anticipate the market. Traders read the report at
the beginning of their trading day and before they begin to trade. The
report, condensed from wire service and internal analyses, attempts to
define the day's market context. The report lists scheduled headlines
for the day and week ahead, consensus predictions about scheduled
headlines, and summaries of market activity during the previous day
and week.

Consensus predictions about scheduled headlines can seriously skew
a market's opinion. When actual events turn out to differ from consensus prediction, the market response can be draconian. In the previous
excerpt, the actual event, the situational cue (WPI up 0.6%), differed
from the prior cue (WPI to rise 0.4%). The disparity led the trader to
expect a sharp market response.

Situational, behavioral, and prior cues are the initial input to the ascription process depicted in Figure 3.2. Ascription is decomposed into
two related subprocesses. First, the cues are used to generate attribution-
relevant categories (identification). In turn, categories are used to generate dispositions (dispositional inference). The next subsections discuss
the components of Trope's model in the context of currency trading.

The Identification Process. Identification is the first stage of processing in
Trope's general model for ascription. At the trading desk, identification

defines membership of an instance in a class. In the previous example, the trader associates the headline about the U.S. WPI with the class of news Inflation (a situational category). Trope describes the identification process as *automatic*. This description, though facile, appears to apply to spot currency traders. None of the traders in Smith's study ever paused to determine what kind of news a particular headline was. The apparent automaticity of the identification process is the product of years of experience at the trading desk.

Attribution-Relevant Categories. Based on his study of currency traders at the trading desk and in laboratory scenarios, Smith proposed that traders invoke 10 categories of news to interpret headlines in order to anticipate the market. The categories, listed in Table 3.1, are intended to be mutually exclusive and exhaustive. They are both a source of generality for the ascription process and a principled account of the traders' knowledge about the impact of world events on the market's behavior.

The first column in Table 3.1 contains the names given to the 10 categories. The second column contains illustrative members of the categories. Each member represents a generic headline topic, that is, the WPI rather than a specific headline (e.g., the U.S. WPI for March). The third column specifies the appropriate algorithm for comparing situational and prior cues that are members of that category. The fourth column lists the values of implicit standards to be invoked in the absence of prior cues.

The first four categories – economic growth, political uncertainty, inflation, and central bank monetary/government fiscal policy – are the most common. Arguably, these are situational categories. News about economic growth and central bank policy are both assessed using the specification for comparison "positive change is good for the relevant currency," that is, the market can be expected to react favorably to news of increasing growth and to news of rising interest rates. The two categories are distinguished by the implicit market standards the traders invoked to anticipate the market. The traders assessed news about economic growth by checking for a positive or negative value; they acted as if the standard for comparison was zero percent. In contrast, the traders assessed news about central bank policy by checking for positive or negative change regardless of value; they acted as if there were no absolute standard for comparison.

The traders consistently inferred that the market would respond quickly and strongly to devalue the currency of a country that broadcast

Table 3.1. *Categories of News Heeded by Currency Traders*

Category	Sample Topics (Members of the Category)	Specification for Comparison	Market Standards (Implicit Standards for Comparison in the Absence of Priors)
Situational			
Economic growth	Gross domestic product	Positive change is bullish for the relevant currency (good when up)	Bullish when above 0%
Political uncertainty	President rushed to hospital	Necessarily bearish for the relevant currency; for priors: buy the rumor, sell the fact	
Inflation	Wholesale price index (WPI)	Negative change is bullish for the relevant currency (good when down)	Bullish when below 2% year-on-year
Central bank monetary policy/ government fiscal policy	Interest rates Foreign trade	Positive change is bullish for the relevant currency (good when up)	
Unemployment	Nonfarm payroll data	Negative change is bullish for the relevant currency (good when down)	Bullish when below 6% year-on-year
Immaterial	Yeltsin to visit Minnesota	Ignored	
Prior			
Old news	Central bank bought paper	Ignored	
Forecasts	Estimate of next quarter's WPI	Ignored	
Behavioral			
Up trend	Currency strong Peace accord	Necessarily bullish for the relevant currency	
Down trend	Currency weak	Necessarily bearish for the relevant currency	

news of political uncertainty. The basis for their decision was not so much a true comparison as an outright classification of political uncertainty as bad news. There is no market standard for news about political uncertainty. The diversity of potential topics – from beheadings to oil embargos – precludes a single market standard.

The third category of news is inflation. Topics in this category are dominated by indices released monthly by government agencies, such as the WPI. Headlines about these topics invariably contain a quantitative value, such as "The U.S. consumer price index rose by 0.6% in March." The traders responded to headlines about inflation by (1) comparing the value announced in the headline to a standard for comparison and by (2) inferring that the market will believe the headline is beneficial for the relevant currency if and only if the announced value is less than or equal to the standard. When a prior cue told them the value the market was said to expect, the expected value acted as the standard for comparison. For example:

Session Time (GMT)
      14:00 Washington, 18 May – The U.S. consumer price index rose by 0.6 pct in March, up by 9.7 pct year on year, Commerce Department reported.
15:48   "The US CPI is up point 6. That is as expected."

The trader proceeded to take no action. His (lack of) behavior suggests that he invoked knowledge that the market does not punish the relevant currency when its expectations are met.

The traders responded to topics in the fifth category of news – unemployment – in much the same was as they responded to news about inflation. They (1) compared the gist of the headline to an expected value (if they had one) or to an implicit market standard and (2) inferred that the market would believe the headline was beneficial for the relevant currency if and only if the announced value was less than the standard. Traders use prior cues to infer what the market expects, and in turn use the ascribed expectations as standards for comparison with subsequent information.

The immaterial category contains headlines about political events that drew no response from the traders. Membership in the category is unexpectedly large. Roughly half of the headlines were written to investigate the traders' response to news of political uncertainty. The common theme uniting these headlines is bluster, diatribe, or innuendo unlikely to lead to action. A student of political science might be able to use the distinctions the traders drew between material and immaterial political topics to inform a model of the materiality of news. This research goes no further than to suggest that the traders treated the market as a keen judge of the support behind the rhetoric.

The old news category contains headlines that revise historic (prior) data about topics in the categories economic growth, inflation, central bank policy, and unemployment. Although traders read headlines that contain revisions to data, they give no indication that they use them to anticipate the market. Similarly, traders appear to ignore forecasts, headlines that project future values for news about economic growth, inflation, central bank policy, and unemployment. The traders' specification for comparison was, in effect, to ignore old news and forecasts.

The last two categories – up trend and down trend – are used to assess behavioral cues. Up trend provides the specification for dispositional inference based on rising prices. Down trend provides the specification for dispositional inference based on falling prices.

The Dispositional Inference Process. The specifications for comparison shown in Table 3.1 indicate the appropriate algorithm for making an inference about the belief the market will form given a situational cue (headline) with or without an associated prior cue (expectation). The knowledge contained in the 10 categories of news reduces the process of dispositional inference to a straightforward comparison of evidence. This knowledge supports the comparison of situational and prior cues (and the assessment of behavioral cues) and is one of the foundations of competent decision making in spot currency trading.

Ascription in Second Partner Review

Johnson, Grazioli, Jamal, and Berryman (2001) have recently argued that understanding how Others think and act is a key for success in detecting financial manipulations. Their work has applied Dennett's intentional stance strategy to the field of auditing (1992, 1993) and includes the development and testing of several information processing models of second partner review.

The 1992 and 2001 studies have examined the responses of auditors engaged in the second partner review of a set of financial statements. Unknown to the auditors, some of the reviewed statements were fraudulent. The auditors were asked to "think aloud" as they reviewed the statements. Their verbal protocols were tape-recorded, transcribed, and coded with reliable coding techniques (Johnson et al., 1992).

The coded protocols were the basis for developing a process model (a computer program) of competent detection of financial manipulations in second partner review. At its core, the model embodies two main skills: (1) the ability to interpret cues in the financial statement in light of what management might want to accomplish and (2) the ability to combine these cues to form a final opinion. The 1992 study showed that experimentally enabling or disabling the expression of these two skills in the model allowed the model to generate a range of behavior that is similar to the range observed in the auditors who participated in the experiments.

In particular, it was found that the models (and auditors) that ascribe goals to the management of a client company are more successful in detecting financial manipulations than the models that do not. As was done for the currency traders, we illustrate this point by commenting on one of the auditor's concurrent verbal report and by using Trope's general model as a frame of reference.

Experimentation. The data presented here are derived from the 2001 study. Twenty-four senior partners from the major accounting firms were asked to perform a second partner review of five sets of financial statements. All five sets described companies for which the partner in charge of the audit intended to issue an unqualified (i.e., "clean") opinion.

All the statements described real companies. Four of the five statements were fraudulently manipulated by the company's management for the purpose of making the company appear more profitable than it actually was. The following example is excerpted from the protocol of subject S17.

Example. S17 examined the financial statements of "Surgical Products," a fictitious name for a company operating in the medical products industry. The company severely misstated its earnings by means of several manipulations, including overstating its inventory, opportunistically changing the accounting treatment of its research and development expenses, and recording shipments of products to wholesalers and customers as sales (Johnson et al., 1992, 2001).

S17 began his analysis by reading the general description of the company's products and markets as provided by management.

Figure 3.4 The instance of ascription seen in the auditor's concurrent verbal report.

S17   ...Okay, they've got a line of products that has one very good characteristic to them from the standpoint of a successful company and that is that they are disposable, so they sell and the user only gets one use out of them.

...Sales of their "autosuture" products which is one line [...] account for all, substantively all, or 99% of company profits, so those other products are not necessarily doing um that well... either that or that they are brand new products and they haven't [...] achieved their market share yet, but that's something to look at in terms of realizability of whatever investment they have in them.

...Okay, attributes its growth in profits this year to three elements. [...] Ah – one is selling price increases of 10% which is pretty strong increase and then growth in volume and ah new products....

[reading about the competition]...It is basically a small player in this particular market for wound closure [...] which makes it surprising that they have been able to sustain a 10% price increase but ah it could be that their products are unique in the marketplace.

The instance of the ascription process presented in the protocol within the context of Trope's process model is graphically summarized in Figure 3.4. In Trope's terms, the company's products, markets, and competition are situational cues that the auditor uses to identify corresponding situational ("small player," "one-product company") and behavioral ("highly innovative, risky") categories.

More generally, *situational cues* are information about the company's internal and external economic environment. For instance, the amount of inventory is a situational cue describing the company's internal environment; the level of market competition is a situational cue describing the company's external environment. Most of the current balances in the income statement and balance sheet are situational cues. The past balances are *prior cues*. The following is an excerpt from S17's analysis of the inventory balances:

S17   . . . Large increase in inventories, primarily in the finished goods area . . .
cost of goods sold is up 48% . . .
inventories are up 76% . . .
again that includes quite a bit of raw materials, which means that the grossed invent[ory] . . . the grossed up inventories after completion are up substantially greater than 76% [. . .]
so I'd like to understand what the strategy is in terms of building inventory and why so much finished goods isn't being sold
this goes back to the issue of getting a breakdown by product since, as noted earlier, only 1% of the company's sales comes from a number of different products. . . .
make sure that they do not have any realizable value problems or any excess inventory problem.

S17 exploits the fact that data are organized in terms of current versus prior reporting years to compute percentages of change, which in turn allows him to generate the situational category "inventory is too high," as well as the behavioral categories "they are not selling their product" and "they are not managing inventory well." The chronological structure of the financial statements offers a rich, well-organized set of prior and situational cues from which to infer situational and behavioral categories.

S17   . . . Now reading the um accounting policy on molds and dies well they've got um what is either a correction of an error accounted for in the current period or a change in accounting which they are calling . . .

which they're calling a development of improved information
it's a ... basically capitalization of engineering labor
certain raw material costs ... hum ... it is really quite significant
since the company's pretax income is essentially flat [...] so
you've got a fairly dramatic change in accounting which affects
the consistency of the costs elements in the income statement
without that change the earnings would have apparently been
down significantly in the current year

In this passage, S17 uses a behavioral cue (the changes made to the
accounting policy) and a situational cue (the impact on the bottom
line) as a basis to derive a behavioral category "aggressive accounting
changes that make the company look more profitable." More generally,
behavioral cues are information on management's actions and reporting
choices.

S17   ... Now reading the Research and Development accounting
         policy and R and D cost are down dramatically ... which is odd
         considering their statements about developing new products
         and the tremendous investment they are making in molds and
         dies associated with the new products

The comparison of a prior cue with a situational cue (past and present
R&D costs) generates the behavioral category "lowering research spend-
ing." However, this category is in stark contradiction with a previously
identified behavioral cue, that is, the development of new products.
S17 solves the contradiction between cues and categories by combining
them with the "aggressive accounting changes" category previously
generated:

S17   ... Could very well be that they have shifted over some of their
         effort to ah actually get these products into production ...

which is one the manipulations actually perpetrated by the company's
management to increase reported net income. This ascribed goal is consistent with other cues and previously generated dispositions:

S17   The company's got a strong equity position – increased from
         54 million to 100 million ... substantial part of the increase is
         coming from a public offering
         they had public offerings both in 19X1 and 19X2
         again suggest they are very sensitive to maintaining good earn-
         ings trends and good earnings.

By the end of his review, S17 identified many other items in the financial statements of Surgical Products that he interpreted as manipulated or as evidence that manipulations took place. In his concluding remarks he stated:

S17   ... It is unlikely that we would issue an unqualified report [...] if everything is a problem, then I'd say that they've got a pervasive problem with the entire financial statements and I would say that it should be an adverse opinion

which is the correct way to manage the risk posed by management of Surgical Products.

The Identification Process. Johnson et al. (1992, 1993, 2001) argue that auditors identify ascription-relevant categories by means of a comparison between observed cues (i.e., the available financial information) and expectations about these cues. Some of these expectations are independent of the financial information provided by the company and are the result of the auditor's knowledge of his or her domain. Other expectations are generated as a function of the information presented in the financial statement.

There is both deliberate and automatic information processing in the identification process used by the auditors. S17 began his review of the inventory balance by deliberately calculating a percentage of change between past and current values of the inventory balance. A more automatic comparison of the percentage of change and its expected value led him to categorize the balance as too high.

The Dispositional Inference Process. The cited studies also specify algorithms by which the dispositional inference process may work. Auditors generate hypotheses about the manager's goals and actions in response to the concurrent presence of three cognitive representations: (1) a violated expectation (an anomaly), (2) an assessment that management might have caused the anomaly, and (3) an assessment of the relevance of the anomaly to possible managerial goals.

For example, the observed value of inventory violated S17's expectation of what that value should be. This anomaly prompted the explanation that the difference may have resulted from a mishandling of the accounting procedures that determined the current balance for inventory, and specifically from neglecting "realizable value problems or any excess inventory problem." In addition, the anomaly contributed to the general goal of "maintaining good earnings trends and good earnings."

Jointly, these three elements led to an ascription to management of the specific goal of intentionally overstating inventory. This ascription was a critical component in the final outcome of S17's review of the financial statements presented by Surgical Products.

The experimental data presented thus far have illustrated how professionals who need to manage risk in social exchanges succeed at their tasks by ascribing goals and beliefs to Others. The next section deepens our investigation of the ascription process by experimenting with information processing models of currency traders and auditors.

The Role of Ascription in Managing Social Exchange Risk

The behavioral data elicited by our simulated market scenarios (spot currency trading) and financial reports (second partner review) provided the basis for constructing models of the information processes underlying the performance of experienced traders and auditors. A description of the models allows us to move beyond the anecdotal analyses presented so far and forces us to be specific about the processing that supports ascription. It also sets the stage for the creation of two *ablated* models. The ablated models are the original models with the implementation of ascription removed or modified. As a last step, we assess the critical role of ascription in managing social exchange risk by contrasting the behavior of the full and ablated models with that of our experimental subjects.

A Model of Spot Currency Trading

The development of the model of currency trading borrows the paradigm of process control from human factors psychology and industrial engineering (Broadbent, 1977; Edwards & Lees, 1974; Moray, 1986; Parasuraman, 1986). The goal of the process control Agent is to keep a process within operational limits as its environment continually changes. The Agent makes decisions about whether, when, and how to take action to control a dynamic process (Wiener, 1984). A familiar example is driving a car; the driver's goal is to keep the car on the road and at a safe distance from Others as traffic conditions vary. The driver's decisions are designed to guide the car down the road. The process control Agent's decisions manage the risk engendered by the interaction of the process with its environment.

The process the spot currency trader seeks to control is his or her position – the value of assets exposed in the international markets. As a process control Agent, the trader samples market information and makes decisions about whether, when, and how to make trades that keep that position within limits of acceptable risk.

There are two general algorithms for process control – feedback control and feedforward control (Brehmer, 1992). An Agent who relies on feedback control samples information about the current state of the process and its environment in order to respond to the current risks and take appropriate action. An Agent who relies on feedforward control samples information that affords anticipation of the future state of the process and its environment in order to infer future risks and take appropriate action. In many domains, skilled Agents display a mixture of the two algorithms (e.g., Bainbridge, 1974).

Our model of spot currency trading (Smith, 1996) proposes that traders adopt a mixture of feedback and feedforward control. Their method of feedback control responds to changing prices with an assessment of the risk facing their positions at that instant and with a judgment of whether and when to make a trade. Their method of feedforward control anticipates the market in order to infer the risks their positions are likely to face in the next few minutes. The focus here is exclusively on the traders' method for feedforward control.

Anticipating the Market: Feedforward Control. We argue that traders adopt the intentional stance to anticipate the market. Specifically, we assume that they address the market as if it were a single rational Other that, on average and over the long run, acts in manner that directly or instrumentally increases its profitability. Adopting the intentional stance with respect to a composite Other requires the assumption that individual Others within that composite share the same goal. We assume that all traders in the spot market share the same goal: increased profitability.

Attributing to the market the goal of increasing profits enables a powerful application of the intentional stance. The trader takes the intentional stance to anticipate the beliefs the market will form in order to predict the direction in which it will drive prices. The basis for the market's beliefs and for the trader's ascription of those beliefs is information about global socioeconomic and political events. This information takes the form of situational cues and prior cues. The situational cues are headlines broadcast by wire services to news screens at trading desks around the world. The prior cues are expectations for the information the market will find when it reads headlines.

Anticipating the market's beliefs allows traders to infer how the market will behave given the beliefs it has formed. Attributing beliefs to the market vastly simplifies the traders' task of understanding (predicting) the market's (future) behavior. Understanding and predicting the direction in which the market will drive prices in response to the headlines it reads enables traders to assess the risks the market's behavior may pose to their positions and to make trades that manage those risks.

Performance Model. To test our model of currency trading we developed a rule-based system that trades foreign currencies in six markets (e.g., the U.S. dollar vs. the German mark). The system, called SPOT, responds to the same stimuli presented to the traders in Smith's laboratory experiments (1996). For each of the eight trading scenarios employed in the experiments, SPOT processes sequentially the news in the overnight report, the headlines, the hourly prices for the currencies, and the request for quotes submitted to the human traders. In response to these inputs, SPOT assumes positions in the currency markets in which it operates. Appendix A describes SPOT's algorithms and technical implementation.

Ablated Model. To ascertain the impact on trading behavior of the ability to ascribe beliefs to the market, we created a version of SPOT that does not ascribe beliefs to the market. Specifically, we modified the original program so that it never reads headlines. This ablation makes SPOT blind to situational cues. The inability to respond to situational cues makes it impossible for SPOT to infer the direction in which the market will drive prices and to assess the future risk to its positions. As a consequence, the ablated model operates in a pure feedback-driven mode. Its decisions to make a trade are prompted by comparing its profits (losses) and the rate of change of prices to static thresholds of acceptable risk. The only measure of risk available to the ablated model is the size of its positions. Accordingly, it invariably directs its attention to the larger position rather than the more newsworthy position.

Results. Table 3.2 presents the profits (losses) generated by the full and ablated models and the professional currency traders in the laboratory experiment. The eight large boxes correspond to the eight trading scenarios. The ninth scenario was used as the subjects' warmup task and was dropped from the analysis.

Table 3.2. *Profits (Losses) Incurred by the Traders and the Models*

	German Marks	Italian Lira	British Pounds	French Francs	Japanese Yen	Swiss Francs
Trader 1	$8,171	($2,237)	($4,200)	$121	($53,639)	($4)
Full	$4,966	$148	($7,618)	($2,566)	($26,042)	($3,456)
Ablated	$1,291	($3,447)	($20,750)	($475)	($27,801)	($5,186)
Trader 2	$3,206	($4,961)	$26,678	$4,982	($26,649)	($5,414)
Full	($724)	($3,599)	$15,805	$7,166	($15,476)	($7,664)
Ablated	$1,653	($3,257)	($2,799)	$6,568	($20,966)	($12,574)
Trader 3	($3,086)	($1,102)	$29,606	$3,062	($53,613)	$1,209
Full	($1,874)	($3,029)	$55,323	$4,770	($27,332)	$4,600
Ablated	$1,392	($4,478)	$11,734	$5,139	($35,702)	$4,734
Trader 1	$13,250	$28,748			$27,089	$30,050
Full	$11,574	$20,447			$15,145	$31,680
Ablated	$6,495	$28,217			$6,605	$21,155
Trader 2	$31,086	$33,137			($2,275)	$9,067
Full	$33,470	$16,856			($922)	$15,905
Ablated	$25,363	$4,285			($8,969)	$7,257
Trader 3	$3,877	($6,182)			($16,245)	$686
Full	$7,702	($10,565)			$6,753	$14,936
Ablated	$3,384	($15,543)			($13,139)	$13,283
Trader 1	$13,295	$15,141	($12,775)	$36	($96,990)	($10,915)
Full	$12,602	($5,160)	($5,871)	$2,634	($50,363)	($22,439)
Ablated	($22,076)	$1,991	($12,808)	($5,904)	($81,980)	($13,286)
Trader 2	$17,566	$469			($123,006)	($19,314)
Full	$48,101	($2,423)			($79,963)	($22,007)
Ablated	$14,973	($20,812)			($73,152)	($28,870)
Trader 3	$18,104	($8,359)	($42,190)	$2,464	($40,471)	($10,648)
Full	$12,668	($8,280)	($39,999)	$2,831	($51,049)	($14,835)
Ablated	($4,430)	($8,280)	($29,401)	$2,884	($45,893)	($15,524)

Table 3.3. *Results of the Comparison between Models and Traders*

Result	Interpretation	n	%
Ascription improves predictive accuracy and increases profits	Ascription explains profitable trading by the trader	19	42%
Ascription improves predictive accuracy but lessens profits	Ascription explains relatively unprofitable trading behavior	7	16%
Ascription hurts predictive accuracy but increases profits	Modeling suggests that the trader fails to invoke ascription	11	24%
Ascription hurts predictive accuracy and lessens profits	Ascription does not explain trader performance	8	18%

In each scenario, the traders and the models were responsible for managing positions in the two currencies indicated at the top of each column (e.g., marks and lira, yen and Swiss francs). The box for each scenario is divided into three sections, one for each professional trader. The top row in each division represents the profits (losses) generated by the trader for that scenario. For instance, in scenario 1, Trader 1 made a $8,171 profit in the dollar–mark and took a $2,237 loss in the dollar–lira; Trader 3 lost $3,086 in the dollar–mark and $1,102 in the dollar–lira.

Table 3.3 summarizes the results presented in Table 3.2 by presenting counts of (1) predictive accuracy and (2) effectiveness of the models. Predictive accuracy is assessed by measuring how well the models approximate the profits (losses) realized by the traders at the end of the scenario. Effectiveness compares the profits realized by the two models.

The data in Table 3.3 show that the model that includes the ascription mechanism realizes net profits (losses) that are closer in absolute value to the profits (losses) realized by the traders than the ablated model in 26 out of 45 scenarios (58%).[1] In 30 out of 45 scenarios (66%), the model that includes ascription realizes higher profits than the model that does not.

---

[1] For each of the eight scenarios, there are six comparisons (6 = 2 currencies × 3 traders). Three comparisons are missing from Table 3.3: two for Trader 2 in the lower pound–franc scenario (missing data) and one for Trader 3 in the lira where there was no difference between the two models.

The results in Table 3.3 prompt three conclusions. The first conclusion is that ascription generally helps to explain profitable trading behavior. The most frequent finding (42% of the cases – see Table 3.3) is that the full model is better than the ablated model both in terms of profits and in terms of its ability to approximate the outcomes of the experimental subjects.

The second conclusion is that sometimes the traders either abstain from ascribing beliefs to the market or override the implications of ascription. In our data, this happened in about 40% of the cases (24% plus 18%, as shown in the last two rows of Table 3.3). Interestingly, the impact of this behavior on overall profits and losses is not clear: In 11 cases out of 19 (=11 + 8), the traders who did not ascribe improved their profits, yet they reduced them in the remaining 8 cases.

The third conclusion is that ascription is not always an optimal behavior: It appears that in about one-sixth of the cases (16%, as indicated in the second row in Table 3.3), attempting to ascribe beliefs to the markets is not the course of action that maximizes profits.

In sum, the role of ascription in decision making under risk that emerges from these data is significant, yet more complex than indicated by our initial expectations. To sharpen our understanding, the next pair of models do not assume that the subjects either always ascribe or never ascribe. The model of second partner review introduced in the next section treats the use of ascription by the experimental subjects as an exogenous (e.g., independent) variable. In other words, it ascribes goals and actions to management when the subjects do, and does not when they do not. This model will then be compared with an alternative model of second partner review that always applies ascription.

A Model of Detecting Financial Manipulations

The strategy employed to develop models of detecting financial manipulations in second partner review consists of four steps (Johnson et al., 2001). First, we developed a model of successful detection of financial manipulations, which we call the *competence* model. As a second step, we compared the behavior of the model (a computer program) with the behavior of the auditors in our experiments. The comparison revealed a small number of key deviations from the model of success. We call these deviations *errors* (the list of the errors is provided later).

The error data were the basis for formulating hypotheses on the nature of the (flawed) knowledge that leads to error. As the third step

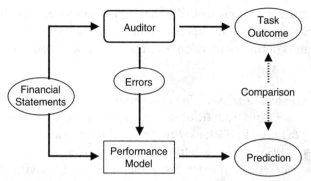

Figure 3.5 Predicting outcomes from observed errors.

in our methodology, we modeled this knowledge as a small number of localized modifications to the competence model. We called these modifications *knowledge bugs* (Van Lehn, 1990) and the model that includes them the *performance model* (Johnson et al., 2001). Individually, each knowledge bug is not sufficient to make the performance model fail the second partner review task. The model (and the subjects) can succeed at the overall task despite making a few errors. The knowledge bugs interact with the characteristics of the task and with each other to determine the final outcome.

Accordingly, the fourth step consists of testing the performance model by using it to predict the outcomes rendered by a new sample of auditors on a set of experimental tasks (Johnson et al., 2001; see also Grazioli, 1997). Given a task and the set of errors made by an individual subject, the model predicts the outcome on the task for that subject. Figure 3.5 shows the technique employed to compute the predictions in step four.

To evaluate the role of ascription in second partner review, we add a fifth analytical step. We omit from the performance model the knowledge bug that causes ascription errors. The resulting *ablated model* takes into account all sources of subject variance from the model of success – that is, all the errors – *except* the variance in ascription behavior (i.e., the ascription errors – more detail is provided later). We expect that this technique will lead to sharper results than the study of currency trading because the performance model of second partner review is a closer approximation to the subjects' ascription behavior. The two alternative versions of the model of currency trading either always ascribe or never ascribe. The performance model of second partner review ascribes goals and actions if and only if the subjects do.

The following sections describe the auditing models, how they ascribe to management the intent to manipulate financial information, and the results of the comparison between the full and ablated versions of the model.

Model of Competent Detection. The development of our model of second partner review draws from theories of deception and its detection (Ceci, Leichtman, & Putnick, 1992; Ekman, 1991; Johnson et al., 1993; Mitchell & Thompson, 1986). Broadly defined, deception is the phenomenon that occurs when an Other – the deceiver – manipulates the environment of an intended victim so that the victim misrepresents the environment and, as a consequence, acts in ways that are more favorable to the deceiver. In second partner review, we look to management as the deceiver and to the auditor as the intended victim of deception. Although the ultimate victim is the public – the users of the manipulated financial statements – management needs the auditor to render a favorable audit opinion.

Deception is detected by realizing that the environment has been manipulated by the deceiver. Our research has proposed that deception is detected by adopting a variation of Dennett's intentional stance. In short, the stance consists of interpreting anomalies in an environment characterized by the presence of a motivated adversary (the potential deceiver) as resulting from the potential deceiver's malicious action.

We have argued that, despite the apparently endless variety of cons and ruses, there is only a small number of general ways to deceive (Bowyer, 1982), which we call *deception tactics*, and that deception is detected by applying a corresponding set of *detection tactics* (Johnson et al., 1993, 2001). Detection tactics are heuristics (cognitive processes and representations) that generate the hypothesis that a specific deceptive manipulation has been attempted by an adversary. Detection tactics are forms of dispositional attribution.

For instance, one general form of deception is *repackaging*, which consists of changing the name or label of an entity (the deception *core*) so that the victim takes it for something else and, as a result, behaves in ways that are more favorable to the deceiver. In the previous example, the management of Surgical Products intended to obtain the auditor's approval of the capitalization (a favorable accounting treatment) of certain expenses by calling these expenses "engineering costs for molds and dies," as opposed to "R&D costs" which have a less favorable accounting treatment.

A list of the detection tactics and further examples in the domain of accounting can be found in Johnson et al. (1993, 2001) and Grazioli (1997).[2] The tactics share features with Trope's model (Figure 3.2). Each tactic is initiated by the observation of an anomaly in the environment and consists of a process that operates on three representations (*categories* in Trope's model): (1) an anomaly is present, (2) the anomaly is functional to the goals of the potential deceiver, and (3) the potential deceiver is capable of generating the anomaly. When all three attribution-relevant categories are present, the intent to deceive (a dispositional attribution) is ascribed to the adversary.

The protocol excerpts presented earlier exemplify the use of the antirepackaging detection tactic. S17 began by noticing that the capitalized molds and dies costs were unusually large, especially in terms of their impact on Surgical's bottom line. In addition, the reduced R&D expense that resulted from the capitalization was functional to one of the ascribed goals of management: showing increasing earnings to the financial markets (Figure 3.4). Finally, S17 commented on the discretionary power of management in labeling those activities one way or another.

The detection tactics have been embedded in a model of successful detection of financial manipulations in second partner review (Johnson et al., 1992, 1993, 2001). The model provides algorithms for the identification of the anomalies that initiate the tactics, algorithms for generating interpretive hypotheses for the anomalies, and algorithms for combining available interpretations of the data.

To test the model, we implemented it as a rule-based system. The system analyzes the same financial statements that were given to the second partner reviewers who participated in our experiments, applies the detection tactics to generate hypotheses about possible manipulations in the statements, evaluates the generated hypotheses, and combines them in an outcome that expresses the extent to which the financial statements are a fair representation of the company's economic condition. Appendix B describes the algorithms of the model and how they were implemented in the rule-based system.

The results of the model's testing have led us to conclude that the competence model hones our understanding of the behavior of the auditors that succeeded in our experimental tasks. However, it is not equally useful for explaining the behavior of the many auditors that did not succeed

---

[2] Grazioli (1997) identifies six deception tactics and six corresponding detection tactics: masking, dazzling, decoying, mimicking, double-play, and repackaging.

in our experiments (Johnson et al., 1992, 2001). To understand the behavior of all subjects, including those who did not detect the manipulated financial information, we developed a model of human performance in second partner review that includes human error.

Performance Model. The comparison of the process traces of the experimental subjects with the process trace of the competence model described in the previous sections identified four types of errors: (A) failing to heed critical cues in the financial statements, (B) generating an incorrect hypothesis (accounting mistake or insufficient disclosure rather than the hypothesis that a manipulation has occurred), (C) dropping correct hypotheses, and (D) failing to combine available evidence.

The errors of interest here are the failures to generate hypotheses that explain identified inconsistencies in financial statements by means of intentional manipulation by management (error B) – which is, as discussed earlier, an ascription. We identified two variants of ascription error B. Error B1 consists of explaining a manipulated cue as an accounting mistake. Accounting mistakes are, by definition, unintentional. Generating such an hypothesis means that the subject correctly identified an anomaly in the accounting process but failed to recognize it as a purposeful manipulation made by management. Error B2 consists of explaining a manipulated cue as an insufficiently disclosed issue. *Insufficient disclosure* refers to the presentation of financial information. The hypothesis of insufficient disclosure is neutral with respect to intentionality. In this case too, the subject falls short of ascribing the intent to manipulate information to management.

We assume that errors occur because of *knowledge bugs* – localized imperfections in a cognitive Agent's processes and representations that manifest themselves as local errors and can lead to ultimate task failure (Grazioli, 1997; Johnson et al., 2001; Van Lehn, 1990). Accordingly, four knowledge bugs (A, B, C, D) were proposed to account for each of the four observed types of error. The performance model adds these knowledge bugs to the competence model described earlier. The purpose of the performance model is to better emulate subject behavior by incorporating capacities for error. It should be noted that no individual bug is sufficient to make the model fail across cases. It is the interaction among bugs that can make the model fail.

Knowledge bug B causes hypothesis generation errors B1 and B2. Bug B is conceptualized as the inability to conceive of a way that management could have caused a detected inconsistency. It is operationalized by inhibiting the performance model's access to specific managerial actions that would explain the inconsistency (Grazioli, 1997). As a result of the modification, the model can still identify manipulated information as an anomaly, but it fails to retrieve a managerial action that could have caused the anomaly. This hampers the model's ability to generate the correct hypothesis that the presented financial information has been manipulated, so that, by default, a weaker *accounting mistake* or *insufficient disclosure* hypothesis is generated.[3]

Ablated Model. To evaluate the role of ascription in second partner review, we created an ablated version of the performance model. The full performance model contains all four bugs and can make all four types of errors that characterize human performance. The ablated model does not contain the ascription bug B (but does contain bugs A, C, and D). Because the ablated model does not contain bug B, it *does not* make ascription errors. Comparison of the ablated and full models reveals how much of the models' effectiveness and predictive accuracy depends specifically on modeling ascription behavior (errors).

Results. The impact of ascription on second partner review is evaluated by comparing the outcomes of experienced auditors with the outcomes of the full and ablated performance models. As before, we use two dimensions of model quality: predictive accuracy and task effectiveness. To measure predictive accuracy, the outcomes of the full and ablated model outcomes were compared with data from experimental subjects engaged in the second partner review of four cases. Task effectiveness was measured by comparing the outcomes of the model with the correct solution for each case.

The subjects used for assessing the models are 24 senior partners from major accounting firms who volunteered for the experiment reported in Johnson et al. (2001). Each subject worked on four manipulated cases describing real companies that perpetrated financial fraud. Because 24 subjects worked on four cases, we have a total of 96 task outcomes. Each subject's response was coded as one of three possible outcomes: "M," assigned when the subject rated the case as misleading; "U+," assigned when the subjects felt that the case needed to be qualified; and "U," assigned when the subject felt that the case was a fair representation of

---

[3] Which one depends on the specific type of the cue (e.g., a cost balance in the income statement or a footnote to the financial statements).

the company's economic condition. Because all cases were fraudulently manipulated, M is the successful outcome, and U and U+ denote failure to detect.

Johnson et al. (2001) report 45 successes and 51 (53%) task failures. As expected, it was found that auditors may succeed in the task despite making some errors (e.g., missing a cue). In the 96 tasks, the 24 subjects made a total of 209 errors. A comparison of the relative frequencies of each type of error shows that error B (the ascription error) was the most frequent, with 114 occurrences (55%).

Table 3.4 presents the ascription errors and the outcomes selected by the subjects in the experiment. For each case submitted to the subjects, we focus on the two major manipulations. Verbal protocol analysis was employed to reveal the types of errors made by each auditor in processing each manipulation (Johnson et al., 2001). For instance, management of the Pharmaceuticals company manipulated their mailing lists and their inventory balances to increase their reported income. The data in the table show that every subject made at least one ascription error B (see, e.g., S2), and some made as many as eight (S12).

An examination of the outcomes selected by each subject in each case shows that the ascription error seems to be frequently associated with failure to detect. About 89% (32/36) of the subjects who made two ascription errors B also failed the task. About 83% (15/18) of the subjects who did not make ascription errors with respect to the major issues in each case succeeded. Error B on the major issues of a case is, however, not fatal: Some subjects identified cases as manipulated despite making two errors B (e.g., S1 on the Pharmaceuticals case). In a related study with a different subject sample, Grazioli (1998) has shown that the occurrence of ascription error B is significantly correlated with the failure to detect.

The error data for each subject, including the error B data presented in Table 3.4, were used to turn "on" or "off" the corresponding bug in the performance model. When the bug was present, the performance model manifested the corresponding error behavior. When the bug was absent, the model defaulted to the competence model and performed correctly. No single error was sufficient to make the model fail: The outcome of the model (i.e., M, U+, or U) on a case was determined by the interaction of the bugs with the characteristics of the specific case.

Table 3.5 presents the results on predictive accuracy of the full and ablated models. Each model predicted the task outcome for each subject on each case in the experiment. The prediction was compared with the outcome selected by the subject as presented in Table 3.4. The full

Table 3.4. *Task Outcomes and Ascription Errors Made by 24 Subjects on Four Fraud Cases*

| | Cases (All Manipulated) | | | | | | | | | | | |
| | Pharmaceuticals | | | Surgical Products | | | Big John's | | | America's Family | | |
Subject	Mailing lists	Inventory	Outcome	Molds & Dies	R&D	Outcome	Pre-opening costs	Inventory	Outcome	Goodwill amortization	Inventory	Outcome
S1	B	B	M	B	B	M		B	M	B		M
S2*			M			M		B	M			M
S3		B	M			M	B	B	U+	B		M
S4		B	M			M	B	B	U+	B	B	U
S5		B	M	B		U		B	M	B	B	U+
S6		B	M	B	B	U+	B	B	U			M
S7		B	M	B		M		B	M	B		U+
S8	B	B	U			U+		B	U+	B	B	M
S9	B	B	U			U+	B	B	M	B		U+
S10		B	M	B	B	U+		B	U+	B	B	U+
S11		B	U	B	B	M			U	B	B	U
S12	B	B	U+	B	B	M	B	B	U+	B	B	U
S13		B	M	B	B	U+		B	M	B	B	M
S14		B	M	B	B	U+		B	M			M
S15			M			U		B	M			M
S16	B	B	U+	B		M		B	M	B	B	U+
S17	B	B	U	B		U+		B	M	B	B	U
S18			U			U+			M	B	B	U
S19			M			M	B	B	U+		B	U+
S20		B	M	B		U+		B	M		B	U
S21			M	B		U		B	U+	B	B	U
S22		B	M	B	B	U+		B	U+			U
S23	B	B	U+	B		U+		B	U	B		U
S24	B	B	U	B		U		B	U+		B	U

Notes: B = the subject made an ascription error in processing the cue. M = the subject rated the case as misleading. U+ = the subject felt that the case needed to be qualified; U = the subject felt that the case was a fair representation of the company's economic condition. Because all cases are fraudulently manipulated, M is the successful outcome; U and U+ denote failures to detect.

Source: Adapted from Johnson et al. (2001).

Table 3.5. *Predictive Accuracy of Alternative Models of the Auditor*

Model Version	Interpretation	Case				
		American Family	Pharma-ceuticals	Surgical Products	Big John's	Total
Full Performance Model	High percentages mean that the outcome agreement of the model that emulates the auditors' ascription errors and the auditors is high.	83% (20/24)	87% (21/24)	83% (20/24)	96% (23/24)	87% (84/96)
Ablated Model (No Bug B)	Lower percentages mean that the outcome agreement of the model that does not emulate the auditors' ascription errors (always ascribes) is lower.	58% (14/24)	75% (18/24)	46% (11/24)	42% (10/24)	55% (53/96)

performance model averaged 87% of correct predictions, the ablated model 55%. The average net loss of predictive power due to ablation is 32%. We conclude that the ability to ascribe goals to a potential adversary explains much of our subjects' overall performance, inclusive of success and failure.

The results on the effectiveness of the full and ablated models are presented in Table 3.6. Effectiveness is defined as the proportion of successes (i.e., selecting an M outcome for each misleading case) over the total number of tasks. For comparison purposes, the first row of Table 3.5 contains the effectiveness of the 24 auditors in the experiment.

The average success rate of the auditors across cases was 48%. The model with the full set of knowledge bugs succeeded 58% of the time across cases; the ablated model succeeded, as expected, much more often: 83% of the time. Table 3.6 prompts the conclusion that ascription errors have a large and negative impact on effectiveness in detecting manipulated financial information. The elimination of flawed ascription knowledge (bug B) increases the average effectiveness of the performance model by 25% (= 83% − 58% in the last column of Table 3.6).

Table 3.6. *Effectiveness of Experimental Subjects and Alternative Models of the Auditor*

Source	Interpretation	American Family	Pharma- ceuticals	Surgical Products	Big John's	Total
Experimental subjects	Auditors' success rate on the experimental cases (used as reference).	33% (8/24)	62% (15/24)	42% (10/24)	54% (13/24)	48% (46/96)
Full Performance Model	The success rate of the model that emulates the auditors' ascription errors is similar to the subjects' success rate.	42% (10/24)	71% (17/24)	54% (13/24)	67% (16/24)	58% (56/96)
Ablated Model (no bug B)	The success rate of the model that does not emulate the auditors' ascription errors (always ascribes) is higher.	75% (18/24)	79% (19/24)	92% (22/24)	87% (21/24)	83% (80/96)

The results in Table 3.6 are fairly uniform across cases, with the exception of Pharmaceuticals, which is characterized by a relatively small net effectiveness gain (from 71% to 79%). One reason for this outlier is a ceiling effect. The case elicited a larger percentage of successes than any other (about 20% more successes than the average of the other three). As a result, there was not much space for improvement when we ablated bug B. We also conducted an inspection of the protocols of the subjects who failed to detect the manipulations in the Pharmaceuticals case. The inspection revealed that these subjects frequently made hypothesis evaluation errors (error C) and evidence combination errors (error D), which we assume indicate the activity of bugs C and D. Ablating bug B in the presence of these other bugs is not sufficient to improve effectiveness.

Overall, the results of the comparison of the full and ablated perfor-mance models support our general argument: (1) ascription is a major determinant of success in a task that requires managing the risk posed by Others, and (2) ascription errors are a major component of the behavioral variance of subjects engaged in a task that requires the management of risk posed by Others.

The results of the auditing data also allow us to strengthen and qualify the conclusions reached from the analysis of the currency traders. Overall, the auditor data show that ignoring ascription behavior (errors B) increases the model's effectiveness and degrades its predictive power. The ablated model of second partner review is more effective be-cause it does not make ascription errors. It can ascribe goals and actions to management and conclude that they have manipulated the financial information. At the same time, as the model gets more successful, its ability to approximate subjects' outcomes accurately worsens, which is consistent with the results obtained in the experiments with the traders' models.

Consistent with the previous analysis, we found that the auditors often failed to (abstain from) ascribe beliefs to the Other. Every subject in our sample made at least one ascription error, and some made as many as eight out of eight opportunities to err. Ascription errors were the most frequently observed type of error in the Johnson et al. (2001) study.

The last conclusion from the analysis of the traders was that ascription is not always an optimal behavior. Although the nature of the second partner review task requires the ascription of the intent to deceive, and therefore a failure to ascribe is tantamount to an error in this domain, we have observed a small number of individuals (3 out of 24) who succeeded at the task despite the fact that their behavior did not show evidence of ascription to management of the intent to deceive. These individuals felt that the cases contained (unintentional) mistakes of such magnitude that the case as a whole was misleading.

Conclusion

In spite of profound differences, spot currency trading and second part-ner review share a defining characteristic: the management of risk posed by others. Both traders and auditors operate in settings where the ac-tions of Others create the possibility for loss. Currency traders manage the risks of holding large sums of foreign currency. Auditors manage the risks of providing assurance that published financial information is free from deceptive manipulations.

We have highlighted two common features of these settings: dynamic interaction with many agents and asymmetric distribution of information under conflict of interest. Under either condition, individuals managing social exchange risk need to understand and predict the actions of others so as to take action to prevent or minimize losses.

Spot currency traders interact in highly dynamic markets that respond to the vagaries of global socioeconomic conditions and political uncertainty. The markets are too large for any one individual to control, and prices can change more rapidly than the trader can respond. Volatility in spot prices creates the possibilities for loss (i.e., risk) or, conversely, opportunities for profit. The highly dynamic nature of the spot markets is the overriding constraint on spot traders' decision making. Understanding and predicting the direction of the market is critical for trading success.

Second partner reviewers do not suffer from time pressure, yet have an equally challenging task: to detect manipulations of financial information that have been designed with the explicit intent to escape detection. Failure to identify these manipulations exposes the auditor to lawsuits and loss of professional reputation. Because the auditors do not have the same access to information that the management of a client company has, understanding the reporting goals of management is critical for auditing success.

Both traders and auditors are engaged in the social exchange of information. However, whereas fraud detection is an adversarial interaction, trading is not. Traders interact repeatedly, often several times a week. The countless iteration of one-on-one exchanges precludes deception and supports the development of trust. A dishonest trader soon has no trading partners and is out of business. In contrast, the auditors have to detect forms of deception: The management of a company in economic distress may deliberately choose to misstate the financial position of the company to obtain more favorable treatment from shareholders, investors, lenders, and regulators.

We have proposed that ascription, the ability to assign goals and beliefs to the Others with whom we interact, plays a major role in decision making in social exchange. We have supported our argument by means of anecdotal evidence from our empirical work and by means of a pair of experiments with two information processing models of the decision making required to manage social exchange risk. Comparison of the process traces of the subjects' and systems' decision making suggests that the systems capture the basis for expert performance. Comparison across subjects and systems demonstrates that identification and processing of attribution-relevant categories mediate competent performance.

We found that experienced professionals involved in managing social exchange risk ascribe goals and beliefs to Others and that ascription is an important determinant of success. However, we also found that there are cases in which ascription does not lead to the best course of action, and that sometimes experienced professionals either do not ascribe or override the implications of ascribing goals and beliefs to Others. Overall, the role of ascription that emerges from these data is more complex than we initially expected.

Reckers et al. (1992) have observed that professional guidelines do not contain operational guidance about how to ascribe goals and beliefs to Others that pose risks. Perhaps some decision makers abstain from ascribing because they believe that ascription is too subjective or unreliable. There is a difference between ascribing and ascribing correctly, and the decisions based on ascription are hard to justify.

March (1988) has proposed that there are higher orders of ascription, which might have decreasing usefulness. We not only ascribe "first-order" beliefs and goals to Others, we also ascribe beliefs and goals that result from them ascribing beliefs and goals to us (see also Dennett, 1987). Indeed, the relationship between accountants and managers has been labeled as "a race to outwit each other." There is little doubt that higher-order ascription quickly becomes very complex.

More broadly, Dennett has argued that there is an evolutionary advantage for Agents who possess cognitive machinery that implements ascription. Recent work in cognitive psychology, neurology, and cognitive ethology supports Dennett's arguments (Baron-Cohen, 1995). We have examined evidence for the operation of such mechanisms in professional settings, and have argued that competent management of risk in social interactions derives part of its power from the cognitive ability to ascribe goals and beliefs to others.

If ascription is a deep cognitive capacity that promotes successful decision making in social settings, yet is not always applied, then there is need for research to better understand its use as well as to determine means to facilitate its exercise. Work by Cosmides, Tooby, and others has already shown that it is possible to elicit extraordinarily high success rates in simple experimental tasks by means of treatments rooted in theories of reasoning about social exchange. What remains to be done is to generalize results obtained in tightly controlled laboratory conditions to more realistic decision-making situations that require managing risks posed by others.

Appendix A: The Currency Trading Model

This appendix describes the implementation of SPOT, the rule-based system that we developed to test our model of spot currency trading. Inputs to SPOT are database files, one for each of the 24 sessions in the laboratory experiment described earlier. The files summarize the events in the trader's experimental session: the news in the overnight report, the headlines the trader read during the trading day, the hourly prices posted on the price screen, and the requests for quotes the trader received. SPOT completes a trading day by cycling through all the lines in a file. The output that SPOT generates includes text files that detail the sizes of the positions it takes and the profits (losses) it creates.

As discussed earlier, SPOT contains methods for both feedback and feedforward process control. The method for feedback control compares the current rate of change in prices and the profits (losses) in a position to thresholds of acceptable risk. The method for feedforward control implements the process of ascription to anticipate the direction in which the market will drive prices whenever it "reads" a headline that the trader read in the experimental session.

Ascribing Beliefs to the Market

SPOT's representation of the market and its environment consists of three classes of objects – *Headlines*, *News Story*, and *World Events* – that constitute attribution-relevant cues and categories. Instances of the class *World Events* specify the algorithm for comparing situational cues either to a market standard or to prior cues when they exist. The comparison yields a value for the object *Market's View* of the appropriate instance of *News Story*. *Market's View of News Story* represents the product of SPOT's ascription of a belief to the market.

SPOT anticipates the direction in which the market will drive prices by reasoning about the beliefs the market forms about headlines. SPOT's limited domain knowledge about headlines (situational cues) is contained in 146 instances of a class of objects called *Headlines*. *Headlines* contain two objects, *topic* and *category*. The values for these objects were set by the developer for each of the 146 instances of the class. The *topic of Headlines* for each instance represents a general type of event (e.g., budget surplus) rather than any particular event (e.g., Swiss budget surplus for February). Each instance is applicable to a large number of potential headlines. The *category of Headlines* for each instance links the associated topic to one of the 10 categories of news listed in Table 3.1. For instance, the *topic* WPI is linked to the *category* inflation.

> CLASS Headlines
> > WITH topic STRING
> > WITH category COMPOUND
> > > Economic growth,
> > > Political uncertainty,
> > > Inflation,
> > > Central bank gov't policy,
> > > Unemployment,
> > > Old news,
> > > Forecast,
> > > Immaterial,
> > > Up Trend,
> > > Down Trend

The 146 instances capture all the knowledge about headlines that SPOT brings to a session. They represent what is undoubtedly a small fraction of the professional trader's knowledge about global socioeconomic and political events. They are the minimum number required to process the headlines in Smith's experiments and suffice to test the sufficiency of SPOT's method for anticipating the market.

The structure of the class *Headlines* finesses Trope's process of identification. The linkage between topics and categories provided by the class *Headlines* removes the need for the system to decide to which category of news each headline belongs. This finesse makes SPOT's identification as "spontaneous" as the traders'.

Whenever SPOT "reads" a headline (an entry in the input database), either in the overnight report or during the trading day, it generates or updates an instance of the class of objects called *News Story*. Instances of the class *News Story* represent SPOT's memory of headlines it has read. For instance, when SPOT read the overnight report for the WPI example, it generated an instance of *News Story* with the objects *city* set to Washington, *topic* set to WPI, *relevant currency* set to the dollar, and *expected value* set to +0.4%. The object *expected value of News Story* represents the information the market was said to expect when it next sampled a related headline.

> CLASS News Story
>> WITH city STRING
>> WITH topic STRING
>> WITH relevant currency STRING
>> WITH expected value NUMERIC
>> WITH index NUMERIC
>> WITH Market's View COMPOUND
>>> bullish,
>>> bearish,
>>> of little concern
>> WITH relative to market standard COMPOUND
>>> below,
>>> above

The knowledge captured by objects in each instance of *News Story* represents all of SPOT's knowledge of prior cues.

SPOT's knowledge of attribute-relevant categories is contained in 10 instances of the class *World Events*. There is one instance for each category of news shown in Table 3.1. The knowledge captured by these 10 instances represents knowledge the trader brings to the trading desk. The values of the two objects, *comparison algorithm* and *market standard*, were assigned by the developer for each instance. The assignments follow the specification given in Table 3.1. For example, the *comparison algorithm* for the *category* inflation is *down is good* (i.e., a decrease in inflation is viewed as beneficial to the relevant currency) and the *market standard* is 2%. The object *market standard* was left blank in the seven instances where it does not apply.

> CLASS World Events
>> WITH category STRING
>> WITH comparison algorithm COMPOUND
>>> Up is good,
>>> Down is good,
>>> Bullish,
>>> Bearish,
>>> Ignore
>> WITH market standard NUMERIC

Figure 3.A1 SPOT's implementation of ascription when it finds a prior cue.

SPOT implements Trope's process of dispositional inference whenever it reads a headline either in the overnight report or during the trading day. It first seeks to match the *category* of the active instance of the class *Headlines* to the *category* of all existing instances of the class *News Story*. If a match is found (e.g., if SPOT had read the overnight report to indicate what the market was said to expect), it updates the *index of News Story* to the information contained in the headline. As shown in Figure 3.A1, SPOT then applies the *comparison algorithm* of the appropriate instance of *World Events* to compare the (new) *index of News Story* to the preexisting *expected value of News Story*. The comparison allows SPOT to attribute a belief to the market based on both the information in the headline and the market's expectation for the headline.

In the example, SPOT found an instance of *News Story* with *city* Washington and *topic* WPI. It updated *index of News Story* to 0.6%, found an *expected value* of 0.4%, and applied the *comparison algorithm of World Events* – down is good – to set the *Market's View of News Story* to *bearish*. The inference of a bearish market view captures SPOT's ascription to the market of the belief that increases in inflation are disadvantageous to the *relevant currency*, in this case, to the dollar.

The search for a matching instance is necessarily unsuccessful the first time SPOT encounters a particular headline during a session (e.g., when it samples the overnight report). Figure 3.A2 shows how SPOT attributes a belief in the absence of a prior cue. When the search is unsuccessful, the system creates a new instance of the class *News Story*. It then matches the *category* of the active instance of the class *Headlines* to the *category* of the 10 instances of the class *World Events* and applies the associated comparison algorithm to compare the (new) *index of News Story* to the preexisting *market standard of World Events*. The

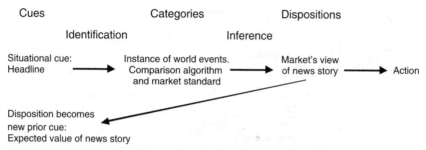

Figure 3.A2 SPOT's implementation of ascription when it does not find a prior cue.

comparison allows SPOT to attribute a belief to the market based on the information in the headline and the default standard for that class of headline.

The result of the comparison is flagged by the object *Market's View of News Story*. The comparison may be either bullish, bearish, or of little concern for the relevant currency. The comparison algorithm for headlines that fall in the categories of news *immaterial*, *old news*, and *forecasts* specifies that the *Market's View of News Story* is of little concern.

The beliefs ascribed to the market are contextually dependent on the presence or absence of a prior cue. For instance, in the absence of a prior cue, a headline that suggests that growth will remain moderate triggers a standard for comparison that supports the inference that the market's response will be tepid. The same headline, in the context of a prior cue that the market expects news of robust growth, triggers a comparison that supports the inference that the market's response will be draconian and swift. Distinguishing between situational and prior cues enables SPOT to capture the contextual sensitivity to expectations that can be critical to success in anticipating the market.

Appendix B: The Model for Detecting Financial Manipulations

To evaluate our model for detecting financial manipulation, we implemented it as a computer program. This appendix provides details on the algorithms contained in the model and on its implementation as a rule-based system. The inputs to the model are the financial statements of the companies included in the experimental materials. The model's output is a diagnostic opinion qualifying the extent to which the

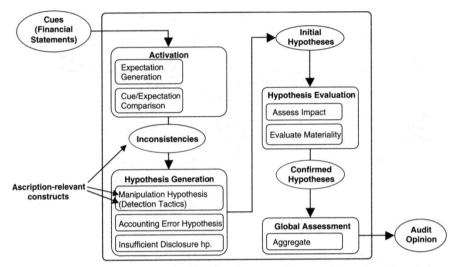

Figure 3.B1 Process model of the detection of financial deception. (Adapted from Johnson et al., 1998.)

financial statements are a fair representation of the company's economic condition (e.g., "the statements are misleading" or "the statements are fair"). The model is based on the assumption that the detection of financial manipulation can be decomposed into four distinct processes: activation, hypothesis generation, hypothesis evaluation, and global assessment.

Activation

The activation process generates expectations for cues in the financial statements, compares each cue with its expectation, and, based on the comparison, flags them as inconsistent (see Figure 3.B1). Expectations are produced by simple linear functions of past values of the target cue, other cues, and industry-characteristic constants (Johnson et al., 1992). As an example, the expected value of inventory is computed by multiplying the past value of inventory by the rate of growth in sales. In the previous protocol excerpt, S17 used a similar technique: He computed the rate of growth in inventory and compared it to a standard (the rate of growth in sales).

Whenever the difference between a cue and its expectation is larger than a specified criterion value (e.g., 2.5% of operating income), the cue is labeled as inconsistent. Inconsistencies (e.g., "the inventory level is too high") are symptoms of possible anomalies in the accounting process that produced the financial statements. Inconsistencies include what Trope calls *ascription-relevant categories*.

Hypothesis Generation and Ascription

Hypothesis generation is the process that implements ascription in the model. The process generates initial hypotheses that explain the inconsistencies detected in the financial statements. Three classes of hypotheses can be generated: The anomaly results (1) from intentional manipulations of the accounting process, (2) from unintentional mistakes in accounting, or (3) from insufficient disclosure of information.

The generation process is activated by the detection of an inconsistency (see Figure 3.B1). First, it attempts to apply the detection tactics to it. If a tactic applies, an hypothesis of intentional manipulation is generated for the inconsistent cue. If no tactic applies, then either an insufficient disclosure hypothesis or an accounting mistake hypothesis is generated. An insufficient disclosure hypothesis is generated when the inconsistent cue is related to a note to the financial statements (e.g., a change in accounting policies). Otherwise, an accounting mistake hypothesis is generated for the cue.

The tactics are fired when three ascription-relevant categories are present: (1) a cue is flagged as inconsistent with its expectation, (2) the inconsistent cue is functional to a possible goal of management, and (3) the inconsistency is feasible, that is, it might have been caused by management. The first two conditions are common to all tactics, and the third distinguishes among them. To establish functionality, the model provisionally ascribes to management the general goal of increasing earnings (similarly to what S17 did) and then examines the cue flagged as inconsistent. If the inconsistent cue is an asset (a liability) and is larger (smaller) than expected, then the model concludes that the inconsistency is functional to the ascribed goal.

The second condition – feasibility – is established when a manipulation of the accounting process that explains the inconsistency is available. The model contains about a dozen manipulations derived from published lists (e.g., Schilit, 1993). Manipulations are associated with specific cues based on each cue's position in the financial statements (e.g., as an asset, an expense, and the like). For instance, capitalized tooling costs are associated with repackaging. The output of the hypothesis generation process is an initial (i.e., subject to evaluation) set of hypotheses. These hypotheses are the input to the next subprocess that evaluates them.

Hypothesis Evaluation

The initial hypotheses generated by the model need to be confirmed. A process of hypothesis evaluation produces confirmed hypotheses on the basis of the relevance (*materiality* in accounting terminology) of the inconsistency associated with each hypothesis.

The type of hypothesis proposed for an inconsistency suggests the nature of the test for materiality of the inconsistency. For instance, insufficient disclosure hypotheses are evaluated on the basis of the magnitude (a dollar value) of the difference between the cue value and its expectation. The repackaging hypothesis prescribes recategorizing the entity that may have been miscategorized under a worst-case scenario assumption. After these dollar values are assigned, the initial hypotheses are individually evaluated against an assumed criterion for materiality (10% of the operating income; Johnson et al., 1992).

Global Assessment

The global assessment process aggregates and evaluates the confirmed hypotheses to produce a final outcome for the second partner review task. The model selects one of three possible outcomes (Grazioli, 1997; Johnson et al., 2001): "Misleading", "Unqualified with additional paragraph," and "Unqualified."

Misleading expresses the conclusion that the reviewed financial statements are an unfair representation of the company's underlying economic conditions. Misleading is the correct solution for all the tasks presented here. Unqualified with additional paragraph means that the model identified some audit issues (e.g., lack of consistency, going concern) in a case, yet these issues are not sufficient for concluding that the financial statements are misleading. An opinion of Unqualified is an indication that the model did not identify any issue or manipulation in a case. This is the outcome desired by the company's management.

Outcome selection is based on either one hypothesis or two or more combined hypotheses. If an individual manipulation hypothesis is material, then the global assessment process selects a Misleading outcome. If a mistake in accounting or an insufficient disclosure hypothesis is material, then the process selects an Unqualified with additional paragraph outcome. Otherwise, an Unqualified outcome is selected. Aggregate evaluation is performed by first cumulating the dollar values associated with each type of hypothesis, and then testing these values against a criterion for aggregate materiality (40% of the operating income). If any aggregate hypothesis is material, the global assessment process selects a Misleading outcome.

References

Albrecht, W. S., Wernz, G. W., & Williams, T. L. (1995). *Fraud: Bringing light to the dark side of business*. New York: Irwin.

Bainbridge, L. (1974). Analysis of verbal protocols from a process control task. In E. Edwards & F. P. Lees (Eds.), *The human operator in process control* (pp. 146–158). London: Taylor & Francis.

Baron-Cohen, S. (1995). *Mindblindness: An essay on autism and the theory of mind*. Cambridge, MA: MIT Press.

Bowyer, J. B. (1982). *Cheating*. New York: St. Martin's Press.

Brehmer, B. (1992). Dynamic decision making: Human control of complex systems. *Acta Psychologica, 81*, 211–241.

Broadbent, D. E. (1977). Levels, hierarchies, and the locus of control. *Quarterly Journal of Experimental Psychology, 29*, 181–201.

Ceci, S. J., Leichtman, M. D., & Putnick, M. E. (1992). *Cognitive and social factors in early deception*. Hillsdale, NJ: Erlbaum.

Cheng, P. W., & Holyoak, K. J. (1985). Pragmatic reasoning schemas. *Cognitive Psychology, 17*, 391–416.

Clark, A. (1987). From folk psychology to naïve psychology. *Cognitive Science, 11*, 139–154.

Cosmides, L. (1985). *Deduction or Darwinian algorithms? An explanation of the "elusive" content effect on the Wason selection task*. Ph.D. dissertation, Harvard University.

Cosmides, L., & Tooby, J. (1992). Cognitive adaptation for social exchange. In J. H. Barkow, L. Cosmides, & J. Tooby (Eds.), *The adapted mind: Evolutionary psychology and the generation of culture* (pp. 163–228). New York: Oxford University Press.

Cosmides, L., & Tooby, J. (1995). Foreword. In S. Baron-Cohen, *Mindblindness: An essay on autism and the theory of mind* (pp. xi–xvii). Cambridge, MA: MIT Press.

Dennett, D. (1987). *The intentional stance*. Cambridge, MA: MIT Press.

Edwards, E., & Lees, F. (1974). *The human operator in process control*. London: Taylor & Francis.

Einhorn, H. J., & Hogarth, R. M. (1986). Judging probable cause. *Psychological Bulletin, 99*, 3–19.

Ekman, P. (1991). *Telling lies: Clues to deceit in the marketplace, politics, and marriage*. New York: W. W. Norton.

Ericsson, K. A., & Smith, J. (1991). *Toward a general theory of expertise.* New York: Cambridge University Press.

Fiske, S. T., & Taylor, S. E. (1991). *Social cognition.* New York: McGraw-Hill.

Grazioli, S. (1997). *Detecting manipulations of financial information.* Ph.D. dissertation, University of Minnesota.

Grazioli, S. (1998). Errors in detecting financial deception: A cognitive modeling approach. *Proceedings of the Fourth Conference of the Association for Information Systems,* 152–154.

Heider, F. (1958). *The psychology of interpersonal relations.* New York: Wiley.

Holland, J. H. (1975/1992). *Adaptation in natural and artificial systems.* Ann Arbor: University of Michigan Press.

Johnson, P. E., Grazioli, S., & Jamal, K. (1993). Fraud detection: Deception and intentionality in cognition. *Accounting, Organization and Society, 18*(5), 467–488.

Johnson, P. E., Grazioli, S., Jamal, K., & Berryman, G. R. (2001). Detecting deception: Adversarial problem solving in a low base rate world. *Cognitive Science, 25*(3), 355–392.

Johnson, P. E., Grazioli, S., Jamal, K., & Zualkernan, I. A. (1992). Success and failure in expert reasoning. *Journal of Organizational Behavior and Human Decision Processes, 53*(2), 173–203.

Jones, E. E., & Harris, V. A. (1967). The attribution of attitudes. *Journal of Experimental Social Psychology, 3,* 1–24.

Kelley, H. H. (1971). *Attribution in social interaction.* Morristown, NJ: General Learning Press.

Keynes, J. M. (1921). *A treatise on probability.* London: Macmillan.

Kruglanski, A. W. (1980). Lay epistemological processes and contents: Another look at attribution theory. *Psychological Review, 87,* 70–87.

Kurtzman, J. (1993). *The death of money.* Boston: Little, Brown.

March, J. G. (1998). *Decisions and organizations.* Oxford: Basil Blackwell.

March, J. G., & Shapira, Z. (1987). Managerial perspectives on risk and risk taking. *Management Science, 33*(11), 1404–1418.

Mitchell, W., & Thompson, N. S. (1986). *Deception: Perspectives on human and non-human deceit.* Albany: SUNY Press.

Moray, N. (1986). Monitoring behavior and supervisory control. In K. R. Boff, L. Kaufman, & J. P. Thomas (Eds.), *Handbook of perception and human performance* (Vol. 2, Chap. 40, pp. 1–51). New York: Wiley.

Newell, A. (1982). The knowledge level. *Artificial Intelligence, 18,* 87–127.

Parasuraman, R. (1986). Vigilance, monitoring, and search. In K. R. Boff, L. Kaufman, & J. P. Thomas (Eds.), *Handbook of perception and human performance,* (Vol. 2, Chap. 43, pp. 1–39). New York: Wiley.

Peters, J. M. (1990). A cognitive computational model of risk hypothesis generation. *The Journal of Accounting Research, 28,* 83–109.

Reckers, P. M. J., Wong-On-Wing, B., & Krull, G. W. (1992). Auditors' assessment of management's disposition: An attributional analysis. *Decision Science, 23,* 957–972.

Schilit, H. M. (1993). *Financial shenanigans: How to detect accounting gimmicks and fraud in financial reports.* New York: McGraw-Hill.

Shanteau, J. (1992). Competence in experts: The role of task characteristics. *Organizational Behavior and Human Decision Processes, 53*(2), 252–266.

Shapira, Z. (1995). *Risk taking: A managerial perspective.* New York: Russell Sage Foundation.

Shoemaker, P. J. H. (1993). Determinants of risk-taking: Behavioral and economic views. *Journal of Risk and Uncertainty, 6,* 49–73.

Smith, K. C. S. (1996). *Decision making in dynamic environments: Trading in the spot currency markets.* Ph.D. dissertation, University of Minnesota.

Thagard, P. (1992). Adversarial problem solving: Modeling an opponent using explanatory coherence. *Cognitive Science, 16,* 123–149.

Trope, Y. (1986). Identification and inferential processes in dispositional attribution. *Psychological Review, 93*(3), 239–257.

Trope, Y., Cohen, O., & Maoz, Y. (1988). The perceptual and inferential effects of situational inducements on dispositional attribution. *Journal of Personality and Social Psychology, 55*(2), 165–177.

Van Lehn, K. (1990). *Mind bugs: The origins of procedural misconceptions.* Cambridge, MA: MIT Press.

von Neumann, J., & Morgenstern, O. (1944). *The theory of games and economic behavior.* Princeton, NJ: Princeton University Press.

Wiener, E. L. (1984). Vigilance and inspection. In J. S. Warm (Ed.), *Sustained attention in human performance* (pp. 207–246). New York: Wiley.

Yates, J. F., & Stone, E. R. (1992). The risk construct. In J. F. Yates (Ed.), *Risk-taking behavior* (pp. 1–25). New York: Wiley.

4   Emergency Decision Making

Jan Skriver, Lynne Martin, and Rhona Flin

Emergency is derived from the Greek word *krisis* and is defined as a situation perceived by a decision maker as "an unforeseen or sudden occurrence especially of danger, demanding immediate action" (*Collins Concise Dictionary*, 1982). In high-hazard industries and the armed forces, emergencies can be expected; thus, emergency response procedures can be drawn up as a means of control. Until recently, the only kinds of theoretical models available for emergency services to work with were normative. Traditional decision-making research used normative models to outline what would be optimal behavior and compared this to actual performance. From this comparison, the services constructed tactical doctrines in the form of operating procedures and guidelines.

Although operational procedures are seldom complete in their coverage of required actions, they are nevertheless available to the person in command. In addition, emergency managers have often, if not always, received some form of training in command and control of incidents. However, in emergencies, normative models cannot be relied on (Brehmer, 1992). Both individual and distributed emergency decision-making research have stressed the importance of context dependencies and have illustrated how the environment impacts on performance (e.g., Flin, Salas, Strub, & Martin, 1998).

Emergency decision making is often a question of applying knowledge and experience to a situation that may have been defined in advance but still contains novel elements. It is important to recognize that one person's emergency may be another's routine. External factors such as time pressure and high risk may not be perceived as such by experienced emergency managers. To them, these may just be two factors that are part of day-to-day work, that is, part of the routine. Here, what may be the defining criterion for an emergency is the number of decision options available to the decision maker and the number of possible developments. For example, the police and military have to consider a large number of possible developments in a wide range of unfamiliar settings. Nuclear power plants, aircraft cockpits, and offshore installations are much more confined and predictable spaces where developments are restricted by environmental constraints. Decision making for police officers could be considered to be more complex and multifaceted than for an emergency manager at the nuclear power plant.

What is common across these domains is that large-scale emergency management is rarely dependent on one individual's decisions. Rather, decision making is distributed among many actors, and no single individual possesses complete knowledge of the current situation. Dowell (1995) suggested that the social organization of cognitive activity is more significant than individual competence in accounting for the performance of collective work. Brehmer (1992) defined distributed decision making as a situation in which a number of agents have to work together toward a common goal in a dynamic context, with each agent having local information about the problem. In such tasks, cooperation between individuals is often problematic, specifically regarding information relay and the rate of change in the system. To perform effectively, the decision makers must communicate to assess the situation and translate the information into an effective action response. Distributed decision-making research has emphasized communication, coordination, teamwork, sharing understanding of the situation, and the imperative of focusing on the decision problem itself (Cicourel, 1990; Hutchins, 1990; Rasmussen, Brehmer, & Leplat, 1991).

Emergency Command and Control

Command and control skills have been a prerequisite for senior personnel in the military and the emergency services for as long as these domains have existed. Recently, however, it has been acknowledged that a similar set of skills is essential for senior site managers in hazardous industries, where the potential for disaster exists in the shape of large-scale loss of life or significant environmental damage. Managers in fields as diverse as sports, entertainment, and the nuclear power industries, as well as transportation, such as merchant navy captains and civil aviation, are in this category (Flin, 1996). The need to train people in these domains to manage emergencies competently is imperative.

One hazardous industry in this category is the offshore petroleum industry – an environment where the potential dangers posed by the presence of volatile hydrocarbon products are exacerbated by the isolated, often hostile, conditions in which exploration and production take place. The potential for disaster and the necessity for efficient, self-sufficient crisis management in the offshore environment are illustrated by the catastrophic loss of the *Piper Alpha* platform in Scottish waters in 1988, which resulted in 167 deaths (Cullen, 1990; or see Flin, Slaven, & Stewart, 1997, for a short summary). As a result, the offshore petroleum industry has made a considerable effort to analyze the environmental conditions and technical specifications for each installation, with every company submitting a formal installation risk assessment to gain operating permission. The industry has also devised a standard of competence for emergency management that equates skilled performance with competence based on a normative model of behavior. The normative approach suggested by the industry does not correspond with the results obtained from a cognitive task analysis of emergency decision making by the offshore installation manager (OIM) (Skriver & Flin, 1997a, 1997b). The main content of this chapter will address how the standard of competence differs from actual behavior.

The Offshore Petroleum Industry

The *Piper Alpha* disaster changed the approach of the offshore petroleum industry to safety and emergency response. The U.K. government introduced legislation to reduce risks to the health and safety of the offshore workforce, known as the *Safety Case regulations* (HSE, 1992). The key feature of the Safety Case is the requirement that operators prepare a formal risk assessment for each of their installations. This includes the identification of all major hazards relating to the installation and their consequences, as well as details of emergency response procedures. The operator, therefore has to preplan emergency responses and provide standard operating procedures for handling the identified hazards in the Safety Case.

The Offshore Petroleum Industry Training Organization's (OPITO) standard of competence, *Controlling Emergencies*, specifies emergency response actions as performance criteria with six separate but interdependent elements. These are the minimum standards[1] of skilled performance for emergency management required by OPITO of OIMs and their deputies (OPITO, 1997). The six performance criteria are (OPITO, 1997, Functional Diagram):

1. Maintain a state of readiness;
2. Assess situation and take effective action;
3. Maintain communications;
4. Delegate authority to act;
5. Manage individual and team performance; and
6. Deal with stress in self and others.

In *Controlling Emergencies*, each element is defined in detail, emphasizing the desired range of behaviors, such as having and maintaining a state of readiness, evidence of emergency procedures and predetermined strategies, communications with relevant sources, and evidence of stress-reduction behavior for the emergency team members. Encompassed in element 2 is decision making. Although the element does not address particular decisions, it provides a structure applicable in all emergencies, as illustrated in Figure 4.1.

Similar competence standards for emergency management have been created for, among others, the emergency services. For example, the U.K. fire service devised a standard of competence for supervision and command (FSAB, 1995). It emphasizes issues such as determining tactical options, maintaining communication links, information gathering, resource allocation, safety of personnel, liaison with external agencies, and dealing with casualties. Flin (1996) noted that there is a clear overlap between the fire brigade's standard of competence and those of other emergency services relating to information gathering, situation assessment, communication, and resource allocation. These elements are significant contributors to effective command and control.

Figure 4.1 describes the optimal approach to emergency decision making according to OPITO. The performance criteria are described in eight steps (OPITO, 1997, p. 4):

2.1 Information from all appropriate sources is obtained, evaluated, and confirmed as quickly possible.

---

[1] There is no statutory qualification or registration for the OIM, but the employer must show in each installation Safety Case submitted to the Offshore Safety Divisions of the Health and Safety Executive that their OIMs have the necessary skills and competence appropriate for this appointment (HSE, 1992).

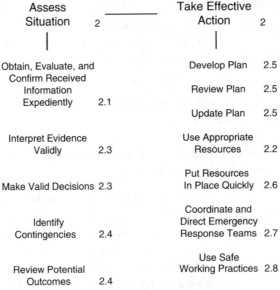

Figure 4.1 Element 2: Assess the situation and take effective action. (OPITO, 1997.)

2.2 Appropriate resources are utilized throughout the emergency.

2.3 Valid interpretations of all evidence are made and valid decisions taken throughout the emergency.

2.4 Potential outcomes of the emergency and possible response actions are reviewed against consequences and probabilities.

2.5 A plan of action including that required to deal with contingency situations is developed in the light of this evidence and is continually reviewed. (This may include doing nothing.)

2.6 Appropriate actions are taken as quickly as possible.

2.7 Emergency response teams are coordinated and directed in an effective manner.

2.8 Working practices are safe and conform to current health and safety legislation.

These elements suggest a decision-making model based on information gathered from all available sources, appropriate resource utilization, valid interpretation of information, and valid action selection based on this information. Additionally, a review of potential consequences and probabilities against possible response actions, the development of a plan of action, and quick interventions are required. The normative approach described by the industry contrasts with research evidence indicating that, in emergencies, decision making is often based on condition-action rules (Rasmussen, 1983) or recognition (Klein, 1989). The main findings have suggested that:

- In a dynamic problem situation, experts tend to generate a single highly likely option and evaluate its appropriateness to the current conditions (Klein, 1989; Lipshitz, 1993). If it is considered to be suitable, it is implemented; if not, it is altered or a different option is created and the process is repeated.

- The main difference between experienced and less experienced decision makers is their situation assessment, not their reasoning ability (Chi, Glaser, & Farr, 1988; Endsley, 1995; Klein, 1989). Situations are assessed quickly using the knowledge base of the decision maker. Identification automatically leads to retrieval of one or more appropriate action alternatives (Orasanu & Connolly, 1993).

- Decision makers usually use a satisficing (Simon, 1955) rather than an optimizing strategy. That is, they select a satisfactory strategy for the situation that may not be the best.

- Rather than being driven by a computational algorithm, expert reasoning is schema-driven. Decision makers use their insight and knowledge to analyze the problem, to decipher the situation, and to define what information is helpful for solution identification (Noble, 1993). This process allows for fast assessment, information gathering and interpretation, and selection of a course of action (CoA), clearly an advantage when under time pressure and faced with the dangers of cognitive overload. An important feature of the schema-driven approach is that people formulate causal models of the circumstances. Understanding is derived from inferences about causal relations (Pennington & Hastie, 1993; Thagard, 1988) based on interpretation of the significance of the events. People attempt to understand the intentions of others and consider suggested actions by anticipating their future consequences (Lipshitz, 1993).

- Reasoning and acting are interwoven rather than segregated (Connolly & Wagner, 1988). People do not analyze every possible detail of a situation but instead think a little, act a little, and then evaluate the outcomes and think and act some more (Gaba & Lee, 1990; Orasanu & Connolly, 1993). This iterative process of reassessment reflects the complexity of dynamic situations.

The OIM's Experience, Role, and Responsibilities

In the U.K. sector of the North Sea, there are approximately 150 installations ranging from large fixed production platforms, with over 300 personnel, to small installations with a crew of 15 or less. As most of the fields are 150 kilometers or more from shore, the installations are designed as self-contained units, having their own power supplies and accommodation for staff. In charge of offshore installations is the OIM,[2] who is responsible for the safety, health, and welfare of the personnel on board. Unlike managers of land-based petrochemical plants or nuclear power plants, OIMs cannot call upon the emergency services for immediate assistance in a crisis. Thus, offshore installations must also be self-sufficient in emergency response. The OIM is the executive decision maker who takes the role of incident commander should an emergency arise. To support the OIM, crew members form several emergency response teams, trained for specific roles such as fire fighting or first aid.

In contrast to the experience of the police and the fire brigade, emergencies are few and far between for the OIM offshore; the OIM must become an expert without extensive real-life practice. Simulator exercises constitute the essence of training and assessment, but when the OIM commences his job on the installation, he seldom reenters the simulator. Experience must be derived from installation exercises held at regular intervals (usually Sunday morning at 07.00 to avoid sleep disturbance). The exercises are often routine and help to reinforce the procedures encompassing the tactical approach. They are limited in time and deal with predefined emergencies according to companies' emergency response manuals. However, time pressure, incomplete information, or life and death issues are not present. These are what make the real emergency more complex and multifaceted. The industry assumes that extensive exercises can provide a framework of sufficient quality to allow the OIM to perform competently in an emergency.

Models of Decision Making

Figure 4.2 illustrates a simple production model of emergency decision making based on the work of Newell and Simon (1972) and Gibson

---

[2] The OIM will be referred to as *he* throughout the chapter, as at present no women hold the post.

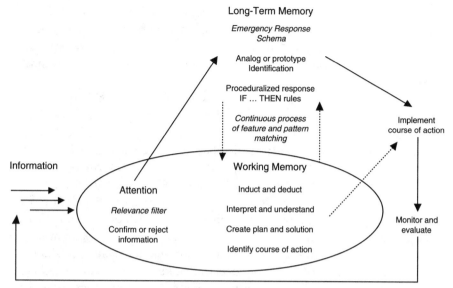

Figure 4.2 A production system model of OIM decision making.

(1979). The model corresponds with research with a wide range of memory experts as participants, which showed that experts were able to utilize preexisting domain-specific knowledge stored in long-term memory (LTM) in the form of predetermined retrieval plans (Chase & Ericsson, 1982). When recall was required, the experts could activate the corresponding retrieval plan and rapidly access the required information.

Neches, Langley, and Klahr (1987) described the fundamental form of a production system as two interacting data structures connected through a simple processing cycle:

1. A working memory (WM) consisting of a collection of symbolic data items called *WM elements*.
2. A production memory consisting of condition-action rules called *productions*, whose conditions describe configurations of elements that might appear in WM and whose actions specify modifications to the contents of WM (Neches et al., 1987, p. 3).

A production can match in several ways, and each way it does match is referred to as an *instantiation*. Instantiations are generated, in an approximate order of plausibility, such that the first production instantiations generated are likely to be the best. Production instantiations are evaluated as they are generated, and the generation of further candidates is terminated as soon as one is found that satisfies. Thus, experienced performers, operating within their domains of expertise, will be able to access the most appropriate solution without complex calculations and computations.

Production rules, as the decision maker's cognitive skills or tools, form the basis of his or her expertise. These are formed over time by the decision maker using more basic human processing skills.

Research on human performance has suggested that people learn through the process of compiling and categorizing information into LTM constructs such as schemata (Neisser, 1976), procedural knowledge (Anderson, 1993), or scripts (Rumelhart, 1975). In 1972, Newell and Simon suggested condition-action rules or IF . . . THEN production rules as the basis of cognitive skills. Similarly, Anderson (1983, 1993), in his architecture of adaptive thought (ACT), suggested that skill acquisition is a gradual process of compiling declarative knowledge into procedural knowledge. The knowledge underlying a skill begins initially in a declarative form, for example as a story, which must be interpreted to produce performance. As a function of its interpreted execution, this skill becomes compiled into a production-rule form. With practice, individual production rules acquire strength and become more attuned to the circumstances in which they apply. This is not surprising; in fact Aristotle stated as far back as 436 BC: "It is from memory that men acquire experience, because the numerous memories of the same thing eventually produce the effect of a single experience" (Aristotle, *Metaphysics*, p. 5).

Production rules account for condition-action responses and explain why serial rather than concurrent generation and evaluation of options are prevalent. However, they do not address why some types of information are preferentially attended to rather than others, how the environment impacts on behavior, and how this helps to define a problem. Ecological psychology (Brunswik, 1956; Gibson, 1979) has emphasized these aspects as paramount to the understanding of human behavior.

Ecological Psychology

Investigating domain-specific behavior should be, as Vicente (1995) stated, a search for environmental constraints that define the rules governing behavior. The ecological approach suggests that in order to understand the rules that govern behavior, it is essential to start by studying the constraints of the task that are relevant to the operator (Vicente, 1995). Gibson (1979) suggested a specificity theory of skill acquisition that views the process of becoming skilled as the education of attention. Cognitive economy and goal relevance both play an important part in this theory. Gibson states that with experience, people learn the strategy that is most economical for the particular task and thereby concentrate on the minimal number of distinctive features that will successfully discriminate among the circumstances of interest. Skill acquisition thus consists of modifying what is attended to, the goal being the identification of diagnostic high-order information that can be used to actualize task goals. The training of attention is achieved by abstraction, filtering, and optimization of perceptual search. Experts have learned to work within and exploit the set of constraints that govern their domain of expertise. For example, Kirlik, Miller, and Jagacinski (1993) found that experts' behavior in complex environments could be modeled by assuming that participants' actions were guided by environmental constraints, despite the fact that the environment did not uniquely constrain behavior. These constraints were perceptually specified rather than chosen by an analytical problem-solving process.

Emphasis on ecological validity underlines the importance of studying the human operator and his or her environment together rather than separately. In the next section, we discuss the main findings from studies of OIM emergency decision making.

A Cognitive Task Analysis of OIM Emergency Decision Making

Two separate studies were conducted to assess whether OIMs made decisions akin to a production model. These studies consisted of knowledge elicitation interviews with 19 OIMs (Skriver & Flin, 1997a) and a protocol analysis of 18 simulated emergencies (Skriver & Flin, 1997b).

The knowledge elicitation interviews were based on hypothetical paper-based scenarios corresponding with the emergency command competence requirements of OPITO (1997). OPITO's risk assessments have led to the identification of six major categories of emergencies for which the offshore petroleum companies have developed standard operating procedures as a tactical framework for the OIM to work within. These are a well control incident, an explosion and fire, an accommodation fire, a helicopter crash, a pipeline incident, and a collision or wave damage causing structural collapse (OPITO, 1997). Decision making in offshore installation emergencies refers to the complete set of activities required to select and execute actions, from information gathering and interpretation, via goal specification, to selection and execution of courses of action.

Three hypothetical paper-based offshore emergency scenarios were used, containing information similar to that which an OIM would receive on arrival at the Emergency Command Center (ECC). The three scenarios were derived from company emergency response training documents and were selected to represent various levels of complexity, danger to the platform, and danger to the personnel on board. Each scenario consisted of a brief description of a crisis incident together with additional information about the time of day, wind speed and direction, sea conditions, and the proximity of helicopters. A sample of 15 experienced OIMs from two companies and 5 deputy OIMs from one company were interviewed. Emphasis was on the initial decisions and the tactical framework applied by the OIMs.

The second study took place at the Montrose Fire and Emergency Training College (MFETC) high-fidelity simulator. The simulator was a realistic copy of an offshore installation command center, containing white boards for checklists, a fire and gas panel, communication links to internal and external sources, and plot plans of the installation.

The installation figuring in the simulator was a medium-size steel production platform with 141 personnel on board. It was set in the northern section of the North Sea. A helicopter with a doctor on board was available in the field. Paramedics could be brought in from an adjacent Norwegian field. Helicopters coming in from Sumburgh, the Shetland Islands, would take approximately 40 minutes to reach the installation.

The installation had four levels of shutdown ranging from stopping processing to total shutdown. Drilling was supposed to be taking place on board the platform at the commencement of the incident. Specific details, such as availability of fire pumps, were presented before the emergencies started and were noted on the white boards. The installation had four fire teams: the white (first response), red (support), green (drilling), and black (night shift) teams. In the command center were four people:

- The *OIM*: Executive decision maker and in overall command. He was responsible for coordinating the approach to the incident and for questioning and directing the command center personnel if he disagreed with their decisions. He also had to make public announcements and phone the onshore emergency command center (known as the *beach*) at regular intervals.

- The *operations supervisor* (OS): Second in command. He was responsible for directing the fire teams and dealing with the specifics of the incident.

- The *maintenance supervisor* (MS): He was responsible for keeping track of people, whether at muster points, missing, or casualties.

- The *radio operator* (RO): He was responsible for external communication with the Coast Guard, helicopters, other installations, ships, and so on. Also kept track of helicopters available, estimated time of arrival, number of seats, and medical support in area.

The OS, MS, and RO roles were played by company or MFETC staff. They acted according to actual roles and responsibilities.

The scenarios started with a yellow (low gas) or red (general platform) alert. The incident command team assembled in the command center and dealt with what they encountered. The task was dynamic and adaptable, that is, developments depended on the OIM's decisions. The emergencies reflected actual time for approximately the first 10 minutes, whereupon time was compressed. The incident lasted until the OIM had regained control and put the status back to green (normal) or the command center staff had abandoned the platform by lifeboat.

Five OIM candidates from one company participated in the study. Analysis of the simulated emergencies was based on transcribed video recordings of communication taking place in 18 incidents, each lasting for about 30 minutes. It was derived from a combination of protocol analysis (Ericsson & Simon, 1993) and content analysis (Krippendorf, 1980) and comprised the five distinctive phases presented in Table 4.1. The analysis was conducted using the qualitative software package Q.S.R. NUD.IST (Qualitative Solutions and Research, 1996). Interrater reliability was $r = .90$. The interviews with 19 OIMs were treated as protocols and were also content analyzed according to Table 4.1.

Decisions Made by OIMs

Table 4.2 depicts the definitions for the decision types identified according to Rasmussen's (1983) skills, rules, and knowledge (SRK)

Table 4.1. *Phases of Analysis*

Step	Brief Description
Data preparation	Transcribe communication on video recordings into protocols.
Functional analysis	Develop coding scheme, encode protocol, and describe components.
Decision type identification	Identify decision type according to Rasmussen's SRK framework (1983).
Condition-action rules	Describe each rule used by the OIMs.
Problem categorization	Identify problem areas and categorize decisions accordingly.

framework. Of the 504 decisions, 255 related to action responses and 249 to communication. The action responses were considered to be the most important, as interventions affected the status of the emergency, whereas communication decisions had minimal impact on the incident itself. The action response decisions were divided according to Rasmussen's SRK taxonomy (Table 4.3). Only the rule-based category (emergency procedures, checklists, condition-action responses, and responding to requests) was utilized, encompassing both tactical decisions that dealt with the overall approach to the incident and operational decisions concerning specific subgoals within the overall structure. A large number of decisions were suggested by other team members and verified by the OIM (48.2%). These were also categorized as rule-based. Knowledge-based decisions consisted of choice problems or novel situations (0%).

The interviews supported this categorization, suggesting that OIMs relied heavily on a tactical framework based on condition-action rules to structure the emergency response process. There was limited evidence that they used the emergency procedures available in the OPITO guidelines and no evidence suggesting that the OIMs' decision making was analytical.

Based on the cognitive task analysis, command and control of an offshore installation emergency can be described as a series of decisions regarding the selection of actions suitable for the current state of the installation. The situation is dynamic, develops over time, and requires continual assessment.

As with most expertise research, the cognitive task analysis in the present study emphasized the OIMs' reliance on condition-action rules.

Table 4.2. *Decision Types*

Type	Definition
Rule-based	
Emergency procedures	Defined in the operating company's manual. Responses depending on IF... THEN rules and prescriptive in the domain, i.e., they do not depend on the decision maker's past experience with similar cases, but rather on the responses prescribed by the industry, the company, etc.
Checklists	List of problem areas used by the OIM to ensure that all aspects of the incident are covered (e.g., shutdown, lifeboat availability). May involve a proactive element, i.e., the checklist could be used to instigate actions before complete assessment had taken place. The checklist also contained time indicators (e.g., when to phone the beach).
Condition-action	Rule-based behavior characterized by controlled actions derived from procedures or subroutines stored in memory. Control of behavior at this level is goal oriented and structured by feedforward control through a stored rule. It does not involve concurrent option generation and evaluation. Stored rules were of the type IF (state) THEN (diagnosis) or IF (state) THEN (remedial action). Identification of the condition could be based on three means of reasoning:
	Problem oriented: the combination of cues into a meaningful condition, which then elicited an appropriate action response. Involved conscious processing and team discussion;
	Recognition primed: No discussion involved; instant decision based on previous experience; and
	Hypothesizing/guessing: involved identification of the condition but lacked a matching action plan. The selected response was based on deductive reasoning.
Responding to request	Decisions made by other emergency response team members. Consisted of verification or responding to requests regarding decisions made on the installation. Decisions could be goal oriented or go/no go.
Knowledge-based	
Analytical	Choice problems. Several legitimate options or CoAs existed from among which one had to be selected. Options had to be evaluated in light of goals and situational constraints; no simple rule applied. Alternatively, novel situations existed for which no existing framework could be applied.

Table 4.3. *Types of Decisions Made by OIMs*

SRK Framework	Decision Level	Decision Type	Percentage of Total Decisions
Rule-based	Tactical decision	Emergency procedures	3.5
		Checklist	4.7
	Operational decision	Goal oriented	35.7
		Recognition	7.1
		Guesses	0.4
		OIM verified	48.2

Each decision was converted into a symbolic condition-action rule. The most predominant condition-action rules were communication decisions. These were compiled, looking at how often the THEN condition remained the same when the IF condition differed. There were 47 rules for which specific THEN conditions were repeated or remained the same for 78 different IF conditions. This accounted for 401 of the 504 decisions or 79.6% of the total number of decisions identified. It included 100% of all communication decisions and 30.6% of all action decisions. The remaining 103 decisions were made on only one occasion.

Processes in OIM Decision Making

The content analysis revealed that the OIM worked concurrently on several problems, continually changing his focus of attention from one to another. Table 4.4 illustrates the distribution of decisions in the problem categories.

Table 4.4. *Distribution of Decisions into Problem Categories*

	Percentage of Decisions	Percentage of Decisions When Featured
Muster	10.6	13.4
Process	9.8	11.8
Incident	23.5	23.5
Medical support	11.0	13.8
Resources	13.7	16.1
Casualties	11.8	17.3
Downmanning	5.5	15.7
Evacuation	14.1	42.4

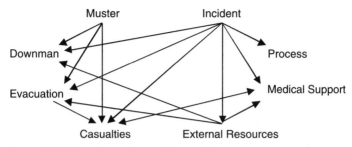

Figure 4.3 The interdependence of key problems.

The distribution of decisions related to the type of emergency; for example, if the installation was abandoned, more than 42% of the decisions focused on the evacuation process. In such a case, the incident (e.g., an explosion) would gradually disappear as the focus of attention, as evacuation became the main concern.

The roles of the emergency crew members were dynamic, shifting to fit the dynamics of the situation with the changes of emphasis. For example, the operations supervisor, who under normal circumstances would take care of fire teams and the incident, would take over the role of directing the evacuation as it became a main concern, whereas the maintenance supervisor, whose role it was to keep track of people and organize removal of the personnel from the platform, would spend time helping the radio operator with external communication instead of directing the evacuation.

From the analysis, the OIM's focus of attention can be divided roughly into three interdependent categories: people, incident, and resources. For example, as an incident evolves, the people category develops from a concern with muster numbers to a need to downman or evacuate, depending on the incident. The *casualties* category is also part of this group but relates to resources through the need for medical support. Figure 4.3 is a path diagram showing the interdependencies of the different problems to which the OIM must attend.

OIMs are aware of the problem areas that comprise the focus of attention and use them as the base for emergency checklists. The checklists, utilized as a reference point, are mostly drawn up by the OIMs themselves. Checklists are installation specific and reinforce the tactical framework suggested by the emergency procedures rather than the production model of decision making. The installation Safety Case risk assessments should ensure that novel emergencies cannot take place. If the problem goes beyond domain-specific knowledge and insight,

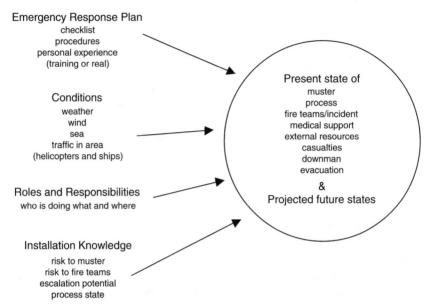

Figure 4.4 A generic model of the OIM's knowledge requirements for an off-shore emergency.

such as a software or hardware failure, the tactical framework can still be followed but decision-making competence may depend on individual differences such as cognitive skills, personality, or the quality of the emergency team's performance. From this identification of problem areas, Figure 4.4 was constructed. This figure specifies the generic knowledge requirements for OIMs.

The OIM must be aware of the platform systems' states, geography, environment, people, and time remaining to perform effectively. The generic model contains information about the present state of:

- The muster: assembly of all personnel at designated points when the alarm is raised.
- The production process: the state of the plant including shutdown, blowdown, and fire pump availability.
- The development of the incident: how the incident is escalating, how it is affecting the installation's structural integrity, and the deployment of the fire-fighting teams.
- Medical support requirements: the need to bring on board extra medical support either from offshore or onshore.
- External resources: the requirements in terms of use of helicopters, fire-fighting vessels, and the Coast Guard.

- Casualties: where they have occurred and what treatment is required.
- Downmanning requirements: the need to evacuate nonessential personnel by helicopter.
- Need to evacuate: means and order of evacuation.

The generic model also encompasses projected future states based on experiential knowledge. Information drawn upon includes, among others, the emergency response plan, the prevailing weather and wind conditions, knowledge of who is doing what and where, and specific installation knowledge such as risk to the muster points and escalation potential.

Team performance is crucial to supply the OIM with information required to make appropriate decisions; in fact, it is the most important role of the offshore emergency team. Offshore emergency response can be seen as a case of distributed competence (Hutchins, 1990). The ECC can be viewed as an information processing system, gathering the details about the state of the incident, the response, and the resources available. The job of the ECC team is to collate the huge amount of information available, using it to build a shared understanding of the incident. This shared understanding is absolutely vital to emergency management because it allows the OIM to coordinate a response plan and put it into action. Responsibility for making decisions about specific problems is distributed to emergency team members; for example, the OS directs the fire teams. Thus, overall emergency performance depends on the coordination of different team members who act according to their own knowledge and understanding. Competent emergency response rests on the ability of the individual team members to perform effectively, both alone and as a group. They operate within a system they know, both in their own roles and responsibilities and in those of the other team members.

The OIM builds his initial mental representation from information received from both the ECC and external sources – for example, people working in the area, the control room, and the standby vessel. The OIM utilizes his knowledge of the geography of the installation to visualize where the incident took place and what is happening (some installations now have closed-circuit cameras as extra support). For all the decision makers in the ECC, information received is filtered through attention, extracting what is of relevance to the ongoing incident, a process described by Gibson (1979) as the *education of attention*. This filtering process is based on pattern or feature recognition. Sternberg (1985) called this *selective encoding* and described the process as one in which a person realizes the relevance of some information at the same time as he or she screens out irrelevant other information. Information the OIM accepts is matched to emergency response schemata stored in LTM. He recognizes it based on either incident training or explicit experience of a similar event. The retrieved schema helps to identify the incident and provide meaning. It also contains information about action plans and means to execute them. The OIM's decisions can be symbolically described in terms of condition-action rules that have been proceduralized (described by Anderson's ACT: 1983, 1993). For example, the first decision to make is to muster, but where to muster depends on the incident:

> IF *the normal muster point is safe*
> THEN *muster at normal muster point.*
> IF *it is not safe.*
> THEN *muster at alternative muster point.*

From Figure 4.4, significant cues are the location of the incident, wind speed and direction, the risk to the normal and alternative muster points, and the risk to route to muster points. The action plan the OIM identifies as appropriate will then be executed and monitored on a continual basis. If the plan fails, a new plan will be retrieved and implemented.

The rules used by OIMs varied significantly in complexity. For example, tactical decisions based on procedures or the checklist were relatively simple, as matching of the condition with the action was available in a visual format and cues were provided by the emergency team members. Operational decisions, such as a decision to attack a fire from a particular direction, were considerably more complex and involved a number of interdependent factors. In most instances they were goal oriented, that is, OIMs identified a goal and then worked toward it. However, operational decisions were less significant and addressed minor problems within the tactical framework.

Although less important than tactical decisions, operational decisions were multifaceted and thus demanded more of the OIM's cognitive abilities, involving inductive and deductive reasoning, interpretation and comprehension of the information available, goal identification, problem solving, and CoA identification and selection. For example, in one scenario a major gas explosion has ripped off some cladding material, which has fallen into the sea. The OIM feared for the platform's structural integrity but could not assess the situation properly because the fire was still raging in the area. Attempting to get near the locus of the emergency would put the lives of the fire team at risk. The standby vessel could not see if there was any structural damage from its present position. Tactically, the OIM decided that because of the unknown effect of the explosion, it was better to start downmanning, that is, removing nonessential personnel from the platform. At an operational level, he moved the standby vessel to a position with a better view of the explosion area and fire in order to gain better information. The rules could be written as:

> *IF there has been an explosion and there is potential for*
> *structural damage*
> *THEN downman nonessential personnel.*

and

> *IF damage to the platform is observable from the sea and*
> *not from the platform*
> *THEN move the standby vessel to a position with a better view.*

The general conclusion drawn from this work is that when OIMs are facing familiar emergencies, actual or simulated, they rely largely on previously memorized solution schemata, such as downmanning, when there is potential for structural damage or for sending people to alternative muster points when the normal musters are unsafe. OIM decision making can be described as a process of pattern matching by accessing rules of thumb stored in LTM. Once the situation is assessed, the appropriate rules are defined and the OIMs know how to proceed, in a forward-driven manner, rather than by reasoning backward from solution to initial state. The value of the OIMs' emergency response schemata is that these can be applied as general strategies to the Safety Case identified emergencies. Reliance on LTM rules of thumb reduces the need for intensive problem solving, thereby releasing WM processing to focus on specific problems, that is, operational decisions.

In this respect, the constrained offshore environment worked in the OIMs' favor. The lack of variability of the potential emergencies means that the six categories of emergency scenarios the industry has defined differ in specifics but share the same framework. That is, the same tactical response is required. For example, a blowout, a fire, and a major gas leak will result in the same procedures being initiated, the same problem areas will receive attention, and the goals will be the same. Figure 4.2

illustrates a generic model of the knowledge requirements for OIMs in an emergency offshore.

Emergency command on offshore installations appears to be a case of domain expertise constrained into a normative tactical framework. Deciding and justifying what the task is and how to do it is defined by emergency procedures devised by the industry. Skilled performance is derived from proceduralization of a tactical framework, with responsibility distributed to emergency team members. The decision-making process observed in and described by OIMs is consistent with a cognitive production model in which the framework is not knowledge-based but rule-based. However, this mismatch is saved from becoming overtly problematic by the nature of the offshore domain. The offshore environment therefore benefits from having a large number of situation constraints. In decision-making terms, the constraints facilitate the emergency response process, as developments are predictable both within a production model and within procedural guidelines.

Conclusion

It is suggested that a simple production system model (Neches et al., 1987; Newell & Simon, 1972) explains the cognitive processing underlying OIMs' emergency decision making on offshore installations, as the processes described are experience based or schema driven. Pattern matching, the recognition process, and the matching of more consciously processed condition-action rules describe the compilation of declarative into procedural knowledge (Anderson, 1993). Production rules capture the normative aspect of *metacognition-others*; they make explicit how decision making should proceed given the context and information at hand. Production rules also explain why serial option generation and evaluation is likely in offshore emergencies and suggest why the decisions made are satisficing rather than optimizing. Symbolically, the emergency decisions taken could be written in terms of IF . . . THEN rules. The two studies also suggested that the OIM had to work toward a number of subgoals, each contributing to the overall approach.

Offshore emergencies are defined by significant environmental constraints. Decision making is bound by the limited number of options available, the small number of cues significant to situation assessment, and the clear and limited number of goals attainable. This has facilitated proceduralization leading to a singular approach to most emergencies. Decisions taken can be divided into tactical (procedures or checklists), dealing with the overall approach to the emergency, and operational (specific to particular subgoals within the tactical framework). Both categories are rule-based, as described by Rasmussen (1983). This contradicts the normative approach taken by the petroleum industry, which sees the decision-making process as mainly knowledge-based. That is, the skilled performance sought through the *Controlling Emergencies* unit does not reflect the rule-based behavior observed. This is not without precedence. Murray (1995) noted that the fire brigade's standards of competence did not appear to reflect actual behavior either. However, as most OIMs lack extensive emergency experience, the provision of a normative framework may be useful for learning the tactical approach.

OIMs cannot be said to be expert emergency managers. The OIM and his team do not have the luxury of extensive real-life practice, like the police or the fire brigade, but must rely on other means to develop skills and knowledge. The offshore environment is a good example of a low base rate domain. Emergencies happen too infrequently to allow compilation of knowledge. However, the limited number of emergencies possible, the predefined emergency procedures, the checklist, and the distribution of responsibilities among emergency team members all enhance the prospects of effective command and control.

Other emergency commanders, such as fire commanders and military officers, work within a system of greater functional variability and fewer environmental constraints. Condition-action responses may still be the prevalent means of making decisions, but the number of situations encountered and the number of options available are higher and the possible outcomes are more varied, yet decisions still have to be made rapidly, based at times on meager situation assessments. In contrast to the OIM, emergency commanders in the police, fire, and military services make decisions in time-pressured, high-risk situations and make them frequently. Thus, the possibilities of environmental attunement (Gibson, 1979) and of compiling declarative into procedural knowledge (Anderson, 1993) are greater. Experienced fire brigade commanders or police officers may have a larger number of condition-action rules stored; however, situation assessment is more complex, involving a greater number of cues, options, and orders by which to apply responses effectively. Drawing conclusions across domains, such as comparing offshore emergency decision making to fire fighting or policing a riot thus seems inappropriate. The competence standards may be similar in their generic shape, but to the experienced emergency manager working in his or her domain of knowledge, what may be significant is not time pressure, stress, and high risk but possibly the number of emergency categories, environmental constraints, problem areas, and action responses available (Martin, Flin, & Skriver, 1997). For example, the fire brigade commander works within a boundless environment where the incident type is unpredictable, limited information is available, the number of cues can be large and contradictory, and the goals can be ambiguous. Thus, we suggest that emergency decision making cannot be discussed as one concept but must be considered on a sliding scale with clearly defined goals, cues, and options at one pole and unclear goals, multiple cues, and multiple options at the other.

References

Anderson, J. R. (1983). *The architecture of cognition*. Cambridge, MA: Harvard University Press.

Anderson, J. R. (1993). *Rules of the mind*. Hillsdale, NJ: Erlbaum.

Aristotle (c. 436 BC, 1937). *The metaphysics*, Books I–IX. London: Heineman.

Brehmer, B. (1992). Dynamic decision making: Human control of complex systems. *Acta Psychologica, 81*, 211–241.

Brunswik, E. (1956). *Perception and the representative design of psychological experiments*. Berkeley: University of California Press.

Chase, W. G., & Ericsson, K. A. (1982). Skill and working memory. In G. H. Bower (Ed.), *The psychology of learning and motivation* (Vol. 16, pp. 1–58). New York: Academic Press.

Chi, M. T. H., Glaser, R., & Farr, M. J. (1988). *The nature of expertise*. Hillsdale, NJ: Erlbaum.

Cicourel, A. V. (1990). The integration of distributed knowledge in collaborative medical diagnosis. In J. Galegher, R. Kraut, & C. Egido (Eds.), *Intellectual teamwork* (pp. 221–242). Hillsdale NJ: Erlbaum.

Collins concise dictionary. (1982). Glasgow, UK: Collins.

Connolly, T., & Wagner, W. G. (1988). Decision cycles. In R. L. Candy, S. M. Puffer, & M. M. Newman (Eds.), *Advances in information processing in organizations* (Vol. 3, pp. 183–205). Stamford, CT: JAI Press.

Cullen, The Hon. Lord. (1990). *The public inquiry into the Piper Alpha disaster*, Vols. I and II. London: HMSO.

Dowell, J. (1995). Coordination in emergency operations and the tabletop exercise. *La Travail Humain, 58*, 85–102.

Endsley, M. R. (1995). Toward a theory of situation awareness in dynamic systems. *Human Factors, 37*, 32–64.

Ericsson, K. A., & Simon, H. A. (1993). *Protocol analysis: Verbal reports as data* (2nd ed.). Cambridge: Cambridge University Press.

Fire Service Awarding Body. (1995). *Emergency fire services. Supervision and command N/SVQ level 3*. Arndale Centre, Luton, UK: Author.

Flin, R. (1996). *Sitting in the hot seat: Leaders and their teams for critical incident management*. Chichester, UK: Wiley.

Flin, R., Salas, E., Strub, M., & Martin, L. (Eds.). (1998). *Decision making under stress*. Aldershot, UK: Ashgate.

Flin, R., Slaven, G. M., & Stewart, K. G. (1997). Emergency decision making in the offshore oil and gas industry. *Human Factors, 38*, 262–277.

Gaba, D. M., & Lee, T. (1990). Measuring workload of the anesthesiologist. *Anesthesia and Analgesia, 71*, 354–361.

Gibson, J. J. (1979). *The ecological approach to visual perception*. Boston: Houghton Mifflin.

Health and Safety Executive. (1992). *A guide to the offshore installations (Safety Case) regulations*. London: HMSO.

Hutchins, E. (1990). The technology of team navigation. In J. Galegher, R. Kraut, & C. Egido (Eds.), *Intellectual teamwork* (pp. 191–220). Hillsdale, NJ: Erlbaum.

Kirlik, A., Miller, R. A., & Jagacinski, R. J. (1993). Supervisory control in a dynamic uncertain environment: A process model of skilled human–environment interaction. *IEEE Transactions on Systems, Man, and Cybernetics, SMC-23*, 929–952.

Klein, G. A. (1989). Recognition-primed decisions. In W. Rouse (Ed.), *Advances in man–machine systems research*, (Vol. 5, pp. 47–92). Greenwich, CT: JAI Press.

Krippendorff, K. (1980). *Content analysis. An introduction to its methodology*. London: Sage.

Lipshitz, R. (1993). Converging themes in the study of decision making in realistic settings. In G. A. Klein, J. Orasanu, R. Calderwood, & C. E. Zsambok (Eds.), *Decision making in action: Models and methods* (pp. 103–137). Norwood, NJ: Ablex.

Marr, D. (1982). *Vision*. San Francisco: W. H. Freeman.

Martin, L., Flin, R., & Skriver, J. (1997). Emergency decision masking – A wider framework? In R. Flin, E. Salas, M. Strub, & L. Martin (Eds.), *Decision making under stress: Emerging themes and applications* (pp. 280–290). Aldershot, UK: Ashgate.

Murray, B. (1995). *Incident command expertise*. Moreton-in Marsh, UK: Brigade Command Course, Fire Training College.

Neches, R., Langley, P., & Klahr, D. (1987). Learning, development, and production systems. In D. Klahr, P. Langley, & R. Neches (Eds.), *Production system models of learning and development* (pp. 1–54). Cambridge, MA: MIT Press.

Neisser, U. (1976). *Cognition and reality: Principles and implications of cognitive psychology*. San Francisco: W. H. Freeman.

Newell, A., & Simon, H. A. (1972). *Human problem solving*. Englewood Cliffs, NJ: Prentice Hall.

Noble, D. (1993). A model to support development of situation assessment aids. In G. A. Klein, J. Orasanu, R. Calderwood, & C. E. Zsambok (Eds.), *Decision making in action: Models and methods* (pp. 287–305). Norwood, NJ: Ablex.

OPITO. (1997). *OPITO approved training standard: OIM (Dep OIM)*. Montrose, UK: Author.

Orasanu, J., & Connolly, T. (1993). The reinvention of decision making. In G. A. Klein, J. Orasanu, R. Calderwood, & C. E. Zsambok (Eds.), *Decision making in action: Models and methods* (pp. 3–20). Norwood, NJ: Ablex.

Pennington, N., & Hastie, R. (1993). A theory of explanation-based decision making. In G. A. Klein, J. Orasanu, R. Calderwood, & C. E. Zsambok (Eds.), *Decision making in action: Models and methods* (pp. 188–201). Norwood, NJ: Ablex.

Qualitative Solutions and Research. (1996). *User's guide for QSR NUD.IST.* London: Sage Publications Software.

Rasmussen, J. (1983). Skills, rules, and knowledge: Signals, signs, and symbols, and other distinctions in human performance models. *IEEE Transactions on Systems, Man, and Cybernetics, 13*, 257–266.

Rasmussen, J., Brehmer, B., & Leplat, J. (Eds.). (1991). *Distributed decision making: Cognitive models for cooperative work.* Chichester, UK: Wiley.

Rumelhart, D. E. (1975). Notes on a schema for stories. In D. Bobrow & A. Collins (Eds.), *Representation and understanding: Studies in cognitive science* (pp. 211–236). New York: Academic Press.

Simon, H. A. (1955). A behavioral model of rational choice. *Quarterly Journal of Economics, 69*, 99–118.

Skriver, J., & Flin, R. H. (1997a). Emergency decision making on offshore installations. In D. Harris (Ed.), *Engineering psychology and cognitive ergonomics* (Vol. 2, pp. 47–54). Aldershot, UK: Avebury.

Skriver, J., & Flin, R. H. (1997b). *Decision making in simulated emergencies.* Presented at the SPUDM 16 Conference of the European Association for Decision Making, Leeds, 17–21 August.

Sternberg, R. J. (1985). *Beyond IQ: A triarchic theory of human intelligence.* New York: Viking.

Thagard, P. (1988). *Computational philosophy of science.* Cambridge, MA: MIT Press.

Vicente, K. J. (1995). A few implications of an ecological approach to human factors. In J. Flach, P. Hancock, J. Caird, & K. Vicente (Eds.), *Global perspectives on the ecology of human–machine systems* (Vol. 1, pp. 55–67). Hillsdale, NJ: Erlbaum.

5   Designing for Competence

Patricia M. Jones

The purpose of this chapter is twofold. First, the notion of competence is discussed as inherently distributed across time, space, people, and artifacts. Thus, because of its distributed nature, an aspect of competent performance is related to communicative competence: how effectively performers can communicate to fellow performers as well as to an intended audience. Second, a methodology for systems design that explicitly takes into account competent performance is described.

This chapter is organized as follows. The first section provides an overview of issues and approaches to distributed competence, with particular attention to cognitive competence (e.g., distributed cognition and transactive memory approaches) and communicative competence (e.g., the cooperative principle and relevance). The second section describes the TEAM (Team Engineering Analysis and Modeling) methodology, a competence-centered approach to the design of information infrastructure to support knowledge work in an organization. The third section describes two examples of the use of the TEAM methodology, and the fourth section provides conclusions and directions for future research.

Distributed Competence

Competence is not solely the property of an actor or a thing; it is an emergent property of that actor or thing in the context of a particular environment and activity. This is the basic premise of human factors engineering: that one envisions effective performance; studies the intended user population, environment, and tasks; and designs technology, procedures, and so on to support competence.

The fields of computer-supported cooperative work and distributed artificial intelligence emerged in part because of the growing recognition that studying single users or agents, although certainly valuable, is insufficient to cope with complex work environments or problem-solving situations. Complex work is inherently social. Similarly, then, the study of competence likewise needs to account for distributed competence, where *distributed* means distributed among multiple agents as well as over space and time.

Two prominent overarching metaphors for the modeling and analysis of distributed, cooperative work view an organization as (1) a distributed information processing system and (2) a sociocultural system (see Jones & Jasek, 1997, for a brief review). A great deal of work in computer-supported cooperative work, enterprise modeling, and distributed artificial intelligence is explicitly grounded in the distributed information processing metaphor in which multiple agents with limited cognitive resources exchange messages, reason about goals, activities, and resources, and engage in joint activity. In contrast, the sociocultural view is less computational and rule-oriented and more negotiated and emergent. Objects of study include situations, breakdowns, tacit knowledge, and group work; how shared meanings emerge in practice; the ways in which action is inherently situated in the local context of particular material and social circumstances (cf. Suchman, 1987); how responsibility, authority, power, status, and "invisible" work are negotiated; and the relations between management and labor.

From these points of view, competence can be interpreted in different ways. We shall make a broad distinction here between cognitive and communicative competence, although these categories clearly overlap. These can be applied to both the information processing and sociocultural views, as shown in Table 5.1.

Competence and Distributed Cognition

Cognitive competence implies the study of expertise, the development of rules and knowledge, and so on. In the sense of distributed cognition, however, competence implies effective transformation of representations and structuring of the environment to support effective performance (Hutchins, 1995). Cognition distributed over time can be analyzed with respect to *precomputations*, including the development of organizational forms and routines (Hutchins, 1995). Thus, the appropri-

Table 5.1. *Perspectives on Competence with Some Example Issues: Cognitive and Communicative Competence as Viewed from the Information Processing and Sociocultural Perspectives*

Competence / Perspective	Information Processing	Sociocultural
Cognitive	Knowledge of other agents and their goals, perspectives, etc. Knowledge of goals and activities	Knowledge of norms Knowledge of cultural rules
Communication	Communication protocols between agents Inference, communicative intentions	Power and status Routinization vs. improvisation (e.g., the emergence of standard forms such as the memo)

ation of cultural and social norms by novices entering a community of practice is also part of the development of competence (Lave & Wenger, 1991).

Hollingshead (1998a, 1998b) offers a view based on transactive memory. In this view, part of distributed competence is knowing what others know and therefore adjusting one's own behavior accordingly, that is, *metacognition-others*. For example, if you and I are driving around Boston, and it's my first time in Boston, and I know that you know the city quite well, then I will allow you to drive or give me directions, as opposed to trying to reason from a map myself. In this example, my knowledge of your expertise allows me to rely on you as a resource, and our joint activity is thus more effective and less effortful.

Communicative Competence

Two perspectives on communicative competence are the cooperative principle and relevance (Jones, 1997). The *cooperative principle* is a general principle that conversational participants are expected to observe: "Make your conversational contribution such as is required, at the stage at which it occurs, by the accepted purpose or direction of the talk exchange in which you are engaged" (Grice, 1975, p. 45, cited in Sperber & Wilson, 1995, p. 33). Grice proposed four associated maxims of quantity, quality, relation, and manner. Mura (1983) summarizes these maxims respectively as "Be succinct, yet complete," "Be truthful," "Be relevant," and "Be clear and orderly." Thus, effective communication means that participants orient themselves to each other and rely on this principle and associated maxims as aids in inferencing. Violation of these maxims leads participants to make inferences to explain why the other actor made that violation. Further related development of these ideas has focused on relevance as the key to effective communication (Sperber & Wilson, 1995).

Clark (1996) discusses language use as a joint activity that emerges from interaction among two or more agents and argues that it is both cognitive and social. Much of his work focuses on the kinds of heuristics that are used to accomplish joint activity successfully; merely explaining communicative competence as effective prediction of another's actions leads to the infinite regress of mutual knowledge (I know that you know that I know that you know, and so on). Hence, a variety of rules of thumb and coordination devices exist or emerge in interaction so that participants can communicate successfully.

Competence-Centered Approach to Design[1]

The design of information technology to support effective work practices is the general aim of human–computer interaction (HCI) and computer-supported cooperative work (CSCW) research. As Newman and Lamming (1995) emphasize, the design of interactive systems should be grounded in a problem statement that articulates the activity to be supported in the context of expected users and their environment. Thus, competent designers create systems to invite competent performance in practice. In particular, competent designers have an explicit model of competent end-user performance that provides guidance and requirements for the design of the system. Furthermore, this explicit normative model is contextual – it takes into account the concrete, specific details of practice.

This competence-centered approach to design can be contrasted with design philosophies that are technology-driven, theory-driven, or user-centered. Table 5.2 differentiates these four approaches to design. Technology-driven design simply seeks to exploit technological advances, with little or no consideration of context and with only implicit ideas about competent performance. Theory-driven design seeks to operationalize a theoretical position that articulates competent

---

[1] These ideas are based on collaborative work with Barbara O'Keefe, Noshir Contractor, Stephen C.-Y. Lu, and Michael Case.

Table 5.2. *Four Design Approaches That Vary by Whether or Not a Competence Model Is Explicit and Whether or Not Context Is Taken into Account*

	Decontextualized	Contextualized
Implicit competence model	Technology-driven	User-centered
Explicit competence model	Theory-driven	Competence-centered

performance but without the notion of context. The COORDINATOR (Winograd & Flores, 1996) is a good example of this approach. Its design was based explicitly on the theory of speech acts that was context-independent. And finally, although user-centered design approaches are concerned with context, they are not necessarily explicit about a normative model. Instead, a common stance is to design for whatever users say they want, as opposed to creating an explicit representation of competent performance, which might differ from current practice.

Thus, the proposed competence-centered approach to design incorporates both an analysis of current practice (a user-centered perspective that is contextual and empirical) and a specification of competence models of HCI and team member interaction (a normative task-centered perspective) (Case, Contractor, Jones, Lu, & O'Keefe, 1992; Jones, Contractor, O'Keefe, & Lu, 1994; Jones et al., 1995). A proposed methodology for competence-centered design is the Team Engineering Analysis and Modeling (TEAM) methodology (Jones, 1995; Jones et al., 1994). The TEAM methodology is a framework for organizing data collection, modeling, design, and evaluation of complex sociotechnical systems into a systematic process in which a model of competence of the organization is central (Jones et al., 1994, 1995). Competence is defined with respect to the particular goals of the organization; in other words, elements of competence are situated and grounded in context, rather than being generic goals such as "be productive." The key features of the TEAM method are its focus on competence and normative modeling of activity and communication of human teams, and the evolving interrelationships between technological affordances and communicative and work practices.

Figure 5.1 summarizes the TEAM methodology. It consists of four major activities organized around a central competence theory. The four activities are user studies and observation, technology application, simulation and modeling, and prototype development. The methodology is applied systematically to the study of individual work practices, group meetings, and organizational communication and workflow

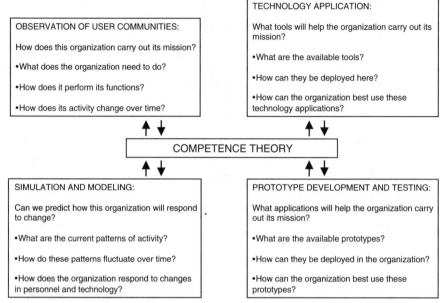

Figure 5.1 The TEAM methodology.

(Case et al., 1992; Jones et al., 1994, 1995), which in turn inform the choice of scenarios and requirements for technology demonstration prototypes.

Examples

Two projects that highlight our competence-centered design approach are the ARMS study and Project CITY. Both projects focus on engineering work contexts in which advanced information technology was deployed to assist in collaborative distributed problem solving. In the case of ARMS, we studied an existing system. In Project CITY, we are designing our own suite of technology tools to support a collaborative engineering process.

ARMS

Our first case study is an analysis of the Automated Review Management System (ARMS), a design review application that was built to support collaborative design between architect/engineering firms and their Army Corps of Engineers clients (Case et al., 1992). In the scenario analyzed by Case et al. (1992), an Air Force base (the end-user AFB) initiated a design project by making a request to the Air Force Strategic Air Command (SAC), which in turn contacted an Army Corps of Engineers design project manager. This project manager was responsible for the design phase of a project and oversaw a number of groups, including engineering design, cost estimation, and design quality assurance. The design work itself was done by an external contractor, an architect/engineering firm (the Architect/Engineer [A/E]). Participants involved in the design process were from SAC itself, from the AFB end-user community, from Corps geotechnical, landscaping, cost estimating, design quality assurance, and construction quality assurance groups, and from the A/E firm. The construction project manager assumed responsibility in the subsequent construction phase.

The design process itself, which was carried out by the A/E and monitored by the design project manager, SAC, and the end user, was structured as a series of sequential phases as follows: project book (2 weeks), project definition (3 weeks), initial submittal review (2 weeks), 60% onboard review (2 weeks), final design (3 weeks), final design late (3 1/2 weeks), first backcheck (1 1/2 weeks), and second backcheck (1 week). During this design process, ARMS was used as a mechanism for reviewers from the Corps, SAC, and the end-user facility to make comments on the A/E's design. Typically, someone from one of the design project manager's groups originated such a comment, and SAC and the end-user AFB facility stated their opinions of the remark using a standard response protocol. The comments were forwarded to the A/E via the design project manager. Also through ARMS, the A/E responded to each comment with a standard response protocol.

We analyzed all the ARMS comments and responses for the entire project with respect to an explicit competence model of feedback in the revision process (Case et al., 1992). According to this model, competent feedback must address the recipient's need for direction and motivation. The recipient must understand what to revise before performing a revision, hence the need for direction. The recipient's need for motivation (or *backing*) follows from the assumption that the recipient is a free agent and may choose not to comply with a revision request unless appropriate motivation is provided. Therefore, a competent performer sends the recipient a message that explicitly states the problem (what is to be revised), the solution (what the revision should accomplish), and the backing (why the revision should take place).

Based on this competence model, comments were classified along three dimensions: (1) specification of the problem; (2) specification of the solution; and (3) specification of the backing. For each dimension, a score of 1 (absent), 2 (general), or 3 (specific) was assigned. For example, a comment that did not specify a problem, but specified a specific solution and some general backing, would be scored as 1 on dimension 1 (problem specification), 3 on dimension 2 (solution specification), and 2 on dimension 3 (backing).

Our analysis examined the relationships of comments to responses by the recipient (typically the A/E) and to the phases in the design process. Some of our findings were that comments were more numerous later in the design process, tended to focus on either problem or solution specification but not both, and, interestingly, that more backing was associated with less agreement or concurrence by the recipient. Further discussion is provided in Case et al. (1992) and Jones et al. (1994).

Project CITY

The management of civil infrastructure systems is a complex process that involves distributed decision making and negotiation among people with heterogeneous agendas, activities, and expertise. Project CITY (Civil Infostructure TechnologY) is a research project intended to support and facilitate public works activities (within the Directorate of Public Works of a major Army installation) via collaborative information technology (Jones & Case, 1996; Jones et al., 1995, 1997).

The mission of the Directorate of Public Works is to provide *mission-ready infrastructure* – buildings, roads, grounds, and utility and energy systems that support the military missions of the base (e.g., training, communications). The Directorate consists of a number of divisions, including the Public Works Division (PWD) and the Environmental and Natural Resources Management Office (ENRMO). In particular, the Public Works Division consists of three branches: Engineering Plans and Services (for design and construction inspection for new construction projects), Facilities Management (for maintenance and repair of buildings, roads, and utilities), and Housing (for managing the housing of soldiers and their families on and off post). ENRMO is responsible for maintaining compliance with regulations dealing with environmental issues ranging from air and water quality to endangered species management to asbestos removal from buildings. All together, the PWD and ENRMO consist of approximately 65 (civilian) employees (Jones & Case, 1996).

Based on extensive studies of the PWD and ENRMO organized around the TEAM methodology (Jones et al., 1994, 1995), we developed a number of representations of the organization (see also Chin, 1997). The methods included ethnographic observation, social network and communication surveys, focus groups, observation of group meetings, and structured and semistructured interviews. The resulting representations included (1) an explicit competence model of ends, means, and outcomes, with associated technology infrastructure prototypes that we used to guide design, (2) an abstraction hierarchy representation of the work domain, and (3) several different kinds of workflow models, focusing on the most ubiquitous workflow process in the organization: the processing of a work request, the Department of Army form 4283. The 4283 process is the most wide-ranging in the organization according to our social network surveys and often the most problematic according to our ethnographic data. The 4283 process is used for jobs requiring more than 40 hours or work or more than $1,000.

The competence model we developed for Project CITY is shown in Table 5.3. It relates specific ends or goals to a description of means and outcomes. Associated with these for the purposes of guiding our design are tools (technology infrastructure such as databases, the Virtual Workspace System [Jones et al., 1997], and the Web) and technology components. All the components in the rightmost column are parts of the CITYSCAPE architecture (Jones et al., 1997). CITYSCAPE (Civil "Infostructure" Technology System for Collaborative Analysis, Prediction, and Evaluation) is a distributed, heterogeneous, modular architecture. The major functions of CITYSCAPE are to support (1) a shared space with a rich variety of data and information to support a wide array of work contexts (CITY-INFO), (2) a flexible workflow support tool for processing work requests (DA 4283) (CITY-WORK), (3) access to spatial data manipulation, particularly for real property, environmental, natural resources, master planning, and computer-aided design functions (CITY-MAP), (4) access to organizational data, particularly for managers and new hires (CITY-KNOW), and (5) a public kiosk allowing members of the community who submit 4283s to the DPW to do so electronically (CITY-DESK).

Conclusions and Directions for Future Research

This chapter has proposed a competence-centered approach to design and illustrated our approach with two studies. The designer who adopts

Table 5.3. *PWD Competence Model.*

Proposed Ends	Proposed Means	Relevant Outcomes	Tools	Use Cases/Demos Prototypes
Reduce time needed for decision making	Concurrent completion of steps for 4283s	Time to decision, estimated cost savings	VWS and database	CITY-WORK
Improve consistency and accuracy of decision making	Make information more accessible	Speed and quality of decisions	Web and Java-based SQL[1] queries	CITY-INFO CITY-MAP
	Support "organizational memory" for generating 4283s and to assist in negotiation	Coherence and ease of decision making, time to decision, estimated cost savings	Web and Java-based SQL queries	CITY-INFO
Unify currently fragmented information about the infrastructure	Centralized, intelligent graphic representation of infrastructure integrated with documentary information	Speed of information retrieval, quality of information, completeness of answers to queries, quality of decision making and planning	VWS, legacy systems of CAD, GIS, and shadow IFS-M database	CITY-INFO CITY-MAP
Allow more systematic and explicit processing of 4283s	Automated support for management of work requests	Time to complete 4283s, efficiency (person-hours), explicitness	VWS	CITY-WORK CITY-DESK
Reduce amount of time for documentation	Automated completion of required reports/forms	Time to complete reports, efficiency	VWS	CITY-WORK
Improve predictability of the PWD/DPW	Computational model of the PWD/DPW organization	Improved predictability of performance of the PWD/DPW; also online performance metrics	IKNOW, Web	CITY-KNOW Blanche demonstration

[1] SQL stands for System Query Language and is widely used in database programming. GIS stands for Geographic Information Systems. IFS-M stands for Integrated Facility System-Micro and is a large database containing real property, environmental, and contractual records related to buildings and civil infrastructure. IKNOW stands for Inquiring Knowledge Networks on the Web and is a Web-based tool for the collection and analysis of social and knowledge networks.

Note: Ends relate to means with associated outcomes, technological tools such as the Virtual Workspace System (VWS) and databases, and prototype technologies that are part of CITYSCAPE.

Source: Jones et al. (1997).

this approach seeks to create an explicit competence model of HCI by taking a normative task-centered perspective that embeds the system within the context of the users' interaction. This normative perspective involves thinking about the users' thinking in the context in which they should think it and has been labeled by the editors of this volume *metacognition-others*. The two example systems illustrate the application of metacognition-others in the design process.

There is still a great need to provide more formal and richer representations to support competence-centered design, and to have these representations and analysis and design methods take into account the rich set of insights from distributed cognition and communication studies discussed in the first section. In this way, the cognitive, social, and engineering disciplines can be fused to provide novel insights into distributed competence systems.

References

Case, M., Contractor, N., Jones, P. M., Lu, S. C.-Y., and O'Keefe, B. J. (1992). Team engineering analysis and modeling: Toward a normative model of team interaction. Proceedings of the 1992 *IEEE International Conference on Systems, Man, and Cybernetics* (pp. 1202–1207).

Chin, G. (1997). *Management of boundary objects in a shared information space for a public works organization.* Ph.D. dissertation, Department of Mechanical and Industrial Engineering, University of Illinois at Urbana-Champaign.

Clark, H. H. (1996). *Using language.* New York: Cambridge University Press.

Grice, H. P. (1975). Logic and conversation. In P. Cole (Ed.), *Studies in Syntax Volume 3: Speech Acts* (pp. 41–58). New York: Academic Press.

Hollingshead, A. B. (1998a). Distributed knowledge and transactive processes in groups. In D. Gruenfeld, M. Neale, & E. Mannix (Eds.), *Research on managing groups and teams* (pp. 103–124). Stamford, CT: JAI Press.

Hollingshead, A. B. (1998b). Retrieval processes in transactive memory systems. *Journal of Personality and Social Psychology, 73*(3), 659–671.

Hutchins, E. (1995). *Cognition in the wild.* Cambridge, MA: MIT Press.

Jones, P. M. (1995). Cooperative work in mission operations: Analysis and implications for computer support. *Computer-Supported Cooperative Work: An International Journal, 3*(1), 103–145.

Jones, P. M. (1997). Human error and its amelioration. In A. P. Sage & W. B. Rouse (Eds.). *Handbook of systems engineering and management* (pp. 687–702). New York: Wiley.

Jones, P. M., & Case, M. P. (1996). *Using the agent collaboration environment for project CITY: From concurrent engineering design to workflow in civil infrastructure management* (Technical Rep. TEC-C-9608). University of Illinois at Urbana-Champaign, Team Engineering Collaboratory.

Jones, P. M., Chin, G., Lucenti, M., Kim, H.-J., Stigberg, D., Sherman, G., Contractor, N., O'Keefe, B. J., Whitbred, R., Grobler, F., Case, M., Heckel, J., Lu, S. C.-Y., & Ganeshan, R. (1997, October). CITYSCAPE: Civil infostructure technology system for collaborative analysis, prediction, and evaluation. *Proceedings of the 1997 IEEE International Conference on Systems, Man, and Cybernetics* (Vol. 3, pp. 2223–2227), Orlando, FL.

Jones, P. M., Contractor, N., O'Keefe, B., & Lu, S. C.-Y. (1994, October). Competence models and self-organizing systems: Towards intelligent, evolvable, collaborative support. *Proceedings of the IEEE 1994 International Conference on Systems, Man, and Cybernetics* (Vol. 1, pp. 367–372), San Antonio, TX.

Jones, P. M., Contractor, N., O'Keefe, B., Lu, S., Case, M., Lawrence, P., & Grobler, F. (1995, October). Workflow and cooperative problem solving in civil infrastructure management. *Proceedings of the IEEE 1995 International Conference on Systems, Man, and Cybernetics* (Vol. 5, pp. 4575–4580), Vancouver, British Columbia, Canada.

Jones, P. M., & Jasek, C. A. (1997, May). Intelligent support for activity management (ISAM): An architecture to support distributed supervisory control. *IEEE Transactions on Systems, Man, and Cybernetics, Special issue on Human Interaction in Complex Systems, 27*(3), 274–288.

Lave, J., & Wenger, E. (1991). *Situated learning: Legitimate peripheral participation.* New York: Cambridge University Press.

Mura, S. S. (1983). Licensing violations: Legitimate violations of Grice's conversational principle. In R. Craig & K. Tracy (Eds.), *Conversational coherence: Form, structure, and strategy* (pp. 101–115). Beverly Hills, CA: Sage.

Newman, W., & Lamming, M. (1995). *Interactive systems design.* Reading, MA: Addison-Wesley.

Sperber, D., & Wilson, D. (1995). *Relevance: Communication and cognition* (2nd ed.). Oxford: Blackwell.

Suchman, L. (1987). *Plans and situated actions: The problem of human–machine communication.* New York: Cambridge University Press.

Winograd, T., & Flores, F. (1986). *Understanding computers and cognition: A new foundation for design.* New York: Addison-Wesley.

Part III

Enablers of Competence

6   Arguments and Decisions

David Hardman and Peter Ayton

Recent work on the psychology of judgment has revived the debate about the nature of probability (Gigerenzer, 1994, 1996; Kahneman & Tversky, 1996). Can we talk about the probability of unique events, or is it only meaningful to talk about probability as the frequency with which certain events occur? Evidence suggests that people are better at making frequentist judgments than unique ones. However, many decisions are made under conditions of relative ignorance, that is, in which there are no historical data on which to base a decision. For example, nothing is known about the carcinogenic potential of the vast majority of chemicals known to exist (e.g. Adams, 1995, pp. 45–50), which raises difficulties when deciding whether to allow novel chemical structures to be used in new products. Knowledge of the nature and biological action of complex chemicals is often so poor that the use of quantitative risk assessment is officially opposed in Britain:

> The [U.K. Department of Health Committee on Carcinogenicity of Chemicals in Food] does not support the routine use of quantitative risk assessment for chemical carcinogens. This is because the present models are not validated, are often based on incomplete or inappropriate data, are derived more from mathematical assumptions than from a knowledge of biological mechanisms and, at least at present, demonstrate a disturbingly wide variation in risk estimates depending on the model adopted. (Carter, 1991, p. 62)

Furthermore, professional toxicologists are subject to biases in their risk assessments (Krause, Malmfors, & Slovic, 1992). A recent approach to the problem of toxicological risk assessment involves an expert system that essentially follows the scheme for arguments proposed by Toulmin (1958). It constructs "arguments" that are, minimally, "for" or "against"

163

propositions (see Green, 1997; Hardman & Ayton, 1997; Tonnelier et al., 1997). These arguments are presented to the user together with a conclusion in the form of a linguistically expressed statement of risk (in order to avoid the spurious sense of certainty that might be associated with a numerical risk estimate). The system has its origins in the work of Fox (1980, 1994), which found that nonprobabilistic decision models were as good as or better than probabilistic ones in accounting for people's behavior in a clinical decision-making task. Subsequently, this work led to the development of a *logic of argumentation* for reasoning under uncertainty (e.g., Krause, Ambler, Elvang-Gøransson, & Fox, 1995).

In the remainder of this chapter, we consider the idea that a natural way for people to think about novel decisions, or decisions where information is lacking, is to construct arguments. We also consider some shortcomings in people's ability to engage in argumentative thinking and what the implications of this may be for important public policy decisions. Unlike the thinking tasks that participants receive in psychological experiments, such real-life situations often involve different groups of people who lack hard facts but who are reasoning from different and conflicting assumptions. To illustrate this, we begin by looking at one such situation, that of the cattle disease bovine spongiform encephalopathy in the United Kingdom. This was a situation in which different participants were unable to reconcile their conflicting arguments, where official advice was that there was no risk to human health from BSE, but where a minority opinion warned that if the worst came to pass, millions could die.

BSE: Decision Making about a Novel Problem Under Conditions of Ignorance

In Britain in the late 1980s, a degenerative brain disease was identified in cattle, and became known as bovine spongiform encephalopathy (BSE) (*mad cow disease*). BSE was spreading through the British herds, and concern grew about the possible effects that might arise from eating beef or bovine by-products. Unfortunately, because this was a new disease, there was no direct evidence about its likely effects on humans. What action should the government have taken? How should they have advised the public?

In the classic decision analytic framework (e.g., Goodwin & Wright, 1998), numerical probabilities are ascribed to all the different possible outcomes identified in a decision tree. The best alternative is then selected by weighting the utilities of outcomes by their probabilities and selecting the course of action with the best expected utility. In the BSE situation, possible courses of action included the destruction of all herds in which infection had been identified, preventing meat from infected cattle from entering the food chain, preventing only certain parts of cattle from entering the food chain, and doing nothing. However, forecasting the possible consequences of each course of action was nearly impossible. At the most basic level, it was unknown whether BSE could even be transmitted to humans. It was also not known initially which parts of cattle carried the infection. Decision making was made even harder by the possible costs of taking action (i.e., the potential devastation of a valuable industry). However, while hard information was largely unavailable, decision making was possible on the basis of assumptions and indirect evidence that were perceived to be relevant. Unfortunately, disagreements about the appropriate assumptions and evidence led to conflict between officialdom and a number of scientists working outside of government (see, e.g., Volume 11 of *The BSE Inquiry* [2000]).

Early on, the official view was adopted that BSE was caused by feeding scrapie-infected sheep to cattle. Scrapie is also a degenerative brain disease, but although it has long been present in some British sheep, there has been no adverse effect on human health. The recent transmission to cattle was attributed to changes in the rendering process following deregulation. On this basis, the officials reasoned that because scrapie was not a danger to humans, BSE would likewise not present a danger and the public was advised accordingly. However, this reasoning was based on the assumption that BSE was just scrapie. In 1990, one high-profile nongovernment scientist, Professor Richard Lacey, told the U.K. Agriculture Select Committee:

> I think the question of sheep scrapie going to man is unproven. The evidence is either uncertain or weak. There is no really good evidence that sheep scrapie goes to man and we have eaten a lot of sheep's brains, nerves, meat for many years. That is not in doubt. Some people say it is, but I believe the evidence of sheep scrapie to man is small. The problem with BSE, we do not know if it has come from sheep in the first place. We do not know where it has come from. We do not know what it is. We do not know its host range. We have to look at BSE as a new disease and I am not going to say it will go to man, I am not going to say it will not, I am saying we do not know. (Quoted in *The BSE Inquiry*, Vol. 11, Sec. 5.15)

However, Lacey added that "if our worst fears are realized, we could virtually lose a generation of people."

Thus, a situation had arisen whereby the official viewpoint was that BSE posed no risk to humans, whereas Professor Lacey – who had a high media profile – was cautioning that millions could be at risk. One of the members of the Agriculture Select Committee "criticized much of Professor Lacey's submission as being 'speculation and supposition and conjecture'" (*The BSE Inquiry*, Vol. 11, Sec. 5.13). Lacey, for his part, claimed that the government was not doing the kind of research that would enable the appropriate questions to be answered.

In their report, the Agriculture Select Committee questioned Lacey's authority, stating that he "showed a tendency to extrapolate sensational conclusions from incomplete evidence in order to publicize his long-standing concerns about food safety." Despite Lacey's having said that nobody knew if BSE could be transmitted to humans, the report added: "When he told us that 'if our worst fears are realized, we could virtually lose a generation of people' he seemed to lose touch completely with the real world" (*The BSE Inquiry*, Vol. 11, Sec. 5.19).[1]

This set the scene for the next few years. The BSE Inquiry report gives a chronological account of some of the interactions between Professor Lacey and his colleague Dr. Stephen Dealler, on the one hand, and officialdom on the other.[2] The report gives "a clear picture of an unhappy relationship. It was one of mutual suspicion verging at times on hostility." Reading the report, one sees that assumptions, speculations, and facts became matters for dispute on both sides. The report adds:

> The nub of the problem was... "the paucity of available evidence."
> Risk evaluation depended to a large extent on individual judgements
> based on results of research into scrapie. The majority of scientists
> judged the risk of transmission to humans to be remote. A minority
> took a less optimistic view, including Professor Lacey and Dr. Dealler.

---

[1] *The BSE Inquiry* says: "We suspect that Professor Lacey must have regretted making this statement, for it was to be quoted as demonstrating that he was alarmist and unreliable. Yet, while extreme, this was a possible worst case scenario. There was a record of a colony of mink being virtually eliminated by infected feed" (Vol. 11, Sec. 5.169).

[2] There were also other figures – Dr. Harash Narang and Mr. Mark Purdey (see Vol. 11 of *The BSE Inquiry*) – who questioned the official government line on BSE. We focus, however, on Professor Lacey and his sometime colleague Dr. Stephen Dealler because Professor Lacey had such a high media profile and forced many issues into the open during the BSE debacle.

> The rival views were to a large extent speculative. (*The BSE Inquiry*, Vol. 11, Sec. 5.166)

We use this example of BSE in order to illustrate the kind of argumentation underlying one of the United Kingdom's most important postwar public policy issues (though the full content of the argumentation is far more complex and voluminous than we can reproduce here). Not only did the various parties involved use arguments, but in the absence of reliable statistical information, arguments were all that was available for decision making. One question that we might ask is, what kind of advice could a decision analyst have provided in this situation? As it happens, we doubt that there is very much that usefully could have been said. By eliciting the views of interested parties, and through discussion, decision analysts attempt to structure a decision such that an option can be found that will be satisfactory to all parties. However, normally one would expect there to be some minimal level of agreement on the actual nature of the problem. In the case of BSE, a fundamental disagreement existed at the outset between those within government and a number of concerned scientists and other individuals outside of government. Because much of this disagreement concerned basic assumptions, it also led to strong disagreement about the appropriate courses of action.

In the rest of this chapter, we review the psychological research on argumentation. The review begins by briefly reviewing evidence that shows how nonroutine decisions proceed via the construction of causal models that attempt to explain the available facts. Next, we show how the evaluation of simple arguments can be influenced by background knowledge. We also consider to what extent people are able to put aside their background beliefs or assumptions when evaluating an argument, and we look at the effect that conflicting evidence has on one's opinions. The review goes on to look at how the availability or nonavailability of a simple reason can influence decision making and the role of reasons in framing effects. Then we consider the way in which people process simple versus complex arguments and, lastly, we look at research concerning people's argument skills. Although we do not suggest that all of these topics were necessarily a factor in the BSE example described earlier, we certainly think that some of them are of relevance – for example, the ability to evaluate arguments whose initial assumptions differ from one's own and the way in which people react to conflicting evidence. We follow this review with some more speculative comments about the nature of argumentation and conclude by suggesting one possible method for thinking about novel decisions such as BSE. However, we do not foresee any panacea for such decisions, but argue that at least we can better understand the way people do think about such decisions by understanding the way in which they process arguments.

The Psychology of Argumentation

Explanation-Based Decision Making

The idea that feeding scrapie-infected meat to cattle caused BSE can be seen as a plausible causal scenario. This is exactly how Hastie and Pennington (2000) regard nonroutine decision making. They argue that decision makers begin the decision process by constructing a causal model in order to explain the available facts, and then subsequent decisions are based on this model. Much research in this domain has been conducted with mock jurors, and the application of Pennington and Hastie's theory in this domain is referred to as the *story model*, following the observation that mock jurors' causal models have a narrative structure (Pennington & Hastie, 1986). Further evidence for the story model comes from the finding that participants more often show false recognition of trial evidence sentences when these are compatible with the story that they have constructed (Pennington & Hastie, 1988). However, in many decisions, the process of argumentation necessarily extends beyond the decision itself in order to assess the desirability and likelihood of alternative outcomes occurring. In this chapter, we are particularly interested in decisions where there is a paucity of evidence, and so decision making is beset by uncertainty and arguments involve assumptions and speculation.

Background Knowledge

In discussing the application of argumentation theory to probabilistic thinking, Kleindorfer, Kunreuther, and Schoemaker (1993) note the possibility that people's deviations from normative models in experiments may be explicable if we can understand the background knowledge (or lack of) that they are bringing to bear on the task. An example of the way that background knowledge can influence thinking is provided by Cummins, Lubart, Alksnis, and Rist (1991). They presented participants with *modus ponens* arguments like the following:

(1)   If my finger is cut, then it bleeds.
        My finger is cut.
        Therefore, it bleeds.

In this case, most subjects were satisfied that the conclusion followed from the premises, and indeed, such problems with abstract content are almost universally accepted (Evans, Newstead, & Byrne, 1993). However, consider the following problem which retains the same logical form but utilizes a different content:

(2)   If I eat candy often, then I have cavities.
        I eat candy often.
        Therefore, I have cavities.

In this case, subjects were much less sure that the conclusion could reasonably be inferred from the premises. Cummins et al. (1991) interpreted their results on this and other problems in terms of the presence of alternative causes and disabling conditions. In this example, it is easy to imagine one or more reasons why eating candy in (2) may not lead to cavities; for example, you might clean your teeth whenever you have eaten something sweet. This, then, is a disabling condition. However, in (1) there is no obvious reason that springs to mind as to why your finger should not bleed if it is cut. In other examples, Cummins et al. show that the frequency of reasoning fallacies is reduced when it is possible to think of more than one reason why a cause should lead to an effect (see also Byrne, 1989; Fairley, Manktelow, & Over, 1999). In the domain of probabilistic thinking, research points to argumentation as forming the basis of judgment, with people apparently constructing mainly causal arguments and often tending to focus only on a subset of whatever information is available (Curley, Browne, Smith, & Benson, 1995).

The Believability of Assumptions, Suppositions, and Conclusions

Arguments do not always proceed from factual premises. Sometimes (as in our BSE example) one needs to evaluate arguments that proceed from assumptions or suppositions. One may or may not believe in the truth of a premise, but one sometimes needs to follow through a train of reasoning when one nonetheless doubts the premise. That is, one needs to be able to identify whether a conclusion follows given that one takes the premise to be true. George (1995) presented participants with *modus ponens* arguments in which the truth of the major premise was questionable. However, participants were asked to *assume* the truth of the premise when evaluating the validity of the conclusion. Some participants endorsed the logically prescribed conclusion even when they thought the major premise was doubtful or untrue. But a majority of participants adopted a *belief-based* mode of reasoning whereby they allocated the conclusion a degree of plausibility concordant with their belief in the major premise.

It is possible to object to an argument in various ways. Shaw (1996) also proposed that some objections are easier to make than others, because they are less cognitively taxing. She predicted that people would be most likely to object to arguments by questioning the truth of the premises or the conclusion. This kind of objection does not require a person to construct or evaluate mental models that represent the ways in which premises and conclusions might be linked, and it does not require them to call upon missing information that could refute the conclusion. Shaw presented student participants with newspaper and magazine editorials, and when asked if they had objections to the arguments therein, the results supported her prediction: The most common objection was to question the truth of the premises or the conclusion. She did find, however, that by drawing people's attention to the link between premises and conclusion, she was able to increase the number of objections based on attacking this link. It could be argued that it is perfectly reasonable to base one's objections to an argument on the questioning of the premises or conclusion. However, in a second experiment, Shaw showed that it was the participants who were best able to identify the premises and conclusions in passages of natural language who were more likely to formulate objections to the link between premises and conclusions. Thus, the less able reasoners were more likely to base their objections on questioning the truth of the premises or conclusions.

Other studies also indicate that the acceptability of conclusions affects one's ability to identify the logic of an argument. Evans et al. (1993) reviewed a number of studies of belief bias in reasoning. In some such studies, participants were presented with arguments of various logical forms and asked to evaluate the validity of conclusions that were sometimes believable and sometimes unbelievable. Typically, an interaction of logic and belief was observed. Participants tended to distinguish valid from invalid arguments, they accepted believable conclusions more than unbelievable ones, and on invalid problems they tended to incorrectly accept believable conclusions more than unbelievable ones.

Belief Perseverance

In the BSE crisis to which we referred earlier, the adherents of different sets of arguments were unable to find common ground and became polarized to the point of hostility. Consider the following two extracts from *The BSE Inquiry* (Vol. 11), which refer to a meeting between Professor Lacey and Dr. Dealler and representatives from the Central Veterinary Laboratory and the Spongiform Encephalopathy Advisory Committee:
Ch. 5.89: Mr. Bradley's minute noted in conclusion:

> Professor Lacey and Dr Dealler were satisfied with the data given to them and certain aspects of their understanding were undoubtedly improved. However, unsound firmly held views were unshakeable.

Ch. 5.90 : Professor Lacey and Dr Dealler, for their part, left the meeting with the feeling that they had not been given a fair hearing. Dr Dealler told the *Inquiry* that

> [i]t seemed initially that Professor Lacey and I were being treated as people who simply did not understand the subject and we had to be taught the truth so that we did understand. It was as if anything that we put forward was treated as invalid if it did not agree with their point of view whereas much of what they were saying the other way was accepted.

Most of us will have faced similar, if less drastic, situations in which people maintain beliefs in the face of opposing evidence and justify this by questioning the veracity of that evidence. Such experiences are amply supported by experimental research (for a review, see Nisbett & Ross, 1980). In some circumstances conservatism can be justified to a degree, because we may have forgotten the evidence that led to our current theory or belief but we still believe it was good evidence. Nevertheless, a classic experiment by Lord, Ross, and Lepper (1979) shows that people do not always respond to evidence in an appropriate way. They presented participants with two purportedly authentic studies on the effectiveness of the death penalty as a deterrent. One study indicated that there was a deterrent effect, whereas the other did not. The prior opinions of these participants on this topic were already known, with one group being in favor of the death penalty and the other against it.

The first main result was that after having read the studies, participants with both opinions reported that the study favoring their opinion was "better conducted" and "more convincing" than the other study. This effect is known as the *biased assimilation* of evidence. The second result was that when participants were asked about their beliefs after having read just one study, their initial belief was strengthened if they had read a supporting study but it was relatively unaffected if they had read an opposing study. Note that these outcomes are defensible *if* it is the case that a participant already has good evidence to support his or her views. A third result is much harder to defend, however. After having read both a supporting and an opposing study, participants were more convinced of the correctness of their initial opinion than they were before having read *any* evidence. This effect is known as *attitude polarization*.

Edwards and Smith (1996) examined the psychological mechanism underlying belief perseveration. Using a variety of controversial topics as their materials, they found that (1) participants spent more time scrutinizing arguments that were incompatible with their prior beliefs, (2) they generated more thoughts and arguments in response to belief-incompatible arguments than to belief-compatible ones, and (3) these thoughts and arguments tended to be refutational in nature when the presented argument was belief-incompatible.

The biased assimilation effect is not confined to laypersons in a given domain but has also been observed in experts. Koehler (1993) replicated the effect with experts on both sides of the extrasensory perception debate, and reported that the effect was actually stronger amongst skeptics than among parapsychologists. McHoskey (1995) found that those who held a conspiracy theory about the Kennedy assassination and their detractors both interpreted the same evidence as supportive of their views. However, in a recent review of the literature on evidence interpretation, MacCoun (1998) reported that both the biased assimilation effect and attitude polarization are subject to boundary conditions. Biased assimilation appears to be a robust effect for those holding extreme attitudes but is difficult to replicate among participants holding moderate views. As regards attitude polarization, some studies have found that this is limited to self-report change ratings. However, MacCoun's comment on the research is worth noting:

> Attitude polarization in response to mixed evidence, if it does exist, is a remarkable (and remarkably perverse) fact about human nature, but the mere fact that participants *believe* it is occurring is itself noteworthy. And even in the absence of attitude polarization, biased assimilation

is an established phenomenon with troubling implications for efforts to ground contemporary policy debates in empirical analysis. (p. 267)

Definite versus Disjunctive Reasons

Shafir, Simonson, and Tversky (1993) analyzed a number of choice problems in terms of whether there were compelling reasons for choosing. One of their findings concerned a *disjunction effect*. This occurs when a disjunction of different reasons appear less compelling than either reason alone. This was illustrated with the 'Hawaiian vacation problem' (from Shafir & Tversky, 1992):

> Imagine that you have just taken a tough qualifying exam. It is the end of the semester, you feel tired and run-down, and you are not sure that you passed the exam. In case you failed you have to take it again in a couple of months – after the Christmas holidays. You now have an opportunity to buy a very attractive 5-day Christmas vacation package to Hawaii at an exceptionally low price. The special offer expires tomorrow, while the exam grade will not be available until the following day. Would you
> (a) buy the vacation package?   [32%]
> (b) not buy the vacation package?   [7%]
> (c) pay a $5 non-refundable fee in order to retain   [61%]
> the rights to buy the vacation package at the same
> exceptional price the day after tomorrow – after you
> find out whether or not you passed the exam?

As the percentage figures show, more subjects preferred to pay in order to defer their decision until the outcome of the exam was known. A second group of subjects was presented with a slightly different version of the problem in which they were told that they already knew the outcome of the exam. Some were told that they had passed and some that they had failed. The responses were as follows:

	Pass	**Fail**
Would you		
(a) buy the vacation package?	[54%]	[57%]
(b) not buy the vacation package?	[16%]	[12%]
(c) pay a $5 non-refundable fee in order to retain the rights to buy the vacation package at the same exceptional price the day after tomorrow?	[30%]	[31%]

In this case, regardless of whether they had passed or failed the exam, most subjects said they would buy the vacation package. From a normative point of view, it is hard to make sense of this finding. If most subjects prefer to take the holiday regardless of passing or failing the exam, then most subjects should also take the holiday even when they don't know the outcome of their exams. From a reasons-based analysis, however, these results are more explicable. It is likely that subjects who fail their exams regard the holiday as a consolation and a period of recuperation before the reexamination, whereas subjects who pass the exams decide they deserve it as a reward. But for subjects who do not know their exam outcome, there is no obvious justification for the immediate purchase of the holiday. Subsequent research has shown that when people decide to wait for information that would not otherwise affect their decision, they may feel obliged to let that information influence their decision (Bastardi & Shafir, 1998).

Reasons as an Explanation for Framing Effects

This emphasis on the *content* of people's thoughts can also throw light on framing effects. Consider the following scenario that Thaler (1985) presented to his participants:

> You are lying on the beach on a hot day. All you have to drink is ice water. For the last hour you have been thinking about how much you would enjoy a nice cold bottle of your favorite brand of beer. A companion gets up to go make a phone call and offers to bring back a beer from the only nearby place where beer is sold, a small run-down grocery store. He says that the beer might be expensive and so he asks you how much you are willing to pay for the beer. (p. 206)

The median price that people were willing to pay was $1.50. Now, one might expect that the price one is willing to pay for a beer should simply reflect how badly one wants that beer. However, when the phrase "run-down grocery store" was replaced with "fancy resort hotel," the median price increased to $2.65.

Most such studies have adopted between-subjects designs, which do not enable us to discover whether or not the subjects themselves would agree that such inconsistencies are irrational, or whether in fact they might have reasons for their different responses. To address this issue, Frisch (1993) distributed both versions of many such framing problems throughout a questionnaire. On the majority of problems, framing effects were replicated. However, after subjects had made their initial responses, Frisch pointed out the two "frames" for each problem and asked whether or not subjects wished to change their responses and what their reasons were. In the preceding beer problem, some people considered the nature of the sales environment to be relevant to the selling price. For example, one argument was that in a run-down store you don't know how long the beer has been sitting on the shelves; therefore, it may be of poorer quality. Responses in such cases clearly involve reasoning beyond the information given.

A particularly well-known framing problem is the Asian disease problem (Tversky & Kahneman, 1981):

> Imagine that the United States is preparing for the outbreak of an unusual Asian disease, which is expected to kill 600 people. Two alternative programs to combat the disease have been proposed. Assume that the exact scientific estimates of the consequences of the programs are as follows:
>
> If Program A is adopted, 200 people will be saved   [72%]
> If Program B is adopted, there is 1/3 probability that   [28%]
> 600 people will be saved, and 2/3 probability that
> no people will be saved

The numbers in brackets show the percentage of subjects choosing each option in Kahneman and Tversky's (1981) study. Clearly, most people prefer Program A. However, the pattern of responses changes when the options are framed in terms of lives lost rather than lives saved:

> If Program C is adopted, 400 people will die   [22%]
> If Program D is adopted, there is 1/3 probability that   [78%]
> nobody will die, and 2/3 probability that 600 people
> will die

C and D are actually the same as A and B, but now people prefer the uncertain option to the surething. Frisch's (1993) study also presented participants with both versions of this problem. This time, participants tended to agree that both versions were the same, and they changed their responses accordingly. However, more recently Jou, Shanteau, and Harris (1996) have shown that framing effects on this and other problems can be eliminated by specifying a simple reason for the nature of the available options. For the disease problem, it was stated that there was only enough vaccine for 200 people, and if a patient did not receive a full dose, then there was a chance that he or she might live or die. Similarly, simple rationales were provided for various other problems that either involved possible loss of life or possible loss of property. Compared to a no-rationale condition, framing effects were eliminated or greatly reduced for all problems. Furthermore, people were risk-seeking on loss-of-life problems but risk-averse on property problems. Jou et al. interpreted their findings as resulting from the activation of a schema. However, we suspect that the key factor in the loss-of-life problems was the perception that it would be unfair to deny treatment to some patients while giving it to others. On the property problems, moral considerations are not paramount, so it is better to try to save something rather than risk losing everything. In short, it appears that people had clear reasons for their choices. Thus, in some framing problems, people possess reasons for considering the frames to be different. In others, a simple rationale eliminates the effects. In either case, people appear to be more rational than researchers had previously considered them to be.

Complex versus Simple Arguments

The research we have reviewed so far has involved fairly simple thinking tasks. Even on these tasks, cognitive limitations seem to affect the way that people think. To what extent do such limitations affect more complex decision situations? Gallhofer and Saris (1996) have analyzed political argumentation underlying the decisions taken in a number of momentous political contexts around the world. Their data were the written documents circulated among politicians. From these documents they were able to identify the courses of action being considered and the potential consequences associated with them. What they found was that arguments tended to be highly simplified. The author of a particular argument often would reduce complexity by considering only a subset of the available strategy options, focusing only on those aspects of outcomes that they judged most important for each strategy and avoiding the use of intensities when describing the probabilities and utilities of those outcomes (i.e., outcomes were represented either as "possible" or "certain" and as "good" or "bad," or with words to similar effect). Although intensities were sometimes used, it is notable that they were rarely used for both probabilities *and* utilities. Thus, depending on the application of intensities to probabilities and utilities, four classes or argument could be identified, with a different set of decision rules applying in each case. For example, where an argument was presented with intensities attached to both probabilities and utilities, a decision rule based on subjective expected utility would be appropriate. But in general, decision makers were simplifying their arguments such that a simple noncompensatory decision rule could be applied and their favored conclusion would "inevitably" follow.

These results were interpreted as supportive of the *dominance structuring* framework proposed by Montgomery (1983). He characterized decision making as a "search for good arguments" and argued that, when faced with a conflict between dimensions, people try to think of a reason to completely ignore one. This is because singleminded arguments are cognitively easier. This results in justifications for actions that can be summarized in statements such as "A good soldier must always obey his commander" (even when told to commit crimes?) or, as Margaret Thatcher stated during the Falklands conflict, "The wishes of the islanders are paramount."

Because numerical probabilities were not present in the arguments analyzed by Gallhofer and Saris (1996), it is not known whether the availability of numerical probabilities would have changed those arguments, although there is no evidence that decision makers even attempted to estimate probabilities. Hogarth and Kunreuther (1995) compared the nature of people's arguments in decisions where probabilistic information was either present or absent. Participants had to decide whether or not to purchase a warranty when buying electrical goods. Under conditions of ignorance they did not receive any information about product reliability or repair costs, but they were asked to provide subjective estimates of these. Under conditions of risk, participants were given quantitative information about reliability and repair costs. The first point to note is that an economic model of decision making was a poor predictor of whether or not people chose to purchase a warranty for electrical goods. Secondly, participants' arguments *did* differ, depending on whether probability information was provided. Under conditions of ignorance, people's arguments tended to be fairly simple and were often nonquantifiable by nature (Hogarth and Kunreuther pointed out that one ought to think *harder* when making decisions in a context of ignorance). By contrast, in the condition of risk, subjects often made trade-off arguments (e.g., between reliability and the cost of a warranty), as well as other multiattribute arguments. The authors suggested that people in the condition of ignorance "may be swayed by the availability of simple arguments that serve to resolve the conflicts of choice" (p. 32).

In summary, it appears that people may reason in a compensatory manner when provided with quantitative information but are less likely to do so in the absence of it. However, this provisional conclusion requires more evidence about people's argumentation in a variety of domains and informational contexts. For example, Montgomery's (1983) dominance structuring theory assumes that ease of justification is a key component in thinking about decisions. Therefore, would political decision makers really think in a more compensatory fashion if quantitative information was available, or does the requirement for justification mean that their thinking will inevitably be simplified? Or is it perhaps the case that on an individual level political decision makers may well construct complex arguments, only to simplify them when trying to persuade colleagues or the public of a particular viewpoint?

The Skills of Argument

Baron (1995) reported an experiment aimed at discovering whether people are more favorably disposed to arguments that consider both sides of a controversial issue (in this case, abortion) or whether one-sided arguments are rated more favorably. A group of students was asked to generate arguments as if they were preparing for a class discussion. The resulting lists of arguments were then classified as one-sided or two-sided, depending on whether the students had presented arguments both pro and con. The same students were then presented with lists of arguments from 24 hypothetical other students and asked to evaluate the thinking of those students. Some of the lists contained only one-sided arguments, whereas other lists were two-sided. When asked to grade the argument lists, participants gave higher grades to lists where they shared the opinion of the writer, but only if the writer had provided more arguments on that side than on the other side. Furthermore, participants gave higher grades to one-sided lists than two-sided ones, even when they disagreed with the arguments presented. When asked to justify their grades, participants frequently cited one-sidedness as a virtue. Two-sided argument lists were often seen as evidence of indecisiveness or of the writer's self-contradiction. However, sometimes participants used both one- and two-sided justifications, thus supporting an earlier suggestion (Baron, 1991) that people can hold both standards simultaneously. It was also the case that students who had themselves generated two-sided argument lists gave higher grades to the two-sided lists of the hypothetical students.

The studies just reviewed have looked at written argumentation from real decision situations (Gallhofer & Saris, 1996), written arguments from a hypothetical consumer task (Hogarth & Kunreuther, 1995), and written arguments presented in an academic context. Only the first of these involved argumentation from an ongoing situation in which different participants were articulating different points of view. One major study that allows us to examine how well people are able to argue their own viewpoint, and to represent alternative viewpoints, is that of Kuhn (1991). In her study, participants verbally articulated their views about the cause(s) of criminal recidivism, school failure, and unemployment. During the course of each interview session, participants were also asked to provide evidence for their views, to consider how they would respond to challenges to their views, and to consider alternative views. In general, people were able to articulate opinions on the topics in question, but at the same time they often were unable to present genuine evidence in support of their opinions. In fact, Kuhn reports that less than half the participants were able to provide genuine evidence, with most forms of evidence being what she termed *pseudoevidence*. When people provide pseudoevidence, they do not provide factual information but rather "a scenario, or script, depicting how the phenomenon might occur" (p. 65). Just under half of the participants were able to generate a counterargument to their own views, and just under half of them were able to generate a rebuttal to counterarguments (although this declines to less than a third if only the most effective forms of rebuttal are considered). Participants were more successful, however, at generating alternative theories, with just over 60% being able to do this. Kuhn states that the most revealing finding of her study is the great certainty that people claim for the opinions they offer, despite the fact that only 26 out of 160 (16%) were able to generate genuine evidence for all three topics. She states that "people confidently 'know' the answers to our questions, but in the naive sense of never having contemplated that the answers could be otherwise" (p. 265).

To summarize the preceding evidence, the thought processes that occur prior to the actual moment of decision appear to be argumentative in nature. However, much of this evidence suggests that the process of argumentation is frequently one-sided (what Baron refers to as *myside bias*). People are often unable or unwilling to consider complex arguments and counterarguments, not just when attempting to persuade others but also when "arguing with themselves." Furthermore, if Baron's (1995) results are representative, then there is a widespread tendency to consider one-sided arguments as better than two-sided ones. These findings are considered further in the following section.

Beyond the Theory of Cognitive Limitations

A traditional cognitive science explanation for a tendency toward simplified arguments is that our limited working memory capacities are ill-equipped to deal with complex arguments. Certainly, it is true that the complexity of decisions increases very quickly as new options and attributes are added, and Simon (1983) has famously argued that "[subjective expected utility] theory has never been applied, and never can be applied – with or without the largest computers – in the real world." Individual differences in working memory capacity may well underlie differences in the ability to make trade-offs in decision making (we are unaware of any studies of working memory and decision making, but working memory does appear to mediate performance on deductive reasoning tasks). As we saw earlier, depending on the information provided, at least some people *can* think in a more analytical manner (Hogarth & Kunreuther, 1995; see also Payne, Bettman, & Johnson, 1993).

There may be more than just cognitive limitation reasons for the way in which people argue, however. Wright (1994) has suggested that people tend to accumulate evidence on only one side of an argument in order to convince themselves as well as others. Indeed, he argues that in certain situations, such as bargaining, you need to be able to convince the other person that you mean what you say – and you can do this most effectively if you have convinced yourself of your own rightness. Presumably, if you start entertaining both sides of the argument, then you are less likely to convince yourself of a particular viewpoint. This seems slightly inconsistent with the findings of Kuhn (1991), who reported that people were poor at producing genuine evidence in support of their views. However, in her study, the topics in question were not personal ones but rather topics of wider social importance on which the relevant evidence can only be accumulated via the media. We suspect that for personal issues, such as whether person A is trustworthy enough to borrow money from person B, people would be much more able to call upon evidence and to produce rebuttals to counterarguments. Indeed, Wright himself (p. 280) cites Trivers (1985), who has written about the kinds of disputes that arise in close relationships:

> [The argument] may appear to burst forth spontaneously, with little or
> no preview, yet as it rolls along, two whole landscapes of information
> appear to lie already organized, waiting only for the lightning of anger
> to show themselves. (p. 420)

Wright adds:

> One might think that, being rational creatures, we would eventually
> grow suspicious of our uncannily long string of rectitude, our unerring
> knack for being on the right side of any dispute over credit, or money,
> or manners, or anything else. Nope. Time and again – whether arguing
> over a place in line, a promotion we never got, or which car hit which –
> we are shocked at the blindness of people who dare suggest that our
> outrage isn't warranted. (p. 281)

However, as we saw earlier, people not only tend to produce simplified forms of argumentation, but they also frequently rate the one-sided
arguments of others more highly. Why might this be? Perhaps we find
it hard to distinguish a clear message when a third party produces arguments on both sides, even though they may attempt to take one line
rather than the other. The British satirical magazine *Private Eye* often
poked fun at the Church of England during the 1980s for using "On the
one hand . . . but on the other . . ." kinds of arguments. During a period
of considerable social upheaval, the Church tried to promote Christian
values while simultaneously trying not to alienate people who may not
have behaved in accordance with (or been interested in) Christian values. The Church's message that we should attempt to understand, for
example, inner-city rioters, while also promoting Christian values, was
clearly perceived by some people as woolly thinking that *had* no clear
message. Similarly, individuals who attempt to argue in an evenhanded
way may give the impression that they lack clarity of thought. One of
the present authors has been collecting data from an Internet personals
site for a project on mate choice and has observed that "decisiveness" is
a quality that women often say they value in men (or, conversely, they
often report "indecisiveness" as an annoying character trait). It is known
that men compete among themselves for status more than women do
(e.g., Buss, 1999), so given that a man is likely to lose status if he cannot
hold his own in a discussion, perhaps the holding of strong opinions
and being decisive are used by women as cues to status.

However, we feel that it would be premature to conclude that presenting the arguments of both sides is always seen in a poor light. What sometimes happens in real life, but did not happen in Baron's study, is that a person will present the arguments of the other side, only to knock them down with counterarguments. In its most extreme form, a person may set up a "straw man" argument that bears a minimal – if any – relation to what the other side really believes. In demolishing this argument, the person is able to present his or her own argument as the obvious viable alternative. Thus, one avenue for future research might be to examine the status of two-sided arguments where the speaker or writer attempts to produce counterarguments to nonfavored arguments.

Conclusions

We believe that the study of argumentation can help enrich our understanding of competent decision making. Indeed, as others have commented (e.g., Montgomery, 1983), an internal process of argumentation seems to underlie individual decision making. In some nonroutine situations, arguments may actually be the only kind of content available for decision making. Furthermore, argumentation can be used as a means of decision support, notably in situations where quantitative approaches may not be useful. However, as we saw in the BSE example, nonroutine decisions may exist where it is difficult to specify what counts as competent decision making (in the sense of behaving normatively). Our review of the psychological literature shows that although people naturally use arguments, they are prone to a number of shortcomings and biases that, we have suggested, may arise from both cognitive capacity limitations and social/evolutionary effects. Although, as Wright (1994) suggests, the brain may be like a lawyer – seeking victory, not truth – many of society's most important decisions require a process of argumentation based on the search for truth, not victory. There is no clear panacea by which conflicting arguments can be reconciled. However, an understanding of the way in which people construct and evaluate arguments and explanations should be of some assistance in understanding why people find it hard to reconcile conflicting arguments. For example, we saw that people find it difficult to evaluate the logical validity of a conclusion when they doubt or do not believe the major premise leading to that conclusion. Yet this is exactly what we need to do when we are attempting to understand the argumentation of someone who has views that conflict with our own. *The BSE Inquiry* states:

> Our conclusion that BSE was probably present in the cattle herd in the 1970s may have implications for past and current assessments of risk which have assumed that the earliest date of infection was around 1980. This illustrates the importance of setting out assumptions and keeping them under review. (Vol. 1, Sec. 14.1289)

Unfortunately, the "BSE-as-scrapie" assumption seems to have gone unquestioned for too long, to the extent that there were no contingency plans for the eventuality that BSE did come to be recognized as a risk to humans (*The BSE Inquiry*, Vol. 1, Sec. 14.1279).

Another real-life example (cited in Goodwin & Wright, 1998) is Saddam Hussein's invasion of Kuwait. Intelligence advice to the first President Bush focused on those events seen as most likely, none of which involved an invasion, with the result that the United States was unprepared for subsequent events. It is interesting to contrast this situation with that of President George W. Bush just after 9/11. According to the reporter Bob Woodward, "Dubya" did *not* fall into the trap of only thinking about what was most likely:

> "We need to plan as if things won't go well," Bush said. What was the scenario if there was no split in the Taliban? "We need to war-game it out, figure out how to keep the pressure on them and effect change, even if things don't go the way we want."
>
> When he commented later in an interview about why he, the perennial optimist, wanted to examine bad scenarios, Bush said, "I think my job is to stay ahead of the moment. A president, I guess, can get so bogged down in the moment that you're unable to be the strategic thinker that you're supposed to be, or at least provide strategic thought. And I'm the kind of person that wants to make sure that all risk is assessed. There is no question what the reward is in this case. But a president is constantly analyzing, making decisions based upon the risk, particularly in war, risk taken relative to the – what can be achieved." He had advisers "who have seen war, who have been in situations where the plan didn't happen the way it was planned." (Woodward, 2002, p. 137)

Ironically, just after this description of analytic thinking, Bush goes on to describe himself as "instinctive" and "a gut player." However, this is probably not as much of a contradiction as it might seem, because one can set out a variety of decision options yet still have a gut feeling about what the best one is.

Systematic ways of thinking about scenarios have been developed and are known as *scenario analysis*. For details, readers are referred to Goodwin and Wright (1998, chapter 14), but in essence, "scenarios focus on key uncertainties *and* certainties about the future and use this information to construct pen-pictures in an information-rich way in order to provide vivid descriptions of future worlds" (p. 359). Rather than attempting to predict the future in a standard decision-analytic way, scenario analysis "assumes that the best that can be done is to identify critical future uncertainties and plan for the range of futures that could, plausibly, unfold" (p. 359). The extent to which scenario analysis can provide a useful tool for thinking about uncertain events deserves further attention from researchers (for an evaluation, see Harries, 2003).

Textbooks on decision analysis often include chapters on how to think creatively (e.g., Clemen, 1996; Goodwin & Wright, 1998). It seems to us that novel decisions involving a paucity of evidence require particularly high standards of open-mindedness and creative thought. Decision makers should not be in too much of a hurry to dismiss thinking that involves assumptions and speculation. The very nature of uncertainty dictates that some of our expectations about the future will be wrong, but at least our imaginations can help us to prepare for that eventuality.

References

Adams, J. (1995). *Risk*. London: UCL Press.

Baron, J. (1991). Beliefs about thinking. In J. F. Voss, D. N. Perkins, & J. W. Segal (Eds.), *Developmental perspectives on teaching and learning thinking skills* (pp. 169–186). Basel: Karger.

Baron, J. (1995). Myside bias in thinking about abortion. *Thinking and Reasoning, 1*(3), 201–288.

Bastardi, A., & Shafir, E. (1998). On the pursuit and misuse of useless information. *Journal of Personality and Social Psychology, 75*(1), 19–32.

Buss, D. M. (1999). *Evolutionary psychology: The new science of the mind*. Boston: Allyn & Bacon.

Byrne, R. M. J. (1989). Suppressing valid inferences with conditionals. *Cognition, 31*, 61–83.

Carter, R. L. (Chairman). (1991). *Guidelines for the evaluation of chemicals for carcinogenicity*. Report of the Committee on Carcinogenicity of Chemicals in Food, Consumer Products and the Environment. London: HMSO.

Clemen, R. T. (1996). *Making hard decisions: An introduction to decision analysis* (2nd ed.). Pacific Grove, CA: Duxbury Press.

Cummins, D. D., Lubart, T., Alksnis, O., & Rist, R. (1991). Conditional reasoning and causation. *Memory & Cognition, 19*(3), 274–282.

Curley, S. P., Browne, G. J., Smith, G. F., & Benson, P. G. (1995). Arguments in the practical reasoning underlying constructed probability judgments. *Journal of Behavioral Decision Making, 8*, 1–20.

Edwards, K., & Smith, E. E. (1996). A disconfirmation bias in the evaluation of arguments. *Journal of Personality and Social Psychology, 71*(1), 5–24.

Evans, J. St. B. T., Newstead, S. E., & Byrne, R. M. J. (1993). *Human reasoning: The psychology of deduction.* Hove, UK: Erlbaum.

Fairley, N., Manktelow, K. I., & Over, D. E. (1999). Necessity, sufficiency and perspective effects in causal conditional reasoning. *Quarterly Journal of Experimental Psychology, 52A*(3), 771–790.

Fox, J. (1980). Making decisions under the influence of memory. *Psychological Review, 87*(2), 190–211.

Fox, J. (1994). On the necessity of probability: Reasons to believe and grounds to doubt. In G. Wright & P. Ayton (Eds.), *Subjective probability* (pp. 75–104). Chichester, UK: Wiley.

Frisch, D. (1993). Reasons for framing effects. *Organizational Behavior and Human Decision Processes, 54*, 399–429.

Gallhofer, I. N., & Saris, W. E. (1996). *Foreign policy decision making: A qualitative and quantitative analysis of political argumentation.* London: Praeger.

George, C. (1995). The endorsement of the premises: Assumption-based or belief based reasoning. *The British Journal of Psychology, 86*, 93–111.

Gigerenzer, G. (1994). Why the distinction between single event probabilities and frequencies is important for psychology and vice-versa. In G. Wright. & P. Ayton (Eds.), *Subjective probability* (pp. 129–162). Chichester, UK: Wiley.

Gigerenzer, G. (1996). On narrow norms and vague heuristics: Reply to Kahneman and Tversky. *Psychological Review, 103*(3), 592–596.

Goodwin, P., & Wright, G. (1998). *Decision analysis for management judgment* (2nd ed.). Chichester, UK: Wiley.

Greene, N. (1997). Computer software for risk assessment. *Journal of Chemical Information and Computer Sciences, 37*(1), 148–150.

Hardman, D. K., & Ayton, P. (1997). Arguments for qualitative risk assessment: The StAR risk adviser. *Expert Systems, 14*(1), 24–36.

Harries, C. (2003). Correspondence to what? Coherence to what? What is good scenario-based decision making? *Technological Forecasting & Social Change, 5561*, 1–21.

Hastie, R., & Pennington, N. (2000). Explanation-based decision making. In T. Connolly, H. R. Arkes, & K. R. Hammond (Eds.), *Judgment and decision making: An interdisciplinary reader* (2nd ed., pp. 212–228). Cambridge: Cambridge University Press.

HMSO. (2000). *The BSE inquiry.* London: Author.

Hogarth, R. M., & Kunreuther, H. (1995). Decision making under ignorance: Arguing with yourself. *Journal of Risk and Uncertainty, 10*, 15–36.

Jou, J. W., Shanteau, J., & Harris, R. J. (1996). An information-processing view of framing effects: The role of causal schemas in decision-making. *Memory & Cognition, 24*(1), 1–15.

Kahneman, D., & Tversky, A. (1996). On the reality of cognitive illusions. *Psychological Review, 103*(3), 582–591.

Kleindorfer, P. R., Kunreuther, H. C., & Schoemaker, P. J. H. (1993). *Decision sciences: An integrative perspective.* Cambridge: Cambridge University Press.

Koehler, J. J. (1993). The influence of prior beliefs on scientific judgments of evidence quality. *Organizational Behavior and Human Decision Processes, 56,* 28–55.

Krause, N., Malmfors, T., & Slovic, P. (1992). Intuitive toxicology: Expert and lay judgments of chemical risk. *Risk Analysis, 12,* 37–43.

Krause, P., Ambler, S., Elvang-Gøransson, M., & Fox, J. (1995). *Computational Intelligence, 11*(1), 113–131.

Kuhn, D. (1991). *The skills of argument.* Cambridge: Cambridge University Press.

Lord, C. G., Ross, L., & Lepper, M. R. (1979). Biased assimilation and attitude polarization: The effects of prior theories on subsequently considered evidence. *Journal of Personality and Social Psychology, 37,* 2098–2109.

MacCoun, R. J. (1998). Biases in the interpretation and use of research results. *Annual Review of Psychology, 49,* 259–287.

McHoskey, J. W. (1995). Case closed? On the John F. Kennedy assassination: Biased assimilation of evidence and attitude polarization. *Basic Applied Social Psychology, 17,* 395–409.

Montgomery, H. (1983). Decision rules and the search for a dominance structure: Towards a process model of decision making. In P. Humphreys, O. Svenson, & A. Vari (Eds.), *Analysing and aiding decision processes* (pp. 343–370). Amsterdam: North-Holland.

Nisbett, R., & Ross, L. (1980). *Human inference: Strategies and shortcomings of social judgment.* Englewood Cliffs, NJ: Prentice Hall.

Payne, J. W., Bettman, J. R., & Johnson, E. J. (1993). *The adaptive decision maker.* Cambridge: Cambridge University Press.

Pennington, N., & Hastie, R. (1986). Evidence evaluation in complex decision making. *Journal of Personality and Social Psychology, 51,* 242–258.

Pennington, N., & Hastie, R. (1988). Explanation-based decision making: The effects on memory structure on judgment. *Journal of Experimental Psychology: Learning, Memory, and Cognition, 14,* 521–533.

Shafir, E., Simonson, I., & Tversky, A. (1993). Reason-based choice. *Cognition, 49,* 11–36.

Shafir, E., & Tversky, A. (1992). Thinking through uncertainty: Nonconsequential reasoning and choice. *Cognitive Psychology, 24,* 449–474.

Shaw, V. F. (1996). The cognitive processes in informal reasoning. *Thinking & Reasoning, 2*(1), 51–80.

Simon, H. A. (1983). *Reason in human affairs.* Stanford, CA: Stanford University Press.

Thaler, R. (1985). Mental accounting and consumer choice. *Marketing Science, 4,* 199–214.

Tonnelier, C. A. G., Fox, J., Judson, P., Krause, P., Pappas, N., & Patel, M. (1997). Representation of chemical structures in knowledge-based systems: The StAR system. *Journal of Chemical Information and Computer Sciences, 37*(1), 117–123.

Toulmin, S. E. (1958). *The uses of argument.* Cambridge: Cambridge University Press.

Trivers, R. L. (1985) *Social evolution*. Menlo Park, CA: Benjamin/Cummings.

Tversky, A., & Kahneman, D. (1981). The framing of decisions and the psychology of choice. *Science, 211,* 453–458.

Woodward, B. (2002). *Bush at war*. London: Simon & Schuster.

Wright, R. (1994). *The moral animal: Evolutionary psychology and everyday life*. New York: Pantheon Books.

7   Representations of Uncertainty and Change: Three Case Studies with Experts

Elke M. Kurz-Milcke, Gerd Gigerenzer,
and Ulrich Hoffrage

Otto Neurath, a driving force behind the Vienna Circle's scientific world-view, once remarked that "it is generally not a good sign when scholars concern themselves too much with the foundations and the history of their discipline, instead of working to find new and exact statements about the topic they are investigating" (1930/1931, p. 107, our translation). Consequently, Neurath thought it advisable to limit such concerns to an occasional "Sunday."

We have not followed Neurath's advice. The three case studies we are presenting have not only benefited from historical research (not necessarily on Sundays), but to some extent owe their existence to it. In our experience, certain aspects of current practice become apparent only in historical perspective; we may study past practices in order to come to an improved understanding of current practices. Hence, in our view, an historical and a scientific perspective need not be rival siblings competing for privileged attention, as they seem to be in Neurath's worldview.

Representational Practices

In this chapter we focus on one particular aspect of practice, namely, experts' representational practices. Experts and, a fortiori, laypeople do

Case Studies I and II were supported by the Deutsche Forschungsgemeinschaft (Ho 1847/1-1). Case Study III was supported in part by a scholarship of the American Psychological Association to the first author and was part of her dissertation research at Bowling Green State University, Ohio. The first author is grateful to Ryan D. Tweney for his advice and support of the research presented in Case Study III. We thank Krishna Bharathi, Seth Bullock, Adam Goodie, Martin Lages, and Laura Martignon for helpful comments and Jill Vyse for her careful editing of the manuscript.

Figure 7.1 Two ways of doing arithmetic. "Dame Arithmetic" from Gregor Reisch, *Margarita Philosophica*, Strassbourg, 1504. (From *The Abacus*, p. 25, by Parry Moon, 1971, New York: Gordon and Breach. Reprinted with permission.)

not always consciously choose a representation, but rely on one that has been established by previous practice and convention. We have chosen a print from the early 16th century to illustrate what we mean by representational practices (Figure 7.1). On the right side of this print, Pythagoras is depicted operating on a calculating board. The left side shows Boethius, one of the earliest and most widely read scholastics, calculating with the symbols of the "new arithmetic." Note their facial expressions.

Dame Arithmetic, in the background, has obviously chosen her favorite. Anyone who has tried division on an abacus, which is but a slight modification of a calculating board, will probably agree with Dame Arithmetic's preference for Arabic numerals and computational symbols that can be represented in writing. However, the new arithmetic does not provide, for all purposes and in all contexts, *the* best representation. Even in our century, abacists have consistently outperformed contestants using calculating machines, at least in terms of speed (Dilson, 1968). On the other hand, the mathematical developments that we refer to later, probability calculus and differential calculus, would not have been possible, as we know them, without written numerical and operational symbols.

One of the criteria by which the usefulness of a particular representation can be judged is computational ease. Consider, for example, a comparison of the Arabic and Roman number systems. Addition and subtraction are easier with Roman numerals (for computation, IIII should be used rather than IV), whereas multiplication and division are much easier with Arabic numerals (see Norman, 1993; Zhang & Norman, 1995, for a detailed comparison of various numeration systems). Furthermore, a representation can help or hinder insight, or highlight certain aspects and make others less easy to see. It is therefore not surprising that at various times mathematical representations have been vehicles of political change. One such occasion was the legal adoption of the metric system in France in 1795 under the motto "for all the people, for all times"; in spite of the motto, "the people" on the streets and in the market squares kept up their old, tried and tested representational practices for many years afterward.

In our case studies, we were interested in the ways in which experts – acquired immune deficiency syndrome (AIDS) counselors, physicians, natural scientists, and mathematicians – represent information in order to draw quantitative inferences. In Case Studies I and II, experts associated with the medical field, AIDS counselors and physicians, had to infer the probability of a disease when a positive test was obtained. The representations employed by the counselors in Case Study I were strikingly uniform and remarkably inefficient, for the experts as well as for their clients (Gigerenzer, Hoffrage, & Ebert, 1998). Case Study II demonstrates an effective way of improving diagnostic reasoning, by using a different representational format (Hoffrage & Gigerenzer, 1998). In Case Study III, experts associated with different academic disciplines (chemistry, physics, mathematics) were asked to solve a problem requiring a differential equation for its exact solution. These scientists relied on very different representations to solve a mixture problem (Kurz, 1997).

Expertise is often discussed in terms of how much information an expert has, and in terms of his or her competence in selecting and processing the relevant information. In this chapter, we argue that experts' reasoning does not simply occur inside the experts' heads, but is performed to a substantial degree by the external representation of information the expert chooses or relies on. Shanteau (1992) has argued that experts' performance cannot be described generically, that is, without taking task

characteristics into account. Our argument is in line with his. Representation is a task characteristic. Our case studies involve experts' use of
a calculus, of the probability calculus in Case Studies I and II, and of
the differential calculus in Case Study III. Finding adequate representations, and also notations was, in fact, central to the inception and the
historical development of these calculi.

Calculi

The Latin term *calculus* means "little stone" and has present-day deriva-
tives in the English words *calculate* and *calculator*. Calculi, or pebbles,
were among the earliest calculation and bookkeeping aids (Damerow,
1995), leading to devices like the counting board, which was used
throughout the Middle Ages, and the abacus (or soroban), which is
still used today, especially in Asia (Moon, 1971). Nowadays we do not
think of a calculus as a material object (except, perhaps, when the term
is used in the medical context), but rather as a set of formalisms to solve
problems concerning, for instance, uncertain events and changing phenomena. This modern sense of the term stems from the 17th century, and
in this sense it relates to the inception of differential and integral calculus (Bos, 1993; Grattan-Guinness, 1980) and of the calculus of probability
(Daston, 1988; Gigerenzer et al., 1989).

In the 17th and 18th centuries, the newly developed calculi of change
and uncertainty had no existence apart from their subject matters. The
same people who worked on problems that we today would consider to
be applied problems also concerned themselves with the analytic aspects
of the mathematics (Bos, 1993, p. 118). Moreover, 18th-century mathematics was dominated by *mixed mathematics*, a category that as such has
ceased to be familiar to us. Mixed mathematics subsumed the study
of topics that we today would consider to be separate fields of study,
if not disciplines, for example, navigation, architecture, or geography.
But no matter which kind of 18th-century mathematics is concerned,
"all of mathematics, including pure mathematics, studied some*thing*"
(Daston, 1988, p. 54). Even today, insofar as mathematical formalisms
are tied to specific representations, be they graphic, verbal, or mental,
mathematics retains a material aspect.

A calculus consists of a fund of basic rules as well as basic concepts.
Thus, a calculus incorporates semantics. G. W. Leibniz's program of a
universal calculus, formulated at the dawn of the Enlightenment, illustrates this point very nicely. Leibniz envisioned an encompassing system

of signs – one for every basic concept – and rules to combine them and its use to record all human knowledge. Then, according to Leibniz's program, it would be possible to settle disputes by computation and, similarly, to acquire new insights based on the application of this calculus. What a daring vision! As Leibniz envisioned it, this formal system was not an end in itself but was meant to serve scientific progress. The calculus's final success, of course, hinged on an important precondition: universal agreement as to its appropriateness. Unsurprisingly, this universal calculus did not materialize on the envisioned scale (which does not lessen Leibniz's computational achievements, which were extraordinary, including, among others, the inception of the differential and integral calculus, contributions to the probability calculus and to logic, as well as the construction of the first calculating machines capable of performing the four basic arithmetic operations).

Leibniz's universal calculus has remained a dream, and the term calculus has lost much of its Leibnizian grandeur. Today, the term is mostly used to refer to particular formal systems, as, for example, the differential calculus or the probability calculus. But even these calculi are not what Leibniz had envisioned, that is, unitary formal systems. Historical scholarship has taught us that these calculi were shaped by alternative, at times competing, proposals. We argue that there are always multiple alternative representations and interpretations in a calculus, and that this variability in representational practice can be functional, allowing a calculus to be relevant for various tasks and in various domains. Our case studies of present-day experts and their representational practices show how this plurality of representation can be a resource. Our case studies are preceded by historical "prisms" that intend to make the spectra of interpretations and representations of the calculi visible.

Representing Uncertainty

Observing Historical Spectra: The Calculus of Uncertainty

According to legend, the calculus of uncertainty is one of the few seminal ideas that has an exact birthday. In 1654, the now famous correspondence between Blaise Pascal and Pierre Fermat first cast the calculus of probability in mathematical form. Ian Hacking (1975) argued that this probability, which emerged so suddenly, was Janus-faced from the very beginning. One face was aleatory, concerned with observed frequencies (e.g., co-occurrences between fever and disease, comets and the death of kings); the other face was epistemic, concerned with degrees of belief or opinion warranted by authority. In his view, the "20th-century" duality between objective frequencies and subjective probabilities existed then as now. Barbara Shapiro (1983) and Lorraine Daston (1988), however, have argued that probability in the 17th and 18th centuries had more than Janus's two faces. It included physical symmetry (e.g., the physical construction of dice, now called *propensity*); frequency (e.g., how many people of a given age die annually); strength of argument (e.g., evidence for or against a judicial verdict); intensity of belief (e.g., the firmness of a judge's conviction of the guilt of the accused); verisimilitude and epistemological modesty, among others. Over the centuries, probability also conquered new territories and created further meanings, such as in quantum physics, and lost old territory, such as the probability of causes (Daston, 1988).

The important point is that the calculus of probability began with several interpretations, and this plurality is still with us. This does not mean that the relationship between these interpretations has remained stable – on the contrary. For instance, the two major faces of probability, subjective belief and objective frequencies, began as equivalents and ended up as diametric opposites. For Jakob Bernoulli and the other Enlightenment mathematicians, belief and frequencies were just two sides of the same coin, and the ease with which the Enlightenment probabilists slid from one interpretation to the other is breathtaking – from today's point of view. Poisson eventually distinguished subjective belief and objective frequencies, and the political economist and philosopher Antoine Cournot (1843/1975) seems to have been the first to go one step further and eliminate subjective belief from the subject matter of mathematical probability: Mathematical probability was not a measure of belief. There is a broader intellectual and social context in which the demise of subjective belief as the subject matter of probability is embedded. The French Revolution and its aftermath shook the confidence of the mathematicians in the existence of a single shared standard of reasonableness. The consensus and the values of the intellectual and political elites fragmented, and degrees of belief became associated with wishful thinking and irrationality. By that time, the calculus of probability had lost its subject matter, the judgment and decision making of reasonable people (Gigerenzer et al., 1989, ch. 1).

By 1840, the calculus of uncertainty was no longer about mechanical rules of rational belief embodied in an elite of reasonable men, but about the observable properties of the *average man* (*l'homme moyen*), the embodiment of mass society, if not of mediocrity. Adolphe Quetelet's (1835) *social physics* determined the statistical distributions of suicide, murder, marriage, prostitution, height, weight, education, and almost everything else in Paris and compared them with the distributions in London or Brussels. The means of these distributions defined the fictional average man in each society. The means and rates of moral behaviors, such as suicides or crimes in Paris or in London, proved to be strikingly stable over the years, and this was cited as evidence that moral phenomena are governed by the laws of a society rather than by the free decisions of its members. In 19th-century France, statistics became known as *moral science*. Quetelet offered a model of human behavior as erratic and unpredictable at the individual level, but governed by statistical laws and predictable at the level of society. This model was independently adopted by James Clerk Maxwell and Ludwig Boltzmann to justify, by analogy, their statistical interpretation of the behavior of gas molecules (Porter, 1986). By this strange route, through analogy with the statistical laws of society, physics was revolutionized.

Throughout most of the 19th and 20th centuries, the *probabilistic revolution* (Krüger, Daston, & Heidelberger, 1987; Krüger, Gigerenzer, & Morgan, 1987) was about frequencies, not about degrees of belief: from the kinetic theory of gas to quantum statistics, and from population genetics to the Neyman–Pearson theory of hypothesis testing. As is well known, subjective probability regained acceptance in the second half of the 20th century with the pioneering work of Bruno de Finetti and Frank Ramsay in the 1920s and 1930s and of Leonard Savage in the 1950s. The reasonable man, once exiled from probability theory, made his comeback. Economists, psychologists, and philosophers now struggle again with the issue of how to codify *reasonableness* in mathematical form – the same issue once abandoned by mathematicians as a thankless task. Before the 1970s, the return of subjective probability still provoked a particularly lively debate between frequentists and subjectivists (whose most prominent species are now called *Bayesians*). Today, both sides pretend to know each other's arguments all too well and seem to have stopped listening. Frequentists dominate statistics and the experimental sciences; subjectivists dominate theoretical economics and artificial intelligence. The territory has been divided up. As Glenn Shafer (1989) complained, "conceptually and institutionally, probability has been balkanized" (p. 15).

To summarize: Since its inception, the calculus of uncertainty has had not one subject matter, but a multitude, that is, there has always been more than one interpretation of this calculus. The two most prominent ones are objective frequencies and subjective degrees of belief. The important point for this chapter is that each of these two interpretations is linked with a specific class of representations. Observed frequencies, for instance, can be represented by discrete elements that are the final tally of a counting process, and which are different from degrees of belief and single-event probabilities. The two representations we will focus on are *natural frequencies* and *probabilities*. The former are pure observed frequencies; the latter are the typical representations of degrees of belief.

Experts' Representations of Uncertainty. In this section, we summarize two case studies that demonstrate how the representation of statistical information – single-event probabilities and natural frequencies – affects human reasoning in Bayesian inference tasks. We first give an example to show how the Bayesian solution can be derived from either of the two representations. Then we report on how AIDS counselors reason in such a task and how they represent the relevant information spontaneously (Case Study I). Finally, we show how performance can be considerably improved by altering the representation of information (Case Study II).

Task Analysis. Consider the situation of a young heterosexual man who has undergone a human immunodeficiency virus (HIV) test. He does not engage in activities considered risky, such as intravenous (IV) drug use or homosexual practices. Yet, the result – after repeatedly applying the enzyme-linked immunosorbent assay (ELISA) and the Western blot test – comes back positive. What is the probability that he actually has HIV? If the test is positive, the probability of being infected – also known as the *positive predictive value* (PPV) – can be computed by Bayes's rule:

$$\text{PPV} = \frac{p(\text{HIV})\,p(\text{pos}|\text{HIV})}{p(\text{HIV})\,p(\text{pos}|\text{HIV}) + p(\text{no HIV})\,p(\text{pos}|\text{no HIV})}, \qquad (1)$$

where $p(\text{HIV})$ denotes the prevalence of HIV in the respective population, $p(\text{no HIV})$ equals $1 - p(\text{HIV})$, $p(\text{pos}|\text{HIV})$ denotes the sensitivity of the test, and $p(\text{pos}|\text{no HIV})$ denotes the false positive rate of the test. Often the specificity rather than the false positive rate of a test is reported; the specificity of a test equals $1 - p(\text{pos}|\text{no HIV})$. To compute the PPV, we consulted the literature for estimates of these probabilities. The prevalence of HIV in heterosexual men with no known risk factors is estimated to be 0.01%. The best estimates for the sensitivity and specificity of the respective testing procedure (repeated ELISA and Western blot testing) is 99.8% for the sensitivity of the test and 99.99%

for its specificity (see Gigerenzer et al., 1998). Inserting these values into Bayes's rule results in a PPV of .50, or 50%, which is consistent with reports in the literature (Deutscher Bundestag, 1990, p. 121; Stine, 1996, p. 338).

Do people understand Bayes's rule and can they infer the PPV from a given prevalence, sensitivity, and false positive rate? There is considerable empirical evidence that suggests the answer is "no" (e.g., Casscells, Schoenberger, & Grayboys, 1978; Eddy, 1982; Gigerenzer & Hoffrage, 1995). The good news is that this negative answer need not be the cause of utter pessimism for the following reason. Note that the statistical information in our HIV example was represented in terms of probabilities. This probability-based format is the information format generally used in medical textbooks and curricula, as well as in the experiments that have demonstrated people's (including physicians') poor performance in Bayesian inference tasks. However, as we saw in the preceding section, probabilities constitute only one way of representing the relevant information; it can also be represented in terms of *natural frequencies*, that is, the absolute frequencies that result from observing cases that have been representatively sampled from a population.

Unlike probabilities, natural frequencies are not normalized with respect to the base rates of disease or no disease. Using natural frequencies, computation of the PPV can be communicated as follows: "Imagine that 10,000 heterosexual men are tested. One has the virus, and he will with practical certainty test positive (sensitivity = 99.8%). Of the remaining uninfected men, one will also test positive (false positive rate = 0.01%). This means that we expect that two men will test positive, and only one of them has HIV. Thus, the chance of having the virus given a positive test is one out of two, or 50%." In general, the PPV is the number of true positives (TP) divided by the number of true positives and false positives (FP):

$$PPP = \frac{TP}{TP + FP}. \tag{2}$$

Figure 7.2 illustrates the fact that Bayesian computations are simpler with natural frequencies than with probabilities or percentages, where the relevant statistical information is inserted in Equation 1 (left-hand side) and Equation 2 (right-hand side).

To compute the formula on the right-hand side, fewer cognitive operations need to be performed. Comparing the two equations yields

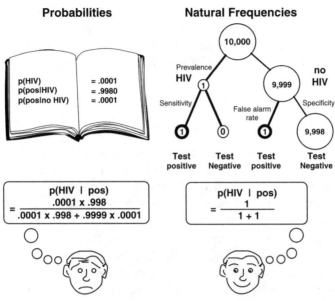

Figure 7.2 Two ways of inferring the predictive value of a positive HIV test. Relevant information is represented either as probabilities or as natural frequencies.

two further (related) results. First, with frequency representation only two pieces of information, the symptom and disease frequencies and the symptom and no disease frequencies (the two bold circles in Figure 7.2), need to be used. Second, and as a consequence of this, the base rate frequency (1 out of 10,000) can be ignored. On balance, in this kind of Bayesian inference task we obtain the same result with less information and fewer cognitive operations. We have chosen our favorite!

As a final example, let us compute the risk of a young homosexual man having HIV, given a positive test result. Assuming that the prevalence for this group is 1.5%, try to compute the PPV by using the probability representation first. (To make a fair comparison, you should think of how you would have dealt with this task before reading the previous pages of this chapter.) Now consider the frequency representation: Out of 10,000 homosexual men, about 150 have the virus and they will probably all test positive. Of the remaining uninfected men, one will also test positive. Thus, we expect that 151 men will test positive and that 150 of these men have HIV. Given a positive test result, the chance of having the virus is therefore 150 out of 151, or 99.3%.

In this way, representing information in terms of natural frequencies can help us "see" the correct Bayesian answer. The numbers can be adjusted; the point is that these numbers have to be represented somehow and that the representation chosen makes the computation more or less easy.

AIDS Counseling for Low-Risk Clients (Case Study I)

How do AIDS counselors communicate the meaning of a positive test result in actual counseling sessions? Do they communicate the risk in probabilities or natural frequencies? The study by Gigerenzer et al. (1998) on AIDS counseling in German public health centers seems to be the only study to have investigated what AIDS counselors tell a low-risk client about the meaning of a positive test. One of the authors of the study visited 20 counseling locations as a client wishing to take an HIV test. He asked the counselor the following questions in the order indicated (unless the counselor provided the information unprompted):

1. Sensitivity of the HIV test	If one is infected with HIV, is it possible to have a negative test result? How reliably does the test identify a virus if the virus is present?
2. Specificity of the HIV test	If one is not infected with HIV, is it possible to have a positive test result? How reliable is the test with respect to a false positive result?
3. Prevalence of HIV in heterosexual men	How frequent is the virus in my risk group, that is, heterosexual men, 20 to 30 years old, with no known risk – such as IV drug use?
4. Predictive value of a positive test	What is the probability that men in my risk group actually do have HIV after a positive test?
5. Window period	How much time has to pass between infection and test, so that antibodies can be detected? (For the present purpose, we will omit the results concerning this question.)

The interview included the following scheme for clarifying questions. If the counselor's answer was a quantitative estimate (a figure or a range), or if the counselor said that he or she could not (or did not want to) give a more precise answer, then the client went on to the next question. If the answer was qualitative (e.g., "fairly certain"), or if the counselor misunderstood or avoided answering the question, the client asked for further clarification and, if necessary, repeated the request for clarification once. If, after the third attempt, there was still no success, the client did not push further and went on to the next question. When the client needed to ask for clarification concerning the prevalence of HIV (Question 3), he always repeated his specific risk group; when asking for clarification concerning the PPV (Question 4), he always referred to the specific prevalence in his risk group, namely, "heterosexual men, 20 to 30 years old, with no known risk-related activity such as IV drug use." If the counselor asked for more information, which happened in only 11 of the 20 sessions, the client explained that he was 27 years old and monogamous, and that neither his current nor his (few) previous sexual partners used IV drugs or engaged in other risky behavior. In 2 of these 11 cases, the client was given a detailed questionnaire to determine his risk; in 1 of these 2 cases, the counselor did not look at the questionnaire and the client still had it in his hands when he left the location. Before turning to the general results of this study, we present excerpts from four typical counseling sessions. The client's questions are abbreviated (e.g., Sensitivity?) and followed by the information provided by the counselors. The counselors' answers to the client's clarifying questions are preceded by a hyphen.

Session 1: A Social Worker

Sensitivity? False negatives really never occur. Although if I think about the literature, there were reports about such cases. – I don't know exactly how many. – It happened only once or twice. *False Positives?* No, because the test is repeated; it is absolutely sure. – If there are antibodies, the test identifies them unambiguously and with absolute certainty. – No, it is absolutely impossible that there are false positives; by repeating the test it is absolutely certain. *Prevalence?* I can't tell you this exactly. – Between about 1 of 500 and 1 of 1,000. *Positive predictive value?* As I have now told you repeatedly, the test is absolutely certain.

Session 2: A Physician

Sensitivity? When there are enough antibodies, then the test identifies them in every case. Two tests are performed; the first test is in its fourth generation and is tuned to be very specific and sensitive. Nevertheless it is tuned in a way that it is more likely to identify positives than negatives. – 99.8% sensitivity and specificity. But we repeat the test, and if it comes out positive, then the result is as solid as cast iron. *False Positives?* With certainty, they don't occur; if there are false results, then only false negatives, occurring when the antibodies have not formed. – If you take the test here, including a confirmatory test, it is extremely certain. In any case the specificity is 99.7%. This is as solid as cast iron. We exclude confusions by using two tests. *Prevalence?* The classification of individuals into risk groups is by now outdated, therefore one cannot look at this that way. – I don't remember this. There is a trend for the virus to spread in the general public. Statistics are of no use for the individual case! *Positive predictive value?* As I already have said: extremely certain, 99.8%.

Session 3: A Physician

Sensitivity? The test is very, very reliable, that is, about 99.98%. *False Positives?* The test will be repeated. After the first test, we do not speak of positive, but only of reactive. When all tests are performed, then the result is sure. – It is hard to say how many false positives occur. – How many precisely? I would have to look up the literature to see if I could find this information there. *Prevalence?* That depends on the region. – Of the approximately 67,000 infected people [in Germany], 9% are heterosexual. – In Munich we have 10,000 infected people, that is, 1% of the population. But these are only numbers, which tell you nothing about whether you have the virus or not. *Positive predictive value?* As I have already have mentioned, the result is 99.98% sure. If you get a positive result, you can trust it.

Session 4: A Social Worker

Sensitivity? Very, very reliable. – No, not absolutely sure, such a thing doesn't exist in medicine, because it may be possible that the virus cannot be identified. – Close to 100%; I don't know exactly. *False Positives?* They exist, but are extremely rare. – On the order of one tenth of 1%. Probably less. However, in your risk group, compared with high-risk groups, false positives are proportionally more frequent. – I don't know the exact value. *Prevalence?* With the contacts you have had, an infection is unlikely. – Generally one can't say. In our own institution, among some 10,000 tests in the last 7 years, there were only three or four heterosexuals, nondrug addicts, or similar non-risk-group persons who tested positive. *Positive predictive value?* As mentioned, the test is not 100% sure. If the test confuses the [HIV] antibodies with others, then other methods such as repeated tests do not help. And if someone like you does not have a real risk, then I could imagine that even 5% to 10% of those who get a positive result will have gotten a false positive result.

How Did the Counselors Represent Statistical Information? The client was provided with information concerning sensitivity by 19 out of 20 counselors. (One of them refused to give any information concerning sensitivity, specificity, or predictive value before the test result was obtained. When the client collected the test result, he didn't receive any information either.) Most counselors gave the client realistic information concerning sensitivity (Table 7.1). However, 5 out of the 19 counselors incorrectly informed the client that even after the window period, it would be impossible to get a false negative result.

The client was informed incorrectly that false positives do not occur by 13 out of 19 counselors (e.g., Session 1). Eleven of the 13 explained this by saying that repeated testing with ELISA and Western blot eliminates all false positives. Five of these 13 counselors told the client that false positives had occurred in the 1980s, but no longer today, and 2 said that false positives occur only in foreign countries, such as France, but not in Germany. In addition to these 13 counselors, 3 other counselors initially suggested that false positives do not occur, but became less certain when the client repeated his question and admitted the possibility of false positives (Sessions 2 and 3). Only the three remaining

Table 7.1. *Summary of the Information Provided in 20 AIDS Counseling Sessions*

	100% Certainty	≥ 99.9%	≥ 99%	> 90%	Range	Best Estimate from the Literature
Sensitivity	5 (of 19)	5	6	3	90–100%	99.99%
Specificity	13 (of 19)	3	3	0	99.7–100%	99.99%
Prevalence	–	–	–	–	0.0075–6%	0.01%
PPV	10 (of 18)	5	1	2	90–100%	50%

Note: Not all the counselors provided numerical estimates. The verbal assertion "absolutely certain" is treated here as equivalent to 100% certain; verbal assertions such as "almost absolutely certain" and "very, very certain" are classified as ≥ 99%, and assertions such as "very reliable" are classified as ≥ 90%.

Source: Gigerenzer et al. (1998)

counselors informed the client right away about the existence of false positives. One of these three counselors (Session 4) was the only one who informed the client of the important fact that the proportion of false positives to true positives is higher in heterosexuals, such as the client.

Recall that the currently available estimates indicate that, of heterosexual German men with low-risk behavior who test positive, only 50% actually have HIV. The information provided by the counselors on this was quite different. Half of the counselors (10 out of 18; 2 repeatedly ignored this question) told the client that if he tested positive, it was absolutely certain (100%) that he had HIV (Table 7.1 and Session 1). He was told by five counselors that the probability is 99.9% or higher (e.g., Session 3). Thus, if the client had tested positive and trusted the information provided by these 15 counselors, he might indeed have contemplated suicide, as many people in this situation have done (Stine, 1996).

How did the counselors arrive at this inflated estimate of the predictive value? They seem to have followed two lines of thought. A total of eight counselors confused sensitivity with the PPV (a confusion also reported by Eddy, 1982, and Elstein, 1988), that is, they gave the same figure for sensitivity as for the PPV (e.g., Sessions 2 and 3). For example, three of these eight counselors explained that, apart from the window period, the sensitivity is 100% and therefore the PPV is also 100%. Another five counselors followed a different line of thought: They erroneously assumed that false positives would be eliminated by repeated testing and, consistent with this assumption, concluded that the PPV is 100%. For both groups, the client's question about the PPV must have appeared to repeat a previous question. In fact, more than half of the counselors (11 out of 18) explicitly introduced their answer to this question with a phrase such as "As I have already said . . ." (e.g., Sessions 1–3).

Table 7.1 shows that two counselors provided estimates of the PPV in the correct direction (between 99% and 90%). Only one of these two (Session 4), however, arrived at this estimate by reasoning that the proportion of false positives among all the positives increases when the prevalence decreases. She was also the only one who explained to the client that repeated testing cannot eliminate all possible causes of false positives, such as a positive test reaction to antibodies wrongly identified as HIV antibodies. The second counselor initially asserted that a positive test result means that an HIV infection is "completely certain," but when the client asked what "completely certain" meant, the physician had second thoughts and said that the PPV is "at least in the upper 90s" and "I can't be more exact."

How Was Statistical Information Communicated? Not one of the counselors communicated the information in terms of natural frequencies, the representation that physicians and laypeople can understand best. Except for the prevalence of HIV, all statistical information was communicated to the client in terms of percentages. The four sessions illustrate this. As a consequence, clients probably did not understand the meaning of what was being communicated to them. Further, some of the counselors did not seem to understand the figures they were communicating. This can be inferred from the fact that several counselors gave the client inconsistent information but did not seem to notice this.

Two examples may serve to illustrate the counselors' unawareness of inconsistency. One physician told the client that the prevalence of HIV in men such as the client is 0.1% or slightly higher and that the sensitivity, specificity, and PPV are each 99.9%. To demonstrate that this information is contradictory, we represent it in natural frequencies. Imagine that 1,000 men take an HIV test. One of these men (0.1%) is infected, and he will test positive with practical certainty. Of the remaining uninfected men, one will also test positive (because the specificity is assumed to be 99.9%, which implies a false positive rate of 0.1%). Thus, two men test positive, and one of them is infected. Therefore, the odds of being infected with HIV are 1:1 (50%), not 999:1 (99.9%). (Even if the physician assumed a prevalence of 0.5%, the odds are 5:1 (84%) rather than 999:1. Note how in this case the odds representation paints a rather more dramatic picture than the probability representation based on percentages.)

Next, consider the information the client received in Session 2. For the prevalence (which the counselor did not provide), assume the median estimate of the other counselors, 0.1%. Again, imagine 1,000 men. One has the virus, and he will test positive with practical certainty (the counselor's estimated sensitivity: 99.8%). Of the remaining uninfected men, three will also test positive (the counselor's estimated specificity: 99.7%). Thus, we expect 4 of the 1,000 to test positive and 1 of these 4 to have the virus. So if the test is positive, the probability of being infected is 25% (one in four), and not 99.8% as the counselor told the client.

This study shows, for a representative sample of public AIDS counseling centers in Germany, that counselors were not prepared to explain to a man with low-risk behavior what it meant if he tested positive for HIV. This is not to say that the counselors were generally ignorant; on the contrary, several counselors gave long and sophisticated lectures concerning immunodiagnostic techniques, the nature of proteins, and the pathways of infection. But when it came to explaining to the client the risk of being infected if he tested positive, they uniformly relied on a representational format that did not serve them well and could have been harmful to their clients.

Diagnostic Insight in Physicians (Case Study II)

To see whether diagnostic reasoning improves when statistical information is represented in terms of frequencies, we decided to manipulate the representational format in an experiment with physicians (Gigerenzer, 1996; Hoffrage & Gigerenzer, 1998). We had previously carried out such an experiment with students as participants, with the result that, when information was presented in natural frequencies (rather than in probabilities), the percentage of Bayesian solutions increased from about 16% to 46% (Gigerenzer & Hoffrage, 1995). Yet, it remained an open (and interesting) question whether this result would generalize to experts such as physicians. Medical textbooks typically present information about sensitivity, specificity, and priors in probabilities (as in Figure 7.2, left-hand side). Medical experts may be so "spoiled" by this common practice that they do not appreciate the advantages of representing the relevant information in natural frequencies.

Forty-eight physicians participated in this study (Gigerenzer, 1996; Hoffrage & Gigerenzer, 1998). The physicians were asked to work on four diagnostic problems: inferring colorectal cancer on the basis of a positive hemoccult test, inferring the risk of breast cancer from a positive mammography test, inferring ankylosing spondylitis on the basis of a positive HL antigen B 27 test, and inferring phenylketonuria from a positive Guthrie test. Two versions of each of the four diagnostic problems were presented to the participants. In one version, the relevant information was presented in a probability format; in the other, in a frequency format. (Which problems were in which format and which format was presented first was systematically varied, with the constraint that the first two problems had the same format.) To illustrate, here are the two versions of the colorectal cancer problem:

> To diagnose colorectal cancer, one of the tests that is conducted to detect occult blood in the stool is the hemoccult test. This test may be used for people above a particular age and in routine screening for early detection of colorectal cancer. Imagine that you are screening in a

certain region using the hemoccult test. For symptom-free people over 50 years old who are screened by the hemoccult test in this region, the following information is available:

The Probability Format

The probability that one of these people has colorectal cancer is 0.3%. If one of these people has colorectal cancer, the probability that he or she will have a positive hemoccult test is 50%. If one of these people does not have colorectal cancer, the probability that he or she will still have a positive hemoccult test is 3%. Imagine a person (aged over 50, no symptoms) who has a positive hemoccult test in your screening. What is the probability that this person actually has colorectal cancer? _____ %

The Natural Frequency Format

Thirty out of every 10,000 people have colorectal cancer. Of these 30 people with colorectal cancer, 15 will have a positive hemoccult test. Of the remaining 9,970 people without colorectal cancer, 300 will still have a positive hemoccult test. Imagine a sample of people (aged over 50, no symptoms) who have positive hemoccult tests in your screening. How many of these people do actually have colorectal cancer? _____ out of _____

The physicians received a booklet containing all four problems, two of which presented information in probabilities and two in natural frequencies. The formats and order of the problems were systematically varied among the physicians, with the constraint that the first two problems were in the same representational format. Participants were invited to make notes, calculations, or drawings while working on the problems; these were analyzed later to reconstruct their reasoning. After the physicians had filled out the booklets, we interviewed them about their reasoning strategies. We only coded answers to the problems as being in accord with Bayes's rule when (1) the numerical estimate was within 5 percentage points of the correct one, and (2) the physician's notes, calculations, or drawings, and the interview confirmed that the answer was neither a guess nor the result of another strategy. Next, we describe the impact of the two representational formats on a physician's reasoning. This physician was a rather typical case, and we therefore call him Dr. Average.

A Physician's Diagnostic Reasoning. Dr. Average is 59 years old, director of a university clinic, and a dermatologist by training. He spent 30 minutes on the four problems and another 15 minutes discussing the results with the interviewer. Like many physicians, he became visibly nervous when working on the problems, but only when faced with the probability formats. At first, Dr. Average refused to write notes; later, he agreed to do so, but only on his own piece of paper and not on the questionnaire. He did not let the interviewer see his notes.

Dr. Average's booklet started with the mammography problem in the probability format. He commented: "I never inform my patients about statistical data. I would tell the patient that mammography is not so exact, and would in any case perform a biopsy." He estimated the probability of breast cancer after a positive mammography as 80% + 10% = 90%, that is, he added the sensitivity to the false positive rate (an unusual strategy). Nervously, he remarked: "Oh, what nonsense. I can't do it. You should test my daughter; she studies medicine." Dr. Average was as helpless with the second problem, ankylosing spondylitis, in a probability format. This time he estimated the posterior probability by multiplying the base rate by the sensitivity (a common strategy in statistically naïve students; see Gigerenzer & Hoffrage, 1995).

Then came the first problem presented in a frequency format. Dr. Average's nervousness subsided visibly. Coming up with the Bayesian answer, he remarked with relief: "That's so easy." He also arrived at the Bayesian answer with the fourth problem, which was also presented in a frequency format. Dr. Average's reasoning evidently turned Bayesian when the relevant information was presented in frequencies. This was the case, despite the fact that he did not know Bayes's rule, as he informed us.

Incidentally, Dr. Average was not the only physician who referred in despair to a daughter or son. In one case, the daughter was actually nearby and was also working on the problems. Her father, a 49-year-old private practitioner, worked for about 30 minutes on the four problems and failed on all of them. "Statistics is alien to everyday concerns and of little use for judging individual people," he declared. He derived his numerical estimates from one of two strategies: base rate only or sensitivity only (both strategies are common with statistically naïve students). His 18-year-old daughter solved all four problems by constructing Bayesian trees (as on the right-hand side of Figure 7.2). When she learned about her father's strategies, she glanced at him and said: "Daddy, look, the frequency problem is not hard. Couldn't you do this one either?" For this private practitioner, even frequency formats didn't help. In contrast, a 38-year-old gynecologist faced with the mammography problem in

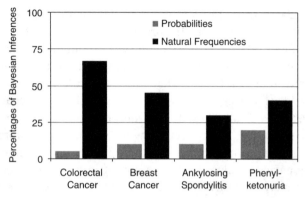

Figure 7.3 The percentage of Bayesian answers is higher when the relevant information is represented as natural frequencies rather than as probabilities.

the frequency format, exclaimed: "A first grader could do this. Wow, if someone couldn't solve this . . .!"

Does Representation Have an Effect on Physicians' Diagnostic Reasoning?
On average, the 48 physicians worked on the four problems for half an hour. When the information was presented in a probability format, the physicians reasoned the Bayesian way in only 10% of the cases, averaged across all four problems. When the information was presented in natural frequencies, this figure increased to 46%.

As can be seen in Figure 7.3, the frequency representation led to higher proportions of Bayesian estimates for each of the four problems. In addition, the natural frequencies turned out to be less time-consuming for the participants. The physicians spent about 25% more time on the probability problems, which indicates that they found them more difficult to solve. As the case of Dr. Average illustrates, the physicians often reacted differently – cognitively, emotionally, physiologically – to the probability format and the natural frequency format. The physicians were more often nervous when information was presented in terms of probabilities. When working on probability problems, they made complaints such as: "I simply can't do that. Mathematics is not my forte." However, with natural frequencies, a typical remark was: "Now it's different. It's quite easy to imagine. There's a frequency; that's more visual." In addition, they were less skeptical about the relevance of statistical information to medical diagnosis when it was communicated in frequencies.

The results of this case study, which have recently been replicated with 96 advanced medical students (Hoffrage, Lindsey, Hertwig, &

Gigerenzer, 2000), show that representing information in natural frequencies is effective in inferring the predictive value of a test. The beneficial effect of natural frequencies is, however, not limited to the field of medicine. In criminal law, judges' and other legal experts' understanding of the meaning of a DNA match could similarly be improved by using natural frequencies instead of probabilities (Hoffrage et al., 2000; Koehler, 1996). It was also found, for example, that legal experts were less likely to support a "guilty" verdict when the statistical information was presented in natural frequencies. An important new finding is that natural frequencies can also facilitate reasoning in complex Bayesian situations characterized either by two or more predictors or by predictors and criteria with more than two values (Krauss, Martignon, Hoffrage, & Gigerenzer, in review).

These results have two implications. First, because information in medical textbooks is routinely communicated in terms of probabilities or percentages, medical students as well as physicians ought to be taught how to translate these figures into natural frequencies. Sedlmeier and Gigerenzer (2001, Study 1) designed a computerized tutorial system that teaches people how to do this. People who were taught to translate probabilities into natural frequencies performed twice as well on Bayesian inference problems as people who were taught the standard method of inserting probabilities into Bayes's rule. Even more striking, performance in the group that translated information into natural frequencies remained stable in a 5-week follow-up test (median performance 90% correct), whereas performance in the standard group showed the usual deterioration due to forgetting (15% correct). Kurzenhäuser and Hoffrage (2002) applied this approach to a typical classroom setting and found that twice as many medical students who learned to actively translate probabilities into natural frequencies (as compared to a control group who learned Bayes's rule) were able to deal with probabilities when tested 2 months later.

A second, equally important implication concerns the communication of risks, not only in medical textbooks but also to patients. For instance, before consenting to medical treatment on the basis of a diagnosis, patients should understand the uncertainties involved, such as the risks of actually having the disease. In order to facilitate accurate assessment of risk, physicians should use the most effective means of representation and thus of communication. As we showed, it is not for lack of contenders that more effective representations are not generally available to medical experts and their patients.

Representing Change

Observing Historical Spectra: The Differential Calculus

Isaac Newton (1642–1727) and Gottfried Wilhelm Leibniz (1646–1716), the two eminent figures credited with the intellectual breakthrough of the differential and integral calculus, had a bitter dispute over priority (Hall, 1980). In the work of both Leibniz and Newton, the inception of the calculus was embedded in a body of questions concerned with natural philosophy, metaphysics, and theology (Bertoloni Meli, 1993; see also the Leibniz–Clarke correspondence in Alexander, 1956). Both of them had arrived at the insight that two old problems could be viewed as inverse to each other: finding tangents to curves and finding areas below curves (quadratures). Since antiquity, these had been distinct problems (Boyer, 1949). Although the calculation of tangents and areas had advanced quite far in the century prior to Newton and Leibniz, it was only through their work that these were seen as inverse and that a general and algorithmic method was established. In the centuries following Newton and Leibniz, some of their concepts were recast and abandoned, and new ones, like the limit concept and the function concept, were introduced. The important point is that the institutionalization of the differential calculus began with rivaling proposals and that this plurality of representation has remained a feature of the calculus. To demonstrate this point, we will ask you, the reader, to look at the graph shown in Figure 7.4 through "Leibnizian glasses," "Newtonian glasses," and "Modern glasses."

Let us start with the *Leibnizian glasses*. Leibniz conceived of smooth curves as polygons with infinitely many sides. If you look at the curvilinear line in Figure 7.4 through Leibnizian glasses you see the smooth curve as a chain of short rectilinear line segments. The "links" in this chain may be infinitely small, but the curve will always remain a chain when you are looking through your Leibnizian glasses. The passage from this imagined chain to the quantification of change can be achieved by the following consideration pertaining to the vertices of the (infinite angular) polygon, or, in other words, to the points at which the (infinitely small) links of the chain meet. The ordinates and abscissas corresponding to the vertices of the polygon can be understood as forming number sequences. To approximate the smooth curve, the differences between the successive terms of such sequences were conceptualized as infinitely small. These infinitesimal differences were called *differentials*

Concentration (kg/liter)

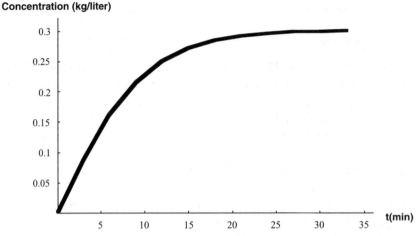

Figure 7.4 Cartesian coordinate system with a graph showing how the salt concentration in the flask changes with time. The line representing the changing concentration can be read in three different ways: a Newtonian, a Leibnizian, or a function-based way.

and denoted by dx or dy, the differentials being assigned to the finite variables x and y, respectively. In other words, the operator d, as in dx, related to a sequence the corresponding difference sequence. Leibniz's operator $\int$, by contrast, related to a sequence the corresponding sum sequence. Thus, Leibniz's insight of the inverse nature of the problem of quadratures and tangents was in the end, or rather in its beginning, based on the inverse operations of summing and finding differences (Bos, 1993).

Now let us try on the *Newtonian glasses*. In Newton's fluxionary calculus, variable quantities, also called *fluents*, were conceived of as changing over time. In Newton's own words (cited from his *Tractatus de quadratura curvarum* of 1704, as translated and reprinted in Struik, 1969, p. 303):

> I consider mathematical quantities in this place not as consisting of very small parts; but as described by a continued motion. Lines are described, and thereby generated not by the apposition of parts, but by the continued motion of points; superficies [surfaces] by the motion of lines; solids by the motion of superficies; angles by rotation of sides; portions of time by a continual flux: and so in other quantities. These geneses really take place in the nature of things, and are daily seen in the motion of bodies.

The velocities or rates of change with respect to time of such variable quantities were called *fluxions*. Newton used *pricked letters* like

$\dot{x}$ to symbolize them. If you look at the graph in Figure 7.4 through Newtonian glasses, you see the curvilinear line as the trace created by a rightward-moving point. Changes in velocity are represented as directional changes on the upward or downward dimension of the rightward-moving point.

The passage from the motion of a geometrical object to the quantification of change was accomplished by considering the change of variable quantities during indefinitely small time intervals, also called *moments* and denoted by the letter o. For instance, Newton determined the momentary change in the area below a curve by adding a moment o to the variable quantity noted on the abscissa and then adding a corresponding term to the variable quantity noted on the ordinate: Consider, for example, the case in which the area underneath a curve is described by the standard equation for a parabola $z = x^2$; adding a moment o to the abscissa corresponds to the expression $z + yo = (x + o)^2$, where z denotes the area, and x and y are the variable quantities denoted on the axes. The computational procedure was then completed by expanding the expression on the right-hand side (applying the binomial theorem), removing the terms without o (because they are equal), dividing by o, and then neglecting terms carrying o as a factor. The result of these computations is $y = 2x$. By this procedure, it was established that the area z underneath the curve $y = 2x$ is x^2. Later, Newton expressed the monetary change of a variable quantity (for example, y) by multiplying its fluxion ($\dot{y}$) by an infinitely small time interval (leading to the expression $\dot{y}o$), but the main idea behind the computational procedure, namely, to consider the change in area by adding very small increments to the variables in an equation, remained the same (see Bos, 1980, pp. 56–59, for a thorough exposition). Newton's insight concerning the inverse nature of the problem of quadratures and tangents was helped by his early work on the binomial theorem and on series expansion in general, and was related to the way in which Newton determined the area underneath a curve.

Lastly, let us switch to the *Modern glasses*. Modern glasses are not part of modern analysis in the same way that Leibnizian and Newtonian glasses had been part of their respective calculi. Geometrical considerations were indispensable for the development, presentation, and justification of Newton's and Leibniz's calculi. The development of modern analysis was accompanied by a distancing from geometrical considerations. The French mathematician Augustin-Louis Cauchy (1789–1857) was a major figure in the reworking of the foundations of the calculus and in its modern formulation. He also introduced the modern notation, in which a prime is used to denote the derivative, for example, $f'(x)$. In Cauchy's definition of limit, and thus of the derivative, no reference was made to geometric figures (Grattan-Guinness, 1980), and his textbook *Cours d'analyse de l'École Royal Polytechnique*, published in 1821, did not contain a single diagram!

However, it is nevertheless possible to construct a visual analogue for the concept of derivative. We ask you to look once again at the graph in Figure 7.4 and to choose a small segment of the curvilinear line. We suggest you imagine that you can move a small open rectangle (rather like a cursor on a computer screen) along the curvilinear line. You could then make it your goal to move the cursor so that the open rectangle frames a segment with particularly strong curvature, but it is up to you. Once you have settled on a segment of the graph, we ask you to imagine that the rectangle and its contents are enlarged so as to fill your entire field of vision, or, in other words, that you are zooming in on the segment. As a result, you see a line with less curvature than the original line segment – you might even see a straight line. Starting with this "new" line, repeat the procedure of choosing a line segment and zooming in on it, and then repeat this procedure as many times as you wish. You will soon get bored because you will be looking at what appears to be the same straight line. With Modern glasses you can thus explore the inner workings of the graph, whereby you will observe that you are approaching a world of straight lines.

To summarize the three different ways of looking at the graph in Figure 7.4: We first looked through Leibnizian glasses and imagined the curvilinear line approximated by a chain with infinitely many infinitely small links; then we looked through Newtonian glasses, imagining the curvilinear line as the trace generated by a moving point; finally, we constructed Modern glasses, zooming in on particular line segments and exploring the inner workings of the graph. The important point for this chapter is that since its inception, the calculus has provided multiple representations of change. This multiplicity is also reflected in the calculus-specific notation. Present-day experts use both Leibnizian notation and Newtonian notation, as well as function-based notation.

Experts' Representation of Change

In this section, we summarize a case study in which calculus experts – a mathematician, a chemist, and a physicist – were asked to solve a problem that requires a differential equation for its exact solution. Next, we introduce the task that these experts were asked to solve, considering first the general model of exponential change.

Task Analysis. What do cell growth, population growth, continuously compounded interest, radioactive decay, cooling of a body, and the decrease in intensity of light when transmitted through a sample have in common? All of these phenomena concern change: an increase or decrease in cell mass, in population size, money, temperature, or light intensity. Furthermore, all of these phenomena have been described, given certain additional assumptions, by a particular mathematical model known as the *law of exponential change*. For example, in an ideal environment, the change in mass of a cell will be proportional to the mass of the cell, at least early on. This relationship can be described by a differential equation (here in Leibnizian notation) of the form:

$$\frac{dx}{dt} = kx, \tag{3}$$

where x is the mass of the cell, t is time, and k is a constant. This differential equation can be solved to determine the mass of the cell at a particular time t or, for that matter, at any time t. Solving the equation, which requires the operation of integration, leads to the following expression:

$$x = x_0 e^{kt}, \tag{4}$$

where x_0 denotes the initial mass of the cell. In words, cell mass grows exponentially. The identical equation has been used to model continuously compounded interest, or radioactive decay, or the change in light intensity when light is transmitted through a sample of a certain thickness. (In the last two cases the constant k has a negative value.)

Now consider a slightly more involved situation as represented by, for instance, the cooling of a body in a surrounding medium of constant temperature. In this case, we have to take into account that the body's temperature adjusts to the temperature of the surrounding medium, so that the difference between its temperature and that of the surrounding medium is crucial. (We assume that the temperature of the body does not affect the temperature of the surrounding medium.) *Newton's law of cooling* (here in Newtonian notation) addresses this situation:

$$\dot{T} = -k(T - T_s), \tag{5}$$

where $\dot{T}$ signifies the change in temperature with time (in Leibnizian notation denoted by dT/dt), k is a constant, and T_s is the temperature of the surrounding medium. In words, the cooling of a body is proportional to the difference between its temperature and that of the surrounding medium. The differential equation describing Newton's law of cooling can also be used to model phenomena other than the cooling and heating of bodies. The expert participants in our third case study worked on a task that can be modeled by an equivalent first-order linear ordinary differential equation.

The following problem, henceforth called the *Flask Problem* (Brenner, 1963), was presented to the expert participants:

> A flask contains 10 liters of water, and to it is being added a salt solution that contains 0.3 kilogram of salt per liter. This salt solution is being poured in at a rate of 2 liters per minute. The solution is being thoroughly mixed and drained off, and the mixture is drained off at the same rate, so that the flask contains 10 liters at all times. How much salt is in the flask after 5 minutes?

This problem can be represented by the following differential equation in Leibnizian notation:

$$\frac{dx}{dt} = 0.2(0.3 - x) = 0.6 - 0.2x \tag{6}$$

or, in Newtonian notation:

$$\dot{x} = 0.6 - 0.2x. \tag{7}$$

Solving the equation and taking into account that initially there is no salt in the flask, the answer to the problem is

$$x = 3 - 3e^{-0.2 \times 5} \text{ kilograms} \tag{8}$$

or 1.9 kilograms (rounded to one decimal position).

A notable feature of this problem is that it requires a conceptualization of instantaneous change. Consider, for example, the following "mutilation" of the problem: "A flask contains 10 liters of water, and to it is being added a salt solution that contains 0.3 kilogram of salt per liter. This salt solution is being poured in at a rate of 2 liters per minute. How much salt is in the flask after 5 minutes?" The answer is, of course, 3 kilograms, little more than a multiplication exercise. In this version, the problem still requires one to consider the rate of change of incoming salt, but there is no need (cognitively speaking!) to operate with the concept of instantaneous change; in the "full" version of the Flask Problem, it is necessary to conceptualize instantaneous change and to operate with it. An exciting feature of calculus is that it provides more than one way to do this.

Representational Practices of Differential Calculus

The experimenter met individually with the experts, usually in the expert's office. The participants were allowed to use paper and pencil and a pocket calculator, but no access to reference books was permitted; they were not told that the problem requires calculus for its solution. The participants were asked to think out loud, using instructional materials adapted from Ericsson and Simon (1993). The protocols were taped and transcribed. The protocols in conjunction with the experts' handwritten notes were analyzed into problem-solving episodes. The analyses of three sessions are summarized in the following (for details see Kurz, 1997).

Session 1: A Mathematician. Participant T is a young, highly productive mathematician whose major field is analysis. He is a faculty member in a doctoral-level mathematics department. He worked on the Flask Problem for about 25 minutes; his protocol consisted of 11 episodes.

After reading the problem statement (Episode I) and drawing a schematic picture of the flask with arrows representing inflow and outflow of mixture (Episode II), Participant T assigned variables and briefly pursued an algebraic approach (Episode III). But then he realized that he "should probably use some calculus, in the sense of rates of change" (Episode IV). More specifically, he realized that a "derivative with respect to time" was needed. But he had to admit, somewhat embarrassed, "not seeing how to do this straightforwardly with calculus either." He proceeded by computing the amount of salt that was added after 1 minute (Episode V). He saw that an extrapolation from there to the solution of the problem was not feasible. As a way out of the dilemma, he introduced the concept of *instantaneous rate of change*, which opened possibilities for computation: In his words, "Instead, I wanna try to figure out what's the instantaneous rate of change of, well, what's the saline solution after any given time. So let me go to 30 seconds."

His new strategy was to "refine until nothing," to choose *decreasing* fixed time increments until the increments would become infinitely small. In actual fact, Participant T's computations concentrated on the first and second 30 seconds (Episode VI), and he only considered, hypothetically, to work with 15-second increments (Episode IX). These computations turned out to be rather laborious, involving checking and rechecking of the results (Episodes VII and VIII). He was clearly feeling uneasy with the progress he was making on the problem.

This rather laborious process of "refining" was not unlike perceptual rehearsal in that Participant T repeatedly carried out very similar computations (Episodes V–VIII) that allowed him to "see" a new pattern (see Ippolito & Tweney, 1995; Tweney, 1996). He noticed that "the *rate in* is always the same" (Episode VIII). This inconspicuous insight enabled a crucial next step in the solution, namely, to "Figure out the *rate out*" (Episode X). He then noticed that "it look[ed] like [he was] coming up with the differential equation here." Once represented in this form, it was only a routine task for him to solve the equation. Unfortunately, however, his differential equation was not entirely correct. The value for the rate out was off by one decimal position because he had not taken into account that the incoming salt was dissolved in 10 liters of fluid. For this reason, his final solution could not be interpreted meaningfully and remained unsatisfactory to him, but at this point, frustrated and pressed for time, he was not prepared to "debug" his solution.

Session II: A Chemist. Participant U is a midcareer physical chemist and a faculty member in a doctoral-level chemistry department. She is very active in research and has published many papers in her field. Participant U spent approximately 40 minutes working on the problem; her protocol consisted of 12 episodes.

Participant U spent considerable time (about 10 minutes) reading (Episode I) and rereading the problem (Episode II). At the end of her second reading she singled out "the critical sentence here," namely, that "the solution is being thoroughly mixed and drained off" (Episode III). From there she reasoned that "the concentration would be increasing over a period of a few minutes, and at some point you'd reach a steady state where you were putting the same amount of salt in as was going out" (Episode IV). This understanding led to a graphical representation (similar to the graph in Figure 7.4). She drew a Cartesian coordinate system with time on the abscissa and salt concentration on the ordinate. Then she constructed a "graph in time" (Episode V) by going to the "1-minute" location in the coordinate system and marking the respective value for the salt concentration, next to the "2-minute" location and again marking the respective value for the salt concentration, and so forth. For the first minute, she explicitly assumed that no salt was leaving the flask; for the 2-minute location she made sure, after adding the same amount of salt than for the first minute that this time she marked a point that was "a little low," because salt loss had to be taken into account. She proceeded to the "3-minute" location, adding twice the amount of the first minute, and again making sure that the value on the ordinate was "low, we'd be even lower." The essential feature of the resulting graph was its asymptotic nature, in her words, that "it's gonna be coming up like this and then it's just gonna be a straight line for the rest of the time" (Episode VI). The change in salt concentration with time had been transformed into the continuous motion of a point, generating a line. In this sense, her graph was a dynamic representation, that is, a representation in which time is necessarily represented in an analog fashion (Freyd, 1987).

Participant U also meant to use her graph to infer a solution to the Flask Problem, but then she noticed that the scale on the ordinate was not right. In fact, the scale was off by one decimal position. She did not read off a solution from the graph but instead assumed that the concentration after 5 minutes would be the steady-state concentration of 0.3 kilogram – the concentration of the incoming salt solution. This assumption gave her 3.0 kilograms as the amount of salt after 5 minutes. The experimenter, somewhat worried that Participant U would quit at this stage, asked whether she could formulate an equation. Immediately she wrote dc/dt (c for concentration, t for time), the "change in the concentration," to represent the left-hand side of an equation (Episode VII). For the right-hand side she reasoned that "first, the concentration is zero," so "the intercept is zero." She added a term denoting "the increase in the concentration," which was 0.6, with the units "kilograms per liter per minute." The "concentration going out," being the "minus part," she approached by making a "linear assumption" (Episode VIII). But she quickly realized that this assumption led to the anomaly of "not getting a steady state." Thus, it had to be a nonlinear function. But what kind of nonlinear "functional form"? This was a difficult question that led her to recapitulate what she knew about the physical process, namely, that "it's increasing at a constant rate" and that "the concentration is increasing linearly," and she was certain "that it's not decreasing at a constant rate," and also that a constant volume of the perfectly mixed solution was pouring out (Episode IX). After silently rereading parts of the problem, she emphasized that she was thinking about the process "in terms of a continuous thing," and that the approximation method she was going to propose next would be a "quickie" way to arrive at a solution (Episode X).

Participant U's approximation method (Episode XI) matched the way she had previously constructed her graph. In the first minute, 0.6 kilogram of salt was added to the flask, and she assumed that no salt was deleted from the flask during this time. In the second minute, another 0.6 kilogram was added and one-fifth of the amount of salt in the flask after 1 minute was subtracted, because the salt was dissolved in 10 liters, 2 of which were withdrawn during the second minute. With the third minute, another 0.6 kilogram of salt was added to the amount in the flask and one-fifth of the amount of salt in the flask after 2 minutes was subtracted. She carried this procedure through to 5 minutes and then announced her solution as "2.14 kilograms in 10 liters; that's approximate!" The experimenter asked what she would do to improve her approximation. She answered promptly (Episode XII): "Well, you have to take smaller time intervals." Finally, the experimenter asked for her best guess of the precise solution. She answered: "Oh, 1.9 kilograms or something at 5 minutes." Certainly, an excellent guess. In a way, she had achieved, what she had proposed earlier (Episode X), namely, that after her solution by approximation she would "try to work back so that [she'd] have an instantaneous picture of what was going on."

Session III: A Physicist. Participant S is a theoretical physicist internationally known for contributions to his field. He teaches undergraduate and graduate physics courses in a masters'-level physics department. Participant S spent about 50 minutes working on the Flask Problem; his protocol consisted of 18 episodes.

After reading the problem statement (Episode I), Participant S determined that his task was to formulate a model, in his words, "to put all this together in some formulas or something and see these relationships" (Episode II). He restated the problem in his words and then computed a "guess," a numerical solution based on simplifying assumptions (Episode III and IV). For his guess, he assumed that salt solution was added to the flask at one instant and deleted at another. He announced 1.5 kilograms to be his answer to the problem, adding that it "may not be right." Fearing that, with this answer, Participant S might end his problem solving, the experimenter asked, "Can you come up with an equation?" "A good question," Participant S agreed, because equations had been "implicit" in what he had been thinking, but now the challenge was to "find what they are." It was clear to him that it would need to be "sort of a rate equation" (Episode V). He started to wonder whether he had missed something before and therefore thought it best to "read this again" (Episode VI).

After rereading the problem, he assigned x to "the amount of salt in the tank" (Episode VII). The left-hand side of his *rate equation* was "the time derivative of x" and was noted in Newtonian notation (see Equation 9). The right-hand side had to be "the rate at which it's added minus the amount that is leaving" (Episode VIII). The "rate at which it's added" was 0.6 kg/min and was followed by a minus sign. He immediately recast the rate of incoming salt as 0.3(2), omitting the units of measurement. Then he proceeded to the part following the minus sign, which had to be "also a function of time." He knew that "the amount of fluid that is flowing out is 2." But how did the amount of salt that was leaving the flask depend upon the concentration of salt solution in the flask? The amount of salt in the tank "is always gonna be x over 10." He had written out the complete differential equation:

$$\dot{x} = 0.3(2) - \frac{x(2)}{10}. \tag{9}$$

After a lengthy pause (of 12 seconds), he came to the conclusion "that this might be the right idea, really," cause this says that the rate at which the amount of salt changes depends upon how fast you add it" (Episode IX). He checked the units of measurement (Episode X) and was just delighted to find that the formulated equation had "the right units, this has the right units!"

He anticipated that solving this equation would take some effort on his part. He restated the equation in Leibnizian notation, which is preferable for solving differential equations. (When he was asked later about this switch in notation, it turned out that he had not been aware of it.) But before actually beginning to solve the equation, he wanted to "see whether [he] like[d] the way this [was] going" (Episode XII), whether this mathematical model matched his process understanding. He determined that "in the extreme future you would reach an equilibrium situation where all of the original water had been replaced and therefore the concentration inside the tank would be 0.3 kilogram per liter." He thus was able to determine the amount of salt in the "extreme future," but the problem asked for "the answer in the middle." He thought that he would find out "the answer to this question by solving this equation," and therefore "it's worth doing" (Episode XII).

Solving his rate equation (Episode XIII; separating variables, then using a substitution procedure, in which he differentiated with respect to a dummy variable y, and then integrating the resulting expression), he arrived at an intermediary result which he evaluated at $t = 0$ and for $t \to \infty$ (Episode XIIV). He found that the equation did not exhibit the right behavior at $t = 0$ when no salt was supposed to be in the flask. But nevertheless, he detected "elements of truth here" because he "saw" that "at long times" the model would reach the appropriate equilibrium. He realized that he had not properly integrated the equation (in his substitution procedure he had used the operations of differentiation and of integration, which made a second integration necessary to solve the differential equation). He integrated, evaluating a definite integral, and computed the general solution (Episode XV). He evaluated the resulting equation at $t = 0$ and for $t \to \infty$ and found what he "thought ought to happen" (Episode XVI). Finally, he substituted $t = 5$ to determine the amount of salt after 5 minutes (Episode XVII) and then used a hand calculator to determine the numerical solution, which was 1.896 kilograms (Episode XVIII).

How Did the Calculus Experts Represent Change?

The solutions worked out by these three experts differed remarkably in many respects. Here the focus is on their use of the differential calculus. In a nutshell, the mathematician's representational use of the calculus was in many respects Leibnizian, the chemist's Newtonian, and the physicist's born out of a genuine modeling approach. Specifically, the mathematician's solution was based on the choice of fixed increments. In the limiting case these decreasing fixed increments are Leibniz's differentials. Limit taking in Leibniz's calculus was global (Bos, 1993, p. 87). With respect to a smooth curve, this global limit taking meant that the curve remained composed of the sides of a polygon even after extrapolation to the infinite case. By contrast, the derivative defines a local limit (see the earlier discussion of the Leibnizian glasses in contrast to the Modern glasses). Participant T knew that a "derivative with respect to time" was necessary, but he did not know how to model the problem using this concept. As a way out of this dilemma, he worked with decreasing fixed increments. In a sense, then, Participant T "approximated" the concept of derivative with his computations rather than the numerical solution of the problem. But even if Participant T's plan to "refine until nothing" was not Leibnizian in intent, the realization in terms of fixed increments was.

The chemist's solution was based on the transformation of the change in salt into the continuous motion of a point, creating a "graph in time." Her approximation method finally paralleled her construction of this graph: First, she determined how much was added; then she made sure that she was "a little low," that she subtracted about the right amount. Next, she extrapolated the appropriate "motion," resulting in her "graph in time." The transformation of change into the motion of a geometrical object was central to Newton's fluxionary calculus (see the previous discussion of the Newtonian glasses). Newton conceived of mathematical quantities as motion of geometrical objects (see the previous quote from the *Tractatus de quadratura curvarum*). Similarly, Participant U provided a successful solution because she was able to utilize a dynamic representation that enabled her to work out an approximation procedure that led to a numerical solution of the problem.

Finally, the physicist engaged in an ongoing process of checking the match between his mathematical model and his physical process understanding, both being constructed simultaneously. In order to consolidate this match, Participant S made the process observable and manipulable. This simulation of the physical process observed a process in time, from "no salt in there to start with" to an "extreme future" in which "you would reach an equilibrium" (Episodes XIIV and XVI). Description was observation in this case; this is, for instance, also parallel to what Nersessian (1992) concluded about thought experiments. And in this case, observation was inextricably coupled with manipulation – a unity that also has been emphasized for experimentation, for instance, in relation to Michael Faraday's experimental investigations (see Gooding, 1992; Tweney, 1992). This unity of observation and manipulation occurred at the interface of Participant S's understanding of the physical process and of his mathematical model. Although it could be argued that the differential equation is the physical process model, the identification of the understanding of the physical process in terms of the mathematical model was the final stage of Participant S's solution process; it was in fact his primary achievement.

This case study shows that there is variability in the representational use of the calculus. Moreover, this variability becomes meaningful when related to the historical development of the differential calculus. In its historical development this variability was also related to differences in the understanding of natural phenomena. Corresponding to their different representations of change, Newton and Leibniz, for instance, also had different notions of accelerated motion (Bertoloni Meli, 1993, pp. 74–91). For Leibniz, accelerated motion was a series of infinitesimal rectilinear motions interrupted by impulses; for Newton, it was a continuous curve where force acts continually. The experts in this case study showed great competence in choosing and developing a representation that was meaningful to them. The plurality of representations provided by the calculus is a feature that experts may use to further their understanding.

Representation Matters

In this chapter, we have argued (1) that the calculi of uncertainty and change provide multiple representations, which bridge the past and present, (2) that the choice of representation is already part of the solution of the problem, and (3) that learning to choose an appropriate representation can help experts to understand uncertainty and change, and to communicate successfully with their clients and students on such topics as how to assess risk. As the studies with AIDS counselors and physicians dramatically demonstrated, the training of experts does not always include learning to choose a suitable representation.

The importance of representations has been emphasized repeatedly, from cognitive science (e.g., Marr, 1982) to physics (e.g. Feynman, 1967). Otto Neurath, who cautioned scientists against wasting their time with history, was in fact a pioneer in designing external representations to help ordinary citizens understand statistical information. Neurath (1939) successfully developed the visual statistical language ISOTYPE – so successfully that in the early 1930s the Soviet government invited him to train specialists to teach the Soviet people ISOTYPE. Unfortunately, he was never paid for his efforts and got into serious financial difficulties (Hegselmann, 1979).

The tools that experts use to quantify risk and change support variability in representational practice. This variability can be beneficial, as we have shown for the case of risk assessment in medical diagnosis, where most experts and laypeople are dramatically helped by representations using natural frequencies. Competence thus can mean knowing how to re-represent a problem so that reasoning is facilitated. Becoming competent in this fashion requires us to acknowledge the possibility of a plurality of alternative representations, in fact, a hallmark of mathematical thinking in general – no matter by whom it is carried out.

In modern terms, the lesson from Neurath, Leibniz, and other students of representation is: Minds do not reason from information, but from representations. Even mathematically equivalent representations can make a difference to the kind of insight experts gain. The power and the indispensable nature of representations was with us in the past, affects us in the present, and will continue to do so in the future.

References

Alexander, H. G. (Ed.). (1956). *The Leibniz–Clarke correspondence*. Manchester, UK: Manchester University Press.

Bertoloni Meli, D. (1993). *Equivalence and priority: Newton versus Leibniz*. Oxford: Clarendon Press.

Bos, H. J. M. (1980). Newton, Leibniz and the Leibnizian tradition. In I. Grattan-Guinness (Ed.), *From the calculus to set theory, 1630–1910* (pp. 49–93). London: Duckworth.

Bos, H. J. M. (1993). *Lectures in the history of mathematics*. Providence, RI: American Mathematical Society.

Boyer, C. B. (1949). *The history of the calculus and its conceptual development*. New York: Dover.

Brenner, J. L. (1963). *Problems in differential equations*. San Francisco: W. H. Freeman.

Casscells, W., Schoenberger, A., & Grayboys, T. (1978). Interpretation by physicians of clinical laboratory results. *New England Journal of Medicine, 299*, 999–1001.

Cournot, A. A. (1843/1975). *Exposition de la théorie des chances et des probabilités*. Paris: J. Vrin.

Damerow, P. (1995). Abstraction and representation: Essays on the cultural evolution of thinking. In R. S. Cohen, Jürgen Renn, & Kostas Gavroglu (Eds.), *Boston studies in the philosophy of science* (Vol. 175, pp. 173–298). Dordrecht: Kluwer Academic.

Daston, L. J. (1988). *Classical probability in the Enlightenment*. Princeton, NJ: Princeton University Press.

Deutscher Bundestag (Ed.) (1990). *AIDS: Fakten und Konsequenzen*. Final report of the Enquete Committee of the 11th German Bundestag, 13/90. Bonn: Bonner Universitäts Buchdruckerei.

Dilson, J. (1968). *The abacus: A pocket computer*. New York: St. Martin's Press.

Eddy, D. M. (1982). Probabilistic reasoning in clinical medicine: Problems and opportunities. In D. Kahneman, P. Slovic, & A. Tversky (Eds.), *Judgment under uncertainty: Heuristics and biases* (pp. 249–267). Cambridge: Cambridge University Press.

Elstein, A. S. (1988). Cognitive processes in clinical inference and decision making. In D. C. Turk & P. Salovey (Eds.), *Reasoning, inference and judgment in clinical psychology* (pp. 17–50). New York: Free Press.

Ericsson, K. A., & Simon, H. A. (1993). *Protocol analysis: Verbal reports as data*. Cambridge, MA: MIT Press.

Feynman, R. (1967). *The character of physical law*. Cambridge, MA: MIT Press.

Freyd, J. J. (1987). Dynamic mental representation. *Psychological Review, 94*, 427–438.

Gigerenzer, G. (1996). The psychology of good judgment: Frequency formats and simple algorithms. *Journal of Medical Decision Making, 16*, 273–280.

Gigerenzer, G., & Hoffrage, U. (1995). How to improve Bayesian reasoning without instruction: Frequency formats. *Psychological Review, 102*, 684–704.

Gigerenzer, G., Hoffrage, U., & Ebert, A. (1998). AIDS counseling for low-risk clients. *AIDS Care, 10*, 197–211.

Gigerenzer, G., Swijtink, Z., Porter, T., Daston, L., Beatty, J., & Krüger, L. (1989). *The empire of chance: How probability changed science and everyday life*. Cambridge: Cambridge University Press.

Gooding, D. (1992). Putting agency back into experiment. In A. Pickering (Ed.), *Science as practice and culture* (pp. 65–112). Chicago: University of Chicago Press.

Grattan-Guinness, I. (1980). The emergence of mathematical analysis and its foundational progress, 1780–1880. In I. Grattan-Guinness (Ed.), *From the calculus to set theory, 1630–1910* (pp. 94–148). London: Duckworth.

Hacking, I. (1975). *The emergence of probability*. Cambridge: Cambridge University Press.

Hall, A. R. (1980). *Philosophers at war: The quarrel between Newton and Leibniz*. Cambridge: Cambridge University Press.

Hegselmann, R. (Ed.). (1979). *Wissenschaftliche Weltauffassung, Sozialismus und Logischer Empirismus*. Frankfurt am M: Suhrkamp.

Hoffrage, U., & Gigerenzer, G. (1998). Using natural frequencies to improve diagnostic inferences. *Academic Medicine, 73*, 538–540.

Hoffrage, U., Lindsey, S., Hertwig, R., & Gigerenzer, G. (2000). Communicating statistical information. *Science, 290*, 2261–2262.

Ippolito, M. F., & Tweney, R. D. (1995). The inception of insight. In R. J. Sternberg & J. E. Davidson (Eds.), *The nature of insight* (pp. 433–462). Cambridge, MA: MIT Press.

Koehler, J. J. (1996). The base rate fallacy reconsidered: Descriptive, normative and methodological challenges. *Behavioral and Brain Sciences, 19*, 1–53.

Krauss, S., Martignon, L., Hoffrage, U., & Gigerenzer, G. (in review). *Bayesian reasoning and natural frequencies: A generalization to complex situations*.

Krüger, L., Daston, L., & Heidelberger, M. (Eds.). (1987). *The probabilistic revolution, Vol. 1: Ideas in history*. Cambridge, MA: MIT Press.

Krüger, L., Gigerenzer, G., & Morgan, M. S. (Eds.). (1987). *The probabilistic revolution, Vol. 2: Ideas in the sciences*. Cambridge, MA: MIT Press.

Kurz, E. M. (1997). *Representational practices of differential calculus: A historical-cognitive approach*. Ph.D. dissertation, Bowling Green State University.

Kurzenhäuser, S., & Hoffrage, U. (2002). Teaching Bayesian reasoning: An evaluation of a classroom tutorial for medical students. *Medical Teacher, 24*, 531–536.

Marr, D. (1982). *Vision*. San Francisco: W. H. Freeman.

Moon, P. (1971). *The abacus: Its history; its design, its possibilities in the modern world*. New York: Gordon Breach.

Nersessian, N. J. (1992). How do scientists think? Capturing the dynamics of conceptual change in science. In R. N. Giere (Ed.), *Minnesota studies in the philosophy of science: Vol. 15. Cognitive models of science* (pp. 3–44). Minneapolis: University of Minnesota Press.

Neurath, O. (1930/1931). Wege der wissenschaftlichen Weltauffassung. *Erkenntnis, 1,* 106–125.

Neurath, O. (1939). *Modern man in the making.* New York: Knopf.

Norman, D. A. (1993). *Things that make us smart.* Reading, MA: Addison-Wesley.

Porter, T. M. (1986). *The rise of statistical thinking, 1820–1900.* Princeton, NJ: Princeton University Press.

Quetelet, L. A. J. (1835). *Sur l'homme et le développment de ses facultés, ou essai de physique sociale.* Paris: Bachelier. [*A treatise on man and the development of his faculties.* Translated by R. Knox (1842), Facsimile edition of translation 1969. Introduction by S. Diamond. Gainesville, FL: Scholars' Facsimiles and Reprints.]

Shafer, G. (1989, November 20). *The unity and diversity of probability.* Inaugural lecture University of Kansas.

Shanteau, J. (1992). Competence in experts: The role of task characteristics. *Organizational Behavior and Human Decision Processes, 53,* 252–266.

Shapiro, B. J. (1983). *Probability and certainty in seventeenth-century England.* Princeton, NJ: Princeton University Press.

Stine, G. L. (1996). *Acquired immune deficiency syndrome. Biological, medical, social and legal issues.* Englewood Cliffs, NJ: Prentice Hall.

Struik, D. J. (Ed.). (1969). *A source book in mathematics, 1200–1800.* Cambridge, MA: Harvard University Press.

Tweney, R. D. (1992). Stopping time: Faraday and the scientific creation of perceptual order. *Physis: Revista Internazionale di Storia della Scienzia, 29,* 149–164.

Tweney, R. D. (1996). Presymbolic processes in scientific creativity. *Creativity Research Journal, 9,* 163–172.

Zhang, J., & Norman, D. A. (1995). The representation of numbers. *Cognition, 57,* 271–295.

8   The Vice of Consensus and the Virtue of Consistency

David J. Weiss and James Shanteau

Our title is adapted from that of an essay by G. B. Shaw (1956), in which he compared two closely related practices, gambling and insurance, and reached opposing conclusions about their merits. In Shaw's view, gambling is fundamentally ruinous, whereas insurance protects the citizenry. Here we criticize the use of consensus as a criterion in science, arguing that it is a poor surrogate for consistency. Consistency, on the other hand, is a necessity.

Consensus is viewed as a pathway to truth. When we receive a disturbing medical evaluation, we rush to seek a second opinion. If the second opinion differs, then we feel justified in questioning the accuracy of the first. If that second judgment is consistent with the first, we are more likely to accept the unhappy situation. If the prognosis is really terrible, we may seek a third opinion, again hoping to disconfirm the opinion. The rationale for this is that at an intuitive level, we are statisticians employing the binomial distribution. The probability that k independent judges reach the same wrong conclusion is q^k, where q is the probability of an individual answer being wrong. If we have confidence in the medical profession, so that we think q is small, then q^k becomes very small as k increases. When the experts agree, they are likely to be right. Meehl (1999) has argued similarly regarding the opinions of different scientists who have given their opinions on the correctness of a theory.

On the other hand, Meehl (1999) has also stressed the necessity of knowing that those expressing the opinions are indeed expert: "on a

Preparation of this manuscript was supported by Grant 98-G-026 from the Federal Aviation Administration in the Department of Transportation. We wish to thank Alice Isen, Gary McClelland, Julia Pounds, and Rickey Thomas for valuable discussions.

disputed point in quantum mechanics I would rely on Dirac's judgment rather than on the pooled judgments of ten psychologists" (p. 284). Similarly, the noted physicist Feynman (1985) recounts his service on a committee to choose a science textbook for elementary schools. A book he considered worthless had been "approved by sixty-five engineers at the Such-and-such Aircraft Company!" Feynman did not want to claim that he was "smarter then sixty-five other guys – but the average of sixty-five other guys, certainly!" (p. 298).

Both quotations illustrate our basic argument: The opinion of 1 highly qualified expert can be far more valuable than the opinion of 100 novices. This issue is fundamental in the identification of the qualified expert (Weiss & Shanteau, 2003).

At the turn of the 20th century, the consensus among physicists was that neo-Newtonian physics offered the best account of the universe. Einstein did not share this belief. Had physics relied on consensus to determine correctness, Einstein's views would have been rejected and many of the conceptual and technological advances of the past 100 years would not have occurred. In psychology, we continue to view research in political (i.e., popularity) terms. That means that our Einstein, should he or she burst onto the scene, will be ignored because of lack of consensus.

Independence

It is important to note that the binomial argument presumes the judgments to be independent. In practice, independence may be violated in several ways. The most blatant way is that judges may reach their decisions in concert. Sharing opinions prior to reaching a decision, as is done in a jury setting, clearly reduces the effective number of independent voices. In some situations, discussion is disallowed. For example, during figure skating competitions, judges are expressly forbidden to interact.

A more subtle form of nonindependence is that decision makers may follow the same rules. For example, figure skating judges are carefully trained to follow specific performance guidelines. Special schools for judges stress the importance of applying uniform criteria. Skating judges are taught how much to value a particular maneuver and how to recognize when it has been carried out properly. Common training thus reduces the independence of evaluations, yet we would consider the scoring chaotic if judges were not looking for the same performance characteristics.

An inherent contradiction in applying the binomial logic is that one kind of independence violation, collusion, is considered inappropriate, yet others are generally deemed desirable. Perhaps the reason is that collusion generally occurs immediately prior to the judgment and is thereby an obvious violation, whereas training typically takes place long before the judgment. We feel that this is a difference of degree rather than kind.

Collusion generates highly correlated judgments. Routine training is likely to yield judgments that are only moderately correlated, because the training is imperfect and the judges forget some of it. People are willing to ignore these moderate correlations in order to justify the use of consensus.

Expert Judgment

The binomial perspective is the basis for Einhorn's (1974) suggestion that agreement with other experts is a necessary characteristic of an expert. That is, the experts in a given field should agree with each other (Ashton, 1985). Einhorn argued that if opinions disagree, then some of the members of the proposed set of experts must not be functioning at the appropriate level. He used this reasoning to disparage several professions, among them clinical psychology and stock brokerage, by showing that agreement among practitioners (as measured by interindividual correlations) was unexpectedly low.

Lack of agreement among peer reviewers for grants and manuscripts has come under a good deal of scrutiny (Cicchetti, 1991). Poor inter-reviewer reliability is the norm across a variety of disciplines. Mixed reviews usually lead to negative decisions. This means disappointment for the submitter. Those whose academic or economic fortunes depend upon the luck of the draw are likely to lose confidence in both their colleagues and the process.

Most respondents to Cicchetti's (1991) target article agreed that reviewer disagreement is undesirable. Rather lonely among the reactions were those of two experienced journal editors (Bailar, 1991; Kiesler, 1991), who argued that reviewers are selected for their complementary perspectives in order to inform the editor's decision. In their view, discrepancy is a healthy sign that reviewers are attending to different aspects of the manuscript, thereby enhancing the validity of the evaluation.

When high consensus does occur, it is because the expert community has largely solved the problems of the domain. Because each individual expert is getting the correct answer, usually with the aid of well-developed technology, their answers agree. It is not agreement that makes the answers correct; rather, it is that answers agree when they are correct.

Laypersons are disturbed when experts do not agree because they overestimate the scientific success achieved by the professional community. Noting that experts often disagree, Shanteau (1999) characterized the "experts should converge" argument as a fundamental misunderstanding of the way experts think. Because the real-world problems that experts tackle seldom have single, stable answers, disagreement is inevitable and even useful. Indeed, one might argue that too much interindividual agreement is a signal that the problem is trivial and scarcely worthy of an expert. Expert judgment may have been replaced by a mechanical device (Weiss & Shanteau, 2003). Certainly, there are manuscripts on which the reviewers agree; but those manuscripts tend to be the ones rated as poor (Cicchetti, 1991).

Structural Reasons for Disagreement among Experts

Analysis of the context in which most experts work provides five structural factors explaining why experts may disagree. These factors reflect the situational constraints under which most experts work.

1. In the domains where experts work, the *ground truth* is often a fiction. Single-point optimal solutions do not exist. Despite the tremendous analytic ability of master players and the incredible computation speed of computer programs such as Deep Blue, for example, the game of chess still does not yield optimal solutions. If this is true for a well-structured game such as chess, how can it be possible to find a "correct answer" in an ill-structured setting? The reason we need experts in the first place is that they offer us answers that we could not obtain any other way (Shanteau, 1999). When there is no single best answer, it should not be surprising that different experts choose different solutions.

2. A distinction can be made between the different levels of decisions made by experts. Using terminology from medicine, it is possible to distinguish between three levels: The first is *diagnosis*

(what is it?) based on categorization and/or classification. The second is *prognosis* (what is the likely outcome?) based on forecasting future scenarios. And the third is *treatment* (what to do about it?) involving selection of a course of action. There are thousands of diagnoses and hundreds of prognoses but relatively few treatments. As pointed out by medical researchers (e.g., Schwartz & Griffin, 1986), experts might disagree at one level (diagnosis) but agree at another (treatment).

3. Despite the assumption made by many researchers, experts are seldom asked to make single-outcome decisions. The concept of a *point prediction* is largely a fiction created for the convenience of the researcher and is not descriptive of the tasks that experts do. As Golde (1969) noted, although "an expert does sometimes make decisions, his [her] role is usually much more that of an advisor . . . [they] let me know the kinds of decisions or actions that I must take" (p. 213). In other words, the job of the expert is to clarify alternatives and describe possible outcomes for clients.

4. As Klein, Orasanu, Calderwood, and Zsambok (1993) emphasized, experts generally work in dynamic situations with frequent updating. Thus, the problems faced by experts are unpredictable, with evolving constraints. In such situations, there are rarely ideal answers. Therefore, whereas outsiders assume a stationary target, the reality faced by experts is generally more like a moving target.

5. A long-term perspective reveals that experts work in realms where the basic science is still evolving. For instance, the rapid changes in medicine mean that the current "best answers" are soon obsolete. Why should we expect experts to agree on a single "correct answer," say for the treatment of the acquired immune deficiency syndrome (AIDS) when new knowledge will likely provide better solutions tomorrow?

Functional Reasons for Disagreement

Five functional factors underlie disagreement among experts. These factors have to do with how experts think about the decisions and judgments they make.

1. Most experts operate as if they have flat loss functions for deviations from optimality. They see small deviations as having minor consequences. In comparison, von Winterfeldt and Edwards

(1986) have observed that researchers often operate as if experts have steep loss functions. That is, researchers view any deviation from optimality, no matter how slight, as having large consequences. Similarly, they see any disagreement between experts, no matter how small, as reason for concern.

2. Whereas those in the heuristics and biases tradition (e.g., Kahneman, Slovic, & Tversky, 1982) view any deviation between behavior and the "correct answer" as an error, experts have a different definition of error. As noted previously, experts are usually more concerned about avoiding big mistakes, whereas researchers are looking for perfection. Thus, the same outcome could well be called an error by the researcher and a success by the expert. In the same situation, experts may see agreement where investigators see disagreement.

3. In many, perhaps most, settings, experts expect to disagree with each other. In a discussion between any two academics, for instance, we know that they invariably will find something about which to argue. Even when they agree on 99% of the issues, they will quickly find the last 1% and disagree about that. Similarly, experts in almost any field bypass points of agreement to focus instead on disagreements. Thus, experts view disagreements as a normal part of doing their job.

4. Disagreements are often the route by which experts increase understanding of their field. By seeking out areas of disagreement between one another, experts explore the limits of their own knowledge and stretch their range of competency. Therefore, experts see disagreements as a key step in increasing their grasp of the field.

5. Once a domain has advanced to the point where all issues are resolved, there will be few disagreements among experts because there is nothing left to argue about. When a field has developed to that extent, however, the answers are known and agreed upon. Thus, total agreement among experts is an indication that there is no longer much of a role for experts to play in that domain.

Domain Differences

We all know that experts in different domains perform different tasks. Yet it is common to treat all experts alike, so that the term *expert* is used generically. For instance, Kahneman (1991) concluded "there is much

Table 8.1. *Progression of Domains from High to Low Performance*

Stability of Domain Stimuli			
High Levels of Performance		Low Levels of Performance	
Aided Decisions	*Competent*	*Restricted*	*Random*
Weather forecasters	Chess masters	Clinical psychologists	Polygraphers
Astronomers	Livestock judges	Parole officers	Managers
Test pilots	Grain inspectors	Psychiatrists	Stock forecasters
Insurance analysts	Photo interpreters	Student admissions staff	Parole officers
Physicists	Soil judges	Intelligence Analysts	Court judges

evidence that experts are not immune to the cognitive illusions that affect other people" (p. 144). On the other hand, it is widely known that at least some experts, such as weather forecasters (Murphy & Winkler, 1977), show little sign of biases or *cognitive illusions* in their professional capacities. Thus, despite the generalizations drawn about experts in general, we know there are many exceptions to the rule.

In an effort to account for these domain differences, Shanteau (2000) constructed Table 8.1 to differentiate between those domains where experts do well and those where experts do not. The table is based on a continuum from high to low competence. In the left column are those domains where experts make aided decisions using decision support systems (DSSs) or other computerized tools (e.g., weather forecasters). The next column contains domains where experts make skilled but largely unaided decisions (e.g., livestock judges). The third column lists domains where experts show limited competence (e.g., clinical psychologists). The behavior of experts in the last column is little better than random (e.g., stockbrokers). Note: Assignment of domains within the table was based on a review of the literature, that is, the assessment of competence is based on the opinions of researchers who study each domain.

There are many ways to describe the differences in this table (see Shanteau, 1992a, 1992b). For present purposes, it makes most sense to note that the domains on the left side possess more stable (*static*) properties. That is, the stimuli and the problem "hold still" for experts to evaluate. The domains on the right side, involve more changeable (*dynamic*) properties. Thus, the stimuli are less stable, harder to specify, and more like moving targets. It makes sense, therefore, that expert agreement will be higher on the left side and lower on the right side.

Table 8.2. *Consensus Values for Experts in Different Domains*

Stability of Domain Stimuli			
High Levels of Performance		Low Levels of Performance	
Aided Decisions	*Competent*	*Restricted*	*Random*
Weather forecasters $r = .95$	Livestock judges $r = .50$	Clinical psychologists $r = .40$	Stockbrokers $r = .32$
Auditors $r = .76$	Grain inspectors $r = .60$	Pathologists $r = .55$	Polygraphers $r = .33$

Note: Values cited in this table were drawn from the following studies (from left to right): Stewart, Roebber, and Bosart (1997), Phelps and Shanteau (1978), Goldberg, and Werts (1966), Slovic (1969), Kida (1980), Trumbo, Adams, Milner, and Schipper (1962), Einhorn (1974), and Lykken (1979).

To test this idea, Table 8.2 summarizes the results from studies of domain experts in the four categories of Table 8.1. Two domains are listed under each category, with the between-expert agreement (consensus) given as average correlations. As can be seen, the average consensus (r) value for weather forecasters is .95, whereas average values for livestock judges, clinical psychologists, and stock forecasters are .50, .40, and .32, respectively. Comparable results appear for other domains on the second line. The values support the trend outlined previously – better-structured domains lead to high consensus and less-structured domains to low consensus.

For comparison, the average within-expert correlations (consistency) for these same domains are listed in Table 8.3. The trends are similar, with

Table 8.3. *Intraindividual (Consistency) Values in Different Domains*

Stability of Domain Stimuli			
High Levels of Performance		Low Levels of Performance	
Aided Decisions	*Competent*	*Restricted*	*Random*
Weather forecasters $r = .98$	Livestock judges $r = .96$	Clinical psychologists $r = .44$	Stockbrokers $r = < .40$
Auditors $r = .90$	Grain inspectors $r = .62$	Pathologists $r = .50$	Polygraphers $r = .91$

Note: Values cited in this table were drawn from the following studies (from left to right): Stewart, Roebber, and Bosart (1997), Phelps and Shanteau (1978), Goldberg and Werts (1966), Slovic (1969), Kida (1980), Trumbo, Adams, Milner, and Schipper (1962), Einhorn (1974), and Raskin and Podlesny (1979).

better-structured domains leading to higher internal consistency. As expected, the consistency (*r*) values (except for pathologists) are higher than the corresponding consensus values in Table 8.2. In two domains (livestock judges and polygraphers), there are notable discrepancies between the consensus and consistency correlations. In these domains, there appear to be "schools of thought" that have produced sizable disagreements among various experts (Shanteau, 2000)

Latent Trait Analysis

A mathematically sophisticated extension of the agreement perspective has been presented by Uebersax (1988, 1992, 1993) using latent class analysis. Acknowledging that although experts might disagree, for example, on the diagnoses of individual patients, his proposal is that generally experts will agree in what they are doing. Experts will consider similar aspects of the situation and employ similar processes, although they may vary in terms of biases and inconsistencies. Uebersax proposed that interobserver agreement at the level of the latent structure underlying the judgments confers validity. Uebersax and Grove (1990) do acknowledge the possibility that the latent trait may not be the trait of interest and may reflect shared, but inappropriate, criteria.

Our view is that high degrees of consensus do not necessarily connote expertise. The history of science is replete with examples of false consensus. Some well-known examples of premature agreement within the scientific community are flat earth, phlogiston, phrenology, and the Rorschach test. Martin Gardner's (1957) compendium gives other illustrations. Groupthink in the Cuban missile crisis (Janis, 1972) is a classic example of how premature consensus retards effective decision making.

A far more important characteristic of expertise, also proposed by Einhorn (1974; see also Weiss & Shanteau, 2003), is consistency. Imagine your consternation if a physician's reports on your medical condition were variable. Inconsistency is virtually unimaginable, and it would be a brave patient who asked the doctor to do an independent reevaluation. In fact, when we do observe inconsistency in an acknowledged expert's opinions, we typically ascribe the variation to changes in the situation. We do not allow for the possibility that the judgments reflect sampled observations from a distribution characterized by high variance. In order to be considered expert, one must be consistent.

In principle, consistency is easy to measure; we need merely ask for repeated responses. But those replications must be independent. This requirement is not merely a statistical nicety. An expert presented with the same stimulus situation will strive to appear consistent, and so will repeat the previous response because of self-presentation considerations (Goffman, 1959). If the stimuli are memorable, as would certainly be the case with a medical patient, the response is likely to be identical. In a research setting, it might be possible to disguise the stimuli to render the judgments more independent. Usually, though, independence is sought by spacing the judgments over time. In the medical setting, delay is not only inconvenient; the passage of time is often accompanied by real changes, and so evaluating consistency is problematic.

Because consistency is hard to ascertain, people rely upon consensus as a surrogate. Presenting the same problem to several experts independently is easy, and therefore seeking consensus is attractive. It is difficult to explore intraindividual agreement, but it is easy to look at interindividual agreement.

The logical error of relying upon consensus remains unexposed because empirically, consensus is usually associated with consistency. In a review of experts across eight domains, Shanteau, Weiss, Thomas, and Pounds (2000) found that intraindividual agreement and interindividual agreement yielded almost identical measures. Reported correlations ranged from .98 for consistency and .95 for consensus for weather forecasters to .40 and .32, respectively, for stockbrokers.

It seems unlikely that consensus can be higher than consistency (except for chance fluctuations), that is, that you can agree with others more than you agree with yourself. The limitation parallels the ceiling placed on the validity of a psychometric test by its reliability. In the fields cited by Shanteau et al. (2000), consensus is about as high as it could be, given the degree of consistency shown by the experts in the domain. The correspondence probably means that the judgments are well prescribed by coherent training across the community or by equipment. However, for two of the expert domains reviewed by Shanteau et al., livestock judging and polygraphy, consistency was much greater than consensus. Apparently, those experts are using rules that are simple enough that they can be consistent, but the rules reflect different schools of thought.

Cultural Consensus Analysis

The cultural consensus approach has been used by anthropologists (Romney, Weller, & Batchelder, 1986) to determine which informants contribute trustworthy information. The technique is mathematically sophisticated and quite elegant, but at its heart is a simple idea: Majority answers to questions are likely to be true.[1] From this premise, the authors derive both estimates of the relative competencies of the informants and assessments of the likelihood that a particular answer is correct. They provide a striking demonstration that it is possible to reconstruct the answer key to an objective test (Batchelder & Romney, 1988).

Generalization of this approach to domains of expertise is problematic. The approach plays on the idea that response clustering implies expertise, because experts must agree on the right way to carry out the task and nonexperts behave idiosyncratically. We consider the premise to be dubious. As we have suggested, for many problems that experts face, there may not be a single right answer. Even if it is granted that experts should be required to agree, it does not follow logically that those who do agree must be experts. Experimentally, the approach suffers from the limitation that it requires the subject population to have sizable numbers of experts as well as nonexperts. The difficulty is that experts tend to be rare. Clustering cannot be demonstrated when only one or two experts are in the sample.

Meta-analysis

Another arena is which consensus supplants consistency is in the evaluation of scientific hypotheses. Though not without its critics (e.g., Chow, 1987), the statistical combination of results using meta-analysis (Cooper & Rosenthal, 1980) has in recent years come to be accepted as the standard method of inquiry. The reviewer exercises judgment in deciding which studies enter the compilation but assiduously tries not to be influenced by data in doing so. Meta-analysis attempts to bring the virtue of quantification to the difficult task of integrating disparate research results. Although minor procedural differences across studies are the norm, effect sizes are combined and essentially averaged. Such combinations are often misleading, especially in studies where there is

---

[1] Wainer (1983) presents an example of the risk in relying upon consensus to define correctness. The Education Testing Service inadvertently designated an incorrect option to a difficult geometry problem on the Princeton Scholastic Aptitude Test (PSAT) as the correct one. Subsequent investigation found that students who scored highest on similar questions were much more likely to have selected the official (but incorrect) answer than the correct one.

experimental control, because effect size depends on the researcher's choice of the levels of the independent variable.[2]

Our deeper objection is on philosophical grounds. Meta-analysts argue that their approach avoids disparaging researchers whose results are outliers, because there is no attempt to invalidate, or even examine, the experiments that yield anomalous results. We believe that such reviews induce the profession to reach premature closure. The outliers are simply overwhelmed by the majority. The following thought experiment illustrates the potential problem. Let us suppose that researchers are trying to decide which way water flows when it is going down the drain. The researchers in Los Angeles, Manhattan, Miami, and Boston, as well as those in Paris and Beijing, all report that the water circles in a clockwise manner. These results are cross-cultural and they agree, so the scientific community happily accepts the result. One lone voice from Melbourne offers a contradictory report, that the water flows in a counterclockwise direction in his laboratory. Although no one says anything uncomplimentary, the Antipodean result scarcely affects the consensually certified answer. The dissenting report is, pardon the expression, washed away.

The point of the thought experiment is that an unknown, powerful effect may be overlooked when the field decides that the question is settled. Indeed, it seems likely that our understanding of behavioral phenomena is often comparable to that of the fictitious hydrologists. Focus on consensus within the scientific community threatens to stifle inquiry. Meta-analysis may be little more than a sophisticated vote-counting scheme (Light & Smith, 1971), one that takes into account sample sizes and effect sizes, but the imprimatur of quantification reifies its results. A large mean effect size is likely to be interpreted as a final statement about the problem.

Instead, we argue that the important determinant of whether a laboratory result should be accepted is its replicability. Significance statements are poor substitutes for repeated results (Fisher, 1925). This is hardly a novel idea, but the current infrastructure of the scientific community does not reward a researcher who seeks to examine the consistency of experimental results.

Our recurrent concerns with independence apply here as well. In order for a replication to strengthen the evidence base for a phenomenon,

---

[2] In general, the farther apart the levels are spaced, the greater the apparent effect size (O'Grady, 1982).

it must provide independent confirmation of the results. Clearly, an experiment that mimics another will yield results that are constrained by the common design.

Conclusion

Reliance upon consensus is ultimately a democratic notion, and democracy is a valued political ideal. We are not arguing that a consensus-based measure is always inappropriate. To determine the most desirable of a set of alternatives, such as the best political leader or most attractive building decor, it is sensible to use a polling system. The mean response reflects how a typical member of the sampled population views the stimulus. It is implicit that everyone's opinion is equally valued.

It is understandable that consensus of opinion and consensus of results have come to be means to scientific validation. However, what works in the world of politics need not work in science. Because consensus and consistency often coincide, the scientific community has been fooled into relying upon consensus when it is reproducibility that is the cornerstone of good science.

References

Ashton, A. H. (1985). Does consensus imply accuracy in accounting studies of decision making? *Accounting Review, 60,* 173–185.

Bailar, J. C. (1991). Reliability, fairness, objectivity and other inappropriate goals in peer review. *Behavioral and Brain Sciences, 14,* 137–138.

Batchelder, W. H., & Romney, A. K. (1988). Test theory without an answer key. *Psychometrika, 53,* 71–92.

Chow, S. L. (1987). Meta-analysis of pragmatic and theoretical research: A critique. *Journal of Psychology, 121,* 259–271.

Cicchetti, D. V. (1991). The reliability of peer review for manuscript and grant submissions: A cross-disciplinary investigation. *Behavioral and Brain Sciences, 14,* 119–186.

Cooper, H. M., & Rosenthal, R. (1980). Statistical versus traditional procedures for summarizing research findings. *Psychological Bulletin, 87,* 442–449.

Einhorn, H. J. (1974). Expert judgment: some necessary conditions and an example. *Journal of Applied Psychology, 59,* 562–571.

Feynman, R. (1985). *Surely you're joking, Mr. Feynman!* New York: W. W. Norton.

Fisher, R. A. (1925). *Statistical methods for research workers.* London: Oliver & Boyd.

Gardner, M. (1957). *Fads and fallacies in the name of science.* New York: Dover.

Goffman, E. (1959). *The presentation of self in everyday life.* Garden City, NY: Doubleday/Anchor Books.

Goldberg, L. R., & Werts, C. E. (1966). The reliability of clinicians' judgments: A multitrait-multimethod approach. *Journal of Consulting Psychology, 30,* 199–206.

Golde, R. A. (1969). *Can you be sure of your experts?* New York: Award Books.

Janis, I. L. (1972). *Victims of groupthink.* Boston: Houghton Mifflin.

Kahneman, D. (1991). Judgment and decision making: A personal view. *Psychological Science, 2,* 142–145.

Kahneman, D., Slovic, P., & Tversky, A. (1982). *Judgment under uncertainty: Heuristics and biases.* Cambridge: Cambridge University Press.

Kida, T. (1980). An investigation into auditor' continuity and related qualification judgments. *Journal of Accounting Research, 22,* 145–152.

Kiesler, C. A. (1991). Confusion between reviewer reliability and wise editorial and funding decisions. *Behavioral and Brain Sciences, 14,* 151–152.

Klein, G. A., Orasanu, J. T., Calderwood, R., & Zsambok, C. E. (1993). *Decision making in action: Models and methods.* Norwood, NJ: Ablex.

Light, R. J., & Smith, P. V. (1971). Accumulating evidence: Procedures for resolving contradictions among different research studies. *Harvard Educational Review, 41,* 429–471.

Lykken, D. T. (1979). The detection of deception. *Psychological Bulletin, 80,* 47–53.

Meehl, P. E. (1999). How to weight scientists' probabilities is not a big problem: Comment on Barnes. *British Journal for the Philosophy of Science, 50,* 283–295.

Murphy, A. H., & Winkler, R. L. (1977). Can weather forecasters formulate reliable forecasts of precipitation and temperature? *National Weather Digest, 2,* 2–9.

O'Grady, K. E. (1982). Measures of explained variance: Cautions and limitations. *Psychological Bulletin, 92,* 766–777.

Phelps, R. H., & Shanteau, J. (1978). Livestock judges: How much information can an expert use? *Organizational Behavior and Human Performance, 21,* 209–219.

Raskin, D. C., & Podlesny, J. A. (1979). Truth and deception: A reply to Lykken. *Psychological Bulletin, 86,* 54–59.

Romney, A. K., Weller, S. C., & Batchelder, W. H. (1986). Culture as consensus: A theory of culture and informant accuracy. *American Anthropologist, 88,* 313–338.

Schwartz, S., & Griffin, T. (1986). *Medical thinking: The psychology of medical judgment and decision making.* New York: Springer-Verlag.

Shanteau, J. (1992a). Competence in experts: The role of task characteristics. *Organizational Behavior and Human Decision Processes, 53,* 252–266.

Shanteau, J. (1992b). How much information does an expert use? Is it relevant? *Acta Psychologica, 81,* 75–86.

Shanteau, J. (1999). Decision making by experts: The GNAHM effect. In J. Shanteau, B. A. Mellers, & D. A. Schum (Eds.), *Decision science and technology: Reflections on the contributions of Ward Edwards* (pp. 105–130). Boston: Kluwer.

Shanteau, J. (2001). What does it mean when experts disagree? In E. Salas & G. Klein (Eds.), *Linking expertise and naturalistic decision making* (pp. 229–244). Mahwah, NJ: Erlbaum.

Shanteau, J., Weiss, D. J., Thomas, R., & Pounds, J. (2000). Performance-based assessment of expertise: How can you tell if someone is an expert? *European Journal of Operations Research, 136,* 253–263.

Shaw, G. B. (1956). The vice of gambling and the virtue of insurance. In J. R. Newman (Ed.), *The world of mathematics (Vol. 3, pp. 154–1533).* New York: Simon & Schuster.

Slovic, P. (1969). Analyzing the expert judge: A descriptive study of a stockbroker's decision processes. *Journal of Applied Psychology, 53,* 255–263.

Stewart, T. R., Roebber, P. J., & Bosart, L. F. (1997). The importance of the task in analyzing expert judgment. *Organizational Behavior and Human Decision Processes, 69,* 205–219.

Trumbo, D., Adams, C., Milner, M., & Schipper, L. (1962). Reliability and accuracy in the inspection of hard red winter wheat. *Cereal Science Today, 7,* 62–71.

Uebersax, J. S. (1988). Validity inferences from interobserver agreement. *Psychological Bulletin, 103,* 405–416.

Uebersax, J. S. (1992). Modeling approaches for the analysis of observer agreement. *Investigative Radiology, 27,* 738–743.

Uebersax, J. S. (1993). Statistical modeling of expert ratings on medical treatment appropriateness. *Journal of the American Statistical Association, 88,* 421–427.

Uebersax, J. S., & Grove, W. M. (1990). Latent class analysis of diagnostic agreement. *Statistics in Medicine, 9,* 559–572.

Von Winterfeldt, D., & Edwards, W. (1986). *Decision analysis and behavioral research.* Cambridge: Cambridge University Press.

Wainer, H. (1983). Pyramid power: Searching for an error in test scoring with 830,000 helpers. *American Statistician, 37,* 87–91.

Weiss, D. J., & Shanteau, J. (2003). Empirical assessment of expertise. *Human Factors, 45*(1), 104–116.

Index